Introduction to Sociolo

C.E. Berkeley Fleming
Roy Hornosty
Cyril Levitt

Contents

1

Auguste Comte

Introductory Note

Throughout this chapter abbreviations are used to refer to other sections of the text. All references to other published materials appear in abbreviated form in parentheses. The following abbreviations have been used:

Pos. Phil.   Auguste Comte. **The Positive Philosophy of Auguste Comte.** 3 vols. Translated by Harriet Martineau. London: G. Bill & Sons, 1896.

Pos. Pol.   Auguste Comte. **System of Positive Polity or Treatise on Sociology, Instituting the Religion of Humanity.** 4 vols. Translated by John Henry Bridges, Frederic Harrison, Edward Spencer Beesly, Samuel Lobb, Fanny Hertz, Vernon and Godfrey Lushington. London: Longmans, Green, and Company, 1875–76.

G.V.   Auguste Comte. **General View of Positivism.** Translated by J.H. Bridges. Edited by Frederic Harrison. London: George Routledge & Sons Ltd., 1908

A Brief Biographical Sketch

Isidore-Auguste-Marie-Francois-Xavier Comte, the first of four children of Louis and Rosalie Comte, was born in Montpellier on January 19, 1798. His father was a humble civil servant whose chief ambition in life was to become tax collector for the district of Montpellier. His mother, née Félicité-Rosalie Boyer, who came from a family of eminent physicians, married his father in 1797 in a secret Catholic cere-

mony (secret because the church was closed by the revolutionary government) and devoted her life to her husband and the family. Both parents were conservative, which in those times meant that they were devout Catholics and ardent Royalists.

At the age of nine, Auguste Comte entered the Lycée at Montpellier which, like all Lycées during the Napoleanic period, was a boarding school designed to prepare young men for the military or the civil service. Comte immediately distinguished himself as an extraordinary scholar. He was not only a brilliant and industrious student, but he could perform remarkable feats of memory—he is said to have repeated a hundred verses after a single reading and to have recited backwards the words of a page he once read. Winning virtually all of the prizes and scholarships open to him, he graduated at the age of 14½ years. He then studied mathematics and wrote the entrance examinations for admission to the Ecole Polytechnique which he passed with the highest marks in all of southern and central France. Not yet sixteen, and therefore ineligible to begin his studies at the Ecole, he remained at the Lycée for another year, during which time he began to teach mathematics.

Comte enrolled in the Ecole Polytechnique in the fall of 1814 and studied mathematics and physics. There he became known as the philosopher (the thinker). He also became known as an ardent Republican, who in the name of liberty, was prepared to rebel against all forms of authority, whether religious, political or academic. Thus he was well prepared to assume a role as a student activist. During his second year of residence, he was a leading figure in a student uprising over the conduct of a geometry instructor. In April of 1816, he, along with fourteen other students, was expelled, and government troops were sent in to close the school. When the Ecole re-opened in mid-August of that year, Comte was not among those who were re-admitted. Still under police surveillance, Comte studied biology for a short while at a medical school in Montpellier.

In September of 1816, at the age of 18 and with all hopes of an academic career dashed, Comte returned to Paris to try to make a living by giving private lessons. There he met the famous French socialist, Claude-Henri de Saint-Simon, under whom he would serve as private secretary for a period of six years. It was during this period that Comte collaborated extensively with Saint-Simon, developed his own social and political ideas, published his "Great discovery of the year 1822"—his **Prospectus of the Scientific Works Required for the Reorganization of Society**, and met Caroline Massin, a nineteen-year-old prostitute with whom he would later share an apartment and whom he would eventually marry.

After a severe and final falling out with Saint-Simon, Comte found himself with no regular employment, a number of debts, and a wife to support. Except for fees received from one private student and small amounts of money which mysteriously found their way into Caroline's hands, the young couple was without means. In 1826, Comte conceived of a plan designed to ease his financial burden and provide him with an opportunity to teach his new philosophy—he would open his home to the public and give a subscription series of seventy-two lectures on what was later to become the Positive Philosophy. The inaugural lecture was enthusiastically received by a number of eminent men of science and letters. However, after the third lecture, Comte, suffering from the strains of an unhappy marriage and becoming increasingly irritable, experienced a severe nervous breakdown (some accounts say that he went insane and never fully recovered). In any event, after an eight-month period of hospitalization and an unsuccessful attempt to have him committed to an insane asylum, Comte was released to the care of his wife and his mother. In 1827, Comte attempted suicide by throwing himself into the Seine River, but he was rescued and henceforth decided that he had a mission to fulfill in life. Gradually restored to his reason, Comte resumed and completed his lecture series in 1829. These lectures were repeated on subsequent occasions and were published between 1830 and 1842 in six volumes as **Cours de Philosophie Positive** (translated and condensed into three volumes in 1853 by Harriet Martineau and published as the **Positive Philosophy of Auguste Comte**).

Things subsequently improved for Comte, and in 1832 he was given a minor appointment at the Ecole as a répétiteur (assistant lecturer). In 1837, he was given another appointment as an entrance examiner, and for the first time Comte had a regular income. But this was not to last. His domestic misery continued and his mental condition grew increasingly worse; he became increasingly irritable and at times violent. This led to a final break with Caroline in 1842, the year he completed the sixth and final volume of the Positive Philosophy. It also led to his writing a scathing attack on Saint-Simon and the official directors of the Ecole which he published as the Preface to this volume. As a result, Comte was relieved of his positions at the Ecole, and he found himself virtually penniless.

The year 1844 marks the beginning of what most believe to be the second phase of Comte's life and career. It was during this year that John Stuart Mill, who was favourably impressed with the positive philosophy, helped to establish a small stipend that would enable the "Father of Positivism" to continue his work. Comte managed with this meagre income by living an ascetic life, eating but two meals a day (one of which was bread and milk) and avoiding all stimulants, tobacco, coffee or alcohol. It was also the year he met Clotilde de Vaux, abandoned by her husband, a tax collector at Meru who stole public monies, falsified the records, set a building on fire and fled to Belgium. Clotilde had come to Paris to seek a living as a writer. Comte immediately fell in love with her, and although they never shared a bed, they developed a deep, intimate personal relationship that lasted until April 5, 1846, when Clotilde died of consumption in Comte's arms. Comte deified her and regarded her as his spiritual wife—his Beatrice. He was deeply inspired by this short-lived love affair and once again began giving public lectures. Confident that his relationship with Clotilde had taught him the full significance of the affective tendencies of our human nature, Comte began to develop his Religion of Humanity. In 1848, he founded the Positive Society, an association devoted to the study of positivism and to the implementation of positive principles in the reorganization of society. In 1849, he established the Universal Church of the Religion of Humanity, along the lines of the Catholic Church which he so vehemently rejected in his earlier life, to ensure the continued development of the spiritual and moral foundation of the new social order.

Comte's second major work, a four volume treatise, later translated into English as the **System of Positive Polity or Treatise on Sociology Instituting the Religion of Humanity**, was published between 1851 and 1854. While the Positive Philosophy focused on basic principles underlying the abstract, theoretical sciences—mathematics, astronomy, physics, chemistry, biology, and sociology, the Positive Polity dealt with normative issues relating to the establishment of a new, durable social order. Many, among them John Stuart Mill, regarded these two works as discontinuous, and dissociated themselves from the latter work. When Comte insisted on absolute discipleship, his following began to erode, and when he supported Louis Napoléon Bonaparte in the Coup d'état of December, 1851, the membership of the Positive Society was significantly reduced. In an "Appeal to the Conservatives" in 1855, Comte attempted to form an alliance between the Positivists and the Catholics to oppose the Liberals and the Communists. Disappointed that his social and political theories received minimal support, Comte died an unhappy man. Cancer claimed his life on September 5, 1857.

Comte's Project

The formative years of Auguste Comte's life were lived in a society marked by extraordinary social chaos, political instability, and moral alienation. The French Revolution had toppled social institutions which had existed for centuries, but it failed to bring about a stable social order based upon the principles of the Enlightenment. Following the ten-year bloodbath of 1789, there remained a significant and powerful minority of monarchists who opposed the democratic principles of the Republic and who, as many historians believe, prevented the Revolution from ever completing itself. France was left divided as the former privileged classes battled liberals, nationalists, and republicans for political power, and, as France was the cultural centre of the Western world, the resulting political instability and social chaos spilled over into the nations of Europe. This was compounded by the social dislocations occasioned by the Industrial Revolution. Thus, in the early part of the nineteenth century, an uneasy peace existed not only in France but in all of Western Europe.

Many historians now attribute this political instability and social chaos to the dramatic transformation of Western European society from the Medieval period into the modern era. The old feudal-Catholic social order was collapsing in the face of an emerging industrial-scientific society which had not yet fully established itself. The foremost problem of the period was the reorganization of social institutions and the reconstitution of a durable social order. This is the problem to which Comte addressed himself early in his life.

After analysing both social orders—the feudal and the industrial—Comte came to the conclusion that underlying each social system was an intellectual and moral base. Just as the feudal order rested upon theological ideas, so the industrial society was based upon scientific thought. Comte reasoned that the key to social reorganization was intellectual reform. Only when social and political thought is informed by true scientific principles will a stable and durable social order be established. The pressing problem for Comte was the construction of a philosophical system that would, on the one hand, replace Catholicism as the moral foundation of society, and, on the other, bring to an end, once and for all, the political instability and social chaos that characterized the age. That system Comte called Positivism.

In the **Cours de Philosophie Positive**, Comte attempts to synthesize the dominant scientific principles underlying the abstract theoretical sciences into a coherent, single system of ideas. These were the ideas that would, in Comte's view, serve as the moral and intellectual foundation of the new social order. But Positivism is not only a philosophy; it is also a Polity—a political and normative system based upon positivistic principles. Thus, Positivism consists of a Philosophy and a Polity which, in Comte's mind, "can never be dissevered; the former being the basis and the latter being the end of one comprehensive system" (**G.V.**, p. 1). In Comte's second major treatise, the **System of Positive Polity**, the contours of the new political and normative order are outlined.

If the state of society is in large measure determined by the character of its intellectual and moral foundation, then a unified, stable, durable social order could only be established upon principles which themselves were internally consistent, permanent, and universal. The search for such principles, as we shall see later, implies a mode of reasoning known as holistic. Holism is a philosophical view which considers the fundamental and determining characteristics of an element in nature to be derived from the whole of which it is a part or from the context in which it occurs. Just as it is impossible to explain the nature and function of a particular organ in a body apart from the living organism as a whole, so it is impossible to explain a particular social phenomenon apart from society as a whole. From this point of view, it is equally impossible to explain a particular society apart from its entire history or the human race taken as a whole. Thus, to achieve his intellectual objective, Comte had to construct a social theory that would account for human behaviour in terms of the development of humanity. And, since the measure of a true science for Comte was its capacity for prevision, such a theory would serve as a guide for the future development of humanity.

The Positivism of Auguste Comte

The Nature of Positivism

In his "Special Preface" to the "General Appendix" to Volume IV of the **System of Positive Polity**, published in 1854, Comte attempts to illustrate the continuity between his early and later works, between his "System of Positive Philosophy" and his "System of Positive Polity." In response to his critics, he republished six early essays, written between 1819 and 1828, to "demonstrate the inconsistency of all who adopting the Positive Philosophy reject those Social Applications which [were] announced from the outset." It is evident from these essays that Comte early in his life committed himself to the development of what later became the Religion of Humanity. Whether these normative works are logically consistent with the scientific writings in the **Cours de Philosophie Positive** we will leave to others to decide. The important point is that in Comte's mind, and this was often the case with early social thinkers, what "ought to be" in social and political life was to be derived from a scientific investigation of the world. The separation of "facts" and "values" that we find in later sociology would have been unacceptable to Comte (Cf. Weber). A correct social science would necessarily lead to the proper social order. Nevertheless Comte did make a distinction between the intellectual and social aspects of positivism, and these can be discussed separately.

a) The Positive Philosophy

The positive philosophy is one of three ways of philosophizing, the others being the theological and the metaphysical. It is based on observation and experience and is anti-speculative in nature. In Comte's view, it is part of the modern revolution of the human mind; it is the true final state toward which human intelligence has been tending. In large measure, it is simply *science*, or natural philosophy, and in this respect it is not particularly new. By the time Comte began giving his lectures on the positive philosophy, natural science had enjoyed at least two centuries of uninterrupted development. What distinguishes the positive philosophy of Comte is its attempt to (a) articulate the fundamental principles of the basic theoretical sciences, (b) synthesize these into a single,

comprehensive system of ideas, and (c) apply the scientific methods that had been so successful in the natural sciences to the study of man and society (It was Comte who coined the word, "Sociology" in 1838).

Positive philosophy distinguishes itself from theological thinking by giving up the vain search for first and final causes, the "real" causes of phenomena, and studies only observable relations between and among things—the "invariable relations of succession and resemblance." These are to be discovered through the application of the scientific method. For Comte, scientific method meant (a) observation of facts with the guidance of a "preparatory theory," (b) experimentation, which in the social sciences most often meant controlled observation, (c) comparison, especially between different societies or different states of a society, and (d) historical method, which is unique to the biological and social sciences and pertains to the study of evolution. Apart from indicating such general scientific approaches to knowledge, Comte is not prepared to outline in detail any logic of scientific analysis. Methodology, for Comte, could not be separated from its application in the various sciences; it could not be examined as a subject in its own right. Comte leaves open the question of whether in the future it will be possible to "construct by *a priori* reasoning a genuine course on method, wholly independent of the philosophical study of the sciences." In the meantime, methodological procedures are to be chosen and evaluated on the basis of their proven results in the sciences. Comte, like many other positivists, had faith in the "givenness" of the phenomenal world.

Like all ways of philosophizing, Comte's positivism rests upon assumptions about the nature of the universe. Many of these are shared with other men of science in Comte's time and are part of the positivistic tradition in social theory. Comte shares with the positivistic tradition the view that the entire universe, including the social world, is governed by invariable natural laws which are external to man and independent of human volition. These laws are accessible to man through the application of the scientific method. Knowledge of man and society is to be derived with the same methods that have been so successful in the natural sciences.

The preceding, although it requires the introduction of another assumption, implies that all knowledge is part of one tree of knowledge, that the various sciences are related one to the other as branches of a common trunk. In Comte's view, the separation of the sciences is useful for analytic purposes and is necessary for their growth and development, but it is important not to lose sight of the unity of all rational knowledge. Early in his career, Comte proposed educational reforms that would lead to the training of a class of generalists whose responsibility it would be to prevent the splintering of knowledge that tends to occur with specialization.

Rational knowledge concerns itself with facts, and the strategy of science is to explain particular facts in terms of general facts, principles, and laws. The goal of science is to discover general laws and, further, to reduce these to the least possible number. The ideal goal would be to express all knowledge in terms of a single principle, such as Newton's law of gravitation. Comte quickly points out that it may never be possible to achieve this ideal, and he cautions against a premature search for an all encompassing single principle. At this stage of development it is necessary to ensure only that the scientific method be applied universally and that the general propositions derived in this manner be logically consistent with one another.

Comte, like all theorists, has to make some assumptions about what constitutes knowledge. For Comte, as well as for other positivists, knowledge is phenomenal, which is another way of saying that man can gain knowledge only about objects and occurrences which are directly observable to the human mind. Further, he can understand only the invariable relations between and among the phenomena observed and not their first, final, or "real" causes. Comte does not deny the existence of a transcendental order, the realm of the other-worldly; he simply regards it as inaccessible to human intelligence.

Only facts can be known, and these are to be discovered through the application of the scientific method. The assumption implicit in this view is that the distinguishing characteristics of phenomena are given in nature; rational knowledge is informed by a natural order, and science is self-correcting. But for Comte, these facts do not disclose themselves directly to the viewing mind; scientific observation is guided by theory. "If in contemplating phenomena we did not immediately connect them with some principles, not only would it be impossible to combine these isolated observations and, therefore, to derive any profit from them, but we should even be entirely incapable of remembering the facts, which would for the most part remain unnoted by us."

In Comte's view, facts are external to the viewing mind; the "human mind can observe all phenomena directly except its own." Mental phenomena can be understood, to be sure, but they are to be understood in terms of their observable results, as for example, in the progress of the sciences. Comte is opposed to all forms of speculative metaphysics and subjectivist psychology.

Facts are also linked to one another in definite ways. As noted, Comte is committed to the belief in the unity of phenomena in space and time. Accordingly, all phenomena, inorganic and organic, but especially the social, are linked in systems; organic and social systems evolve in definite ways in time. What this means is that objects and occurrences are to be explained not only in relation to other objects and occurrences but also, and more importantly, in relation to the whole or system of which they are component parts and in relation to the process that necessarily transforms them over time. Applied to the study of man and society, this means that individual human beings are not to be understood as unique entities but rather are to be considered as units of trans-individual, social wholes, and societies are to be explained not only in terms of their internal structure and organization (social statics) but also in terms of their history (social dynamics).

b) The Positive Polity

The normative and political system which Comte outlined in the **System of Positive Polity** during the second phase of his career brought him considerable disfavour among the same scientific community that had embraced so enthusiastically his positive philosophy. Yet in the opening chapter of the **Cours de Philosophie Positive** Comte makes very clear the social aims to which the positive philosophy is directed.

Comte was convinced that the social world was governed by ideas (Cf. Marx). Thus, the great political and moral crisis that characterized the societies of Western Europe during the early part of the nineteenth century, in Comte's view, was at bottom due to "intellectual anarchy." To put an end to this political instability and social chaos it would be necessary for all to agree upon a common set of general ideas. But, people's minds are confused, largely due to the presence and "simultaneous employment of three radically incompatible philosophies—the theological, the metaphysical, and the positive." While any one of these could sustain a social order, the presence of all three prevents agreement on the essential principles that govern social life.

The question is which philosophy shall it be that governs the lives of men. In Comte's view, it is the positive philosophy that is destined to prevail. "It alone has been making constant progress for many centuries, while its antagonists have been as constantly in a state of decay." The human mind has undergone a dramatic revolution in the course of history; increasingly, all knowledge becomes positive (i.e., scientific). The natural sciences are now based on positive principles; all that remains is to extend the positive philosophy to the study of social phenomena. Because the positive philosophy is rooted in nature, the universal principles derived in this manner will necessarily form a single, coherent set of general ideas which, in turn, will lead to a durable, stable social order.

In Comte's view, positivism would serve as the moral as well as the scientific foundation for the reorganization of society. Thus, Positivism would be the Religion of Humanity, as the subtitle of the **System of Positive Polity** suggests. In this work, Comte argues, among other things, that if positivism were understood and practised, egoism would be subordinated to altruism, and the development of humanity would be guided by universal love as it progressed toward its final resting state in the "Great Being."

Naturally, a Religion of Humanity requires a priesthood. During the latter years of his life, Comte proclaimed himself to be the High Priest of Humanity and with perfect positivistic logic worked out the details of the positive priesthood. It would consist of 20,000 sociologists, one for each ten thousand families in Western Europe, who would report to seven national chief priests, who in turn would be presided over by the High Priest himself. The priesthood would be expanded with the final conversion of the world to positivism.

These sociologist-priests would direct the educational process, advise on civil matters, evaluate candidates for positions in the positive society, foster feelings of love and benevolence in the community, act as moral censors, persuade men to fulfill their obligations and responsibilities, and research, teach, and preach the sociological gospel. To dissuade individuals from entering the priesthood for pecuniary reasons, Comte proposed that these sociologist-priests be paid very low salaries. When today's sociologists receive their monthly pay cheques, they often feel that somehow the works of Auguste Comte are still being read.

The Law of the Three Stages

Early in his career, Comte believed that he had discovered the "great fundamental law" of the "progressive growth of the human mind." Proof of this law could be found in an inductive study of history and/or in a deductive study of human intelligence. "This law consists in the fact that each of our principle conceptions, each branch of our knowledge, passes in succession through three different theoretical states: the theological or fictitious state, the metaphysical or abstract state, and the scientific or positive state." The first state, the theological state is the "necessary starting point of human intelligence" and the third, the positive, represents its "fixed and definite state;" the second state is transitional.

In the theological state, man's speculative faculties are directed toward a search for first and final causes, for absolute knowledge, and causality is attributed to supernatural agents. Comte reasoned that, in the dawning of history, man perceived phenomena and likened their actions to his own. Believing his own behaviour to be self-willed, he imagined these phenomena to be produced by the willful acts of supernatural beings. The seeming anomalies of the universe he attributed directly to the arbitrary intervention of these beings. Comte argues that man could not have developed a natural science in this state, because he lacked a preparatory theory that would guide his scientific investigations. Also, and equally important, primitive man, without a body of scientific truths to use to his advantage, would have been totally demoralized if he had believed that the universe was governed by immutable, natural laws.

The theological state evolves naturally through three stages, from fetishism, to polytheism, to monotheism. In the first stage, all phenomena are perceived to be governed by capricious individual supernatural beings. In the second stage, the mind becomes more organized, and the multitude of gods is divided into categories, each of which governs a certain phase of life. To resolve contradictions among the several gods, the system of deities is eventually organized into a hierarchy, with a single god at its head, a God who creates the universe and controls all phenomena. In the final stages of the theological state, a single God is seen as the creator of Nature. For the human mind it is but one small step from this stage to the next major stage in the development of human intelligence, the metaphysical state.

In the metaphysical state, which is "only a simple general modification of the first state," phenomena are explained in terms of abstract forces, real entities or personified abstractions, which are believed to be inherent in the phenomena themselves. Using this mode of reasoning, an explanation occurs when the phenomenon in question is assigned to its corresponding inherent abstract force or entity. Metaphysical reasoning simply involves the substitution of abstractions for supernatural beings. In Comte's view, the metaphysical state is transitional and serves simply to dislodge thought from the realm of the supernatural. In this state, explanations are still mystical, and man is not yet prepared to give up his search for first and final causes. The latter occurs in the positive state.

In the positive state, knowledge is scientific. The human mind realizes that it is impossible to obtain absolute truth and gives up its vain search for primary and essential causes. In Comte's words, it "endeavours . . . only to discover, by a well-combined use of reasoning and observation, the actual laws of phenomena—that is to say, their invariable relations of succession and likeness." Accordingly, particular phenomena are explained in terms of general facts, "the number of which the progress of science tends more and more to diminish." This inclination to generalize is characteristic of human intelligence and is itself an important factor in the movement of thought through the three stages.

Since the social world is governed by ideas, then it stands to reason that the different stages of the development of human intelligence must necessarily give rise to different forms of social life. Comte indeed argues that society too evolves through three stages—the militaristic, the legalistic, and the industrial. Each is sustained by a different philosophical system, and as philosophical systems change so do the forms of social life.

The militaristic society is hierarchically structured and is dominated by priests and warriors. God as the King of Kings decrees rules and sanctions which are strictly enforced by earthly rulers. The social order is maintained by conquest and military power, and slavery is its principle institution.

The legalistic society is dominated by lawyers, and its government is based on a doctrine of abstract "natural" rights, which replace the divine rights of kings. Social life is legalistic and formal and is characterized by criticism and argument. Industry begins to develop, and slavery becomes more indirect, but society is unstable, because it lacks a durable foundation and gives way to the industrial society.

The industrial society is based on science, and the social order is organized around the production of goods. But while the productive apparatus is governed by men of science and industry, the social order is informed by positive principles. Thus, economic activities are engaged in for the benefit of mankind. Philosophers (sociologist-priests), women, the working class, and the capitalists will each play a role in the maintenance and future development of society.

Comte was convinced that the societies of Western Europe, particularly France, had passed through the metaphysical stage and were about to establish themselves along the lines of the positive doctrine which he espoused. The positive doctrine was not only based upon scientific principles, which in themselves constitute an advancement in human intelligence, but was also a synthesis of the essential features of the two preceding stages of human development. Recognizing these to be "order" and "progress," Comte was convinced that the new philosophy would give rise to a durable and progressive social order.

The Law of the Three Stages also applies to the education and development of the individual. During childhood, the individual engages in theological speculation; during adolescence, his reasoning is metaphysical. When he matures and enters adulthood, he recognizes the true order of the universe and comes to reason like a positivist.

Hierarchy of the Sciences

While all knowledge ultimately passes through the three stages of development, the various branches of knowledge do not evolve simultaneously. Comte classified the abstract theoretical sciences according to (a) their order of evolution through the three stages, (b) their order of increasing dependence upon sciences previously developed, (c) their order of increasing specificity and decreasing generality, (d) their increasing complexity, and (e) their difficulty of scientific measurement and prediction. The result was a hierarchy of six sciences, with the sixth (social physics or sociology) being the latest to pass through the three stages, the most dependent upon the sciences that preceded it, the most specific in nature, the most complex, and the most difficult to study with the methods of science.

Hierarchy of the Sciences

6. Sociology
5. Biology (Physiology)
4. Chemistry
3. Physics
2. Astronomy
1. Mathematics

Comte was not the first to attempt an encyclopedic classification of human knowledge. It was a common practice among men of science during Comte's time, and there were several such schemas in existence during the early part of the nineteenth century. But it was not simply a fashionable thing to do, it was based on a firm belief in the unity of rational knowledge, i.e., that the various branches of knowledge are part of a common trunk. To classify the sciences in this manner would itself constitute a contribution to knowledge.

Comte's classification system is informed by a number of considerations. The system could not be based on any distinction among the various faculties of the human mind. The mind was in a state of disarray, due to the simultaneous presence of theological, metaphysical, and positive conceptions. But even if the mind were in a coherent state, that is, informed by a single philosophy, a classification system based on intellectual faculties would be contrary to the spirit of the positive sciences. In Comte's view: "the classification must proceed from a direct study of the objects to be classified, and must be determined by the real affinities and natural connections that they present." In other words, the classification system itself must be informed by nature, and not by man.

In deciding which branches of knowledge should be included, Comte made two sets of distinctions. First, he distinguished between theoretical and practical or applied knowledge. Applied sciences, such as medicine and engineering, while no less scientific in nature, are based on the theoretical sciences and draw on several of them simultaneously. Since the theoretical sciences are the foundation of rational thought, they alone can be classified rationally. Comte also distinguished between general, abstract sciences and specific, concrete sciences. Specific sciences, such as mineralogy, geology, and even botany, while theoretical in nature, are also based on the fundamental sciences—chemistry, physics, biology, etc. The basic scientific principles are to be found in the latter, and these sciences alone are included in Comte's classification system.

The Nature of Sociology

Sociology is the Queen of the Sciences, but it alone among the abstract theoretical sciences had not yet passed through the metaphysical stage into the positive. This was due largely to the fact that sociology, being the latest of the sciences, could not develop fully until all of the sciences lower in the hierarchy had reached their full potential as positive sciences.

Comte had hoped to make sociology scientific or at least to establish the groundwork for such a transition. The course in positive philosophy was a plea for the extension of the positive method to the study of social phenomena.

To be sure, social phenomena are more complex than the phenomena studied by other sciences. But, in Comte's view, the sciences constitute a "single body of homogeneous doctrine." Therefore, sociology is not qualitatively different from the other sciences and must be studied in the same manner. The main difference between sociology and the other sciences is that sociology, being the latest, is dependent upon the sciences that preceded it through the three stages. In Comte's view, sociology could not be fully understood until the student had acquired an adequate background in the other sciences. By an adequate background, Comte did not mean knowledge of all the highly specialized research in chemistry, physics, biology, etc., but rather, an appreciation of the basic theoretical principles underlying these sciences. Since these principles were discovered in a particular order, according to their dependence upon one another, they would have to be studied in the order of their development. To become a sociologist, one would have to study the theoretical sciences in the order in which they appear in the hierarchy. To Comte, sociology was no "bird" course!

Inspired by observations in the biological sciences, Comte divided sociology into two sub-fields—social statics and social dynamics. Just as we can distinguish the study of the structure of an organism and the functioning of its parts (physiology) from a study of growth and development, so we can distinguish between the study of social organization and the study of social evolution. Social statics is the study of the "laws of action and reaction of the different parts of the social system—apart for the occasion, from the fundamental movement which is always gradually modifying them." Social dynamics is the study of the laws of the "necessary and continuous movement of humanity." In Comte's view, the evolution of society was governed by natural laws, in the same way that the growth and development of an organism followed a definite and predictable course.

Comte was convinced that the natural development of humanity was progressive. Social dynamics then was a study of the laws of human development or, simply put, the Law of Progress. He was also convinced that the natural state of society was one of order. Social statics was a study of this presumed natural order. The dual focus of sociology then would be

Order and Progress. For Comte these are but two aspects of the same reality: in its essence, progress is "identical with order, and may be looked upon as order made manifest."

It is important to note that neither social statics or social dynamics is a study of society as it exists, i.e., as it existed in early nineteenth-century Western Europe. As we noted, the society of Auguste Comte was riddled with political and social crises, and it was difficult for many to see any progress in the developments that had occurred since the Revolution. Comte assumed that this state of affairs was temporary and transitory; it was not the natural condition of mankind. A sociology that began and ended with this state of affairs would be in error. In Comte's view, social anarchy is simply a consequence of the fact that people lacked true knowledge of the fundamental laws of social order and social progress. Comte's sociology would put an end to this anarchy by articulating the authentic social order toward which all societies are naturally tending.

The Theory of Cerebral Functions

Comte rooted his law of human development in the nature of man. In the closing chapters of Volume I of the **System of Positive Polity** he outlines what in essence is a theory of human nature.

Comte's theory of cerebral functions was inspired by Gall's cerebral physiology. According to Gall, the human brain was an assemblage of organs, some with intellectual and some with affective functions. According to this theory, the constituent elements of moral and mental life are direct functions of various differentiated but interrelated anatomical parts of the human brain.

Comte enlarged upon this theory and divided the brain into three broad categories of cerebral organs. Accordingly, the "three kinds of phenomena of which our life consists," variously referred to as "Intellect," "Affection," and "Activity," are innate in man and, although they are subject to some modification due to the interaction of the organism with the environment, they are the spontaneous sources of human action, and they determine those characteristics of our personality that differentiate us from others. According to Comte, the ten affective, five intellectual, and three practical cerebral organs are developed through constant exercise and are diminished and even atrophied by prolonged disuse.

The affective region, located in the posterior portion of the brain, is the chief source of spontaneity

and unity for the human organism. Less dependent upon the environment and virtually cut off from direct contact with external bodies, the affective organs provide the motive force for human action; they also determine the goals toward which the other faculties are to be directed. Intellect and Activity are weaker in intrinsic energy, but they have direct contact with the external world through the mechanisms of sensation and motion and can on occasion arouse the emotions. Though all three categories of cerebral organs have their own inherent tendencies and can stimulate each other, intra-cerebral stimulation is largely in the direction of Intellect and Activity. In Comte's view, intellectual and active faculties are brought into the service of the affective ones.

Unlike the Enlightenment thinkers who exalted the speculative faculties in man, Comte attributes primacy to the affective. When the affective faculties are weakened or inhibited, speculation becomes "vague and incoherent" and activity results in "disorderly agitation." In Comte's view: "We act from affection; we think in order to act."

While the affective faculties are the "wellsprings" of human conduct, they are not of one piece. Comte divides the affective faculties into two broad categories, one consisting of seven personal, "egoist" instincts, and the other made up of three social, "altruistic" drives. While both types provide vital energy for the organism, and while either can serve the purposes of "vital unity," the two types of affective faculties are in a state of constant antagonism.

While the two antagonistic forces exist naturally in the human organism, their coexistence creates disequilibrium in the individual. Personal equilibrium is possible only when one of the two predominates (it matters not which), but social order can be sustained only by a preponderance of the social, altruistic tendencies in our human nature. Comte believed that in the course of human history there has been an ascendancy of the latter. It was the explicit purpose of the Religion of Humanity to accelerate this natural evolutionary process tending toward the Positive Society.

For Comte, the acceleration of the natural historical process did not mean the suppression of personal desires; this was the mistake of the nineteenth-century socialists. For, "if there were no personal wants stimulated by the necessity of preserving life, our collective existence would be as objectless and undefined as the life of the individual." (Pos Pol:I, p. 558) Comte's "great problem" was "to raise social feeling by artificial effort to the position which, in the natural condition, is held by selfish feelings." And this can only be approximated. Positivism "will never, indeed, be able to do away with the fact that practical life must, to a large extent, be regulated by interested motives; yet it may introduce a standard of morality inconceivably higher than any that has existed in the past." (G.V., p. 41)

The Law of Human Progress

In Comtean social theory, the progress of humanity is as probable as any natural law, and men and society are the instruments of progress. While the historical process is not absolutely and totally determined—men can modify the intensity of order and the speed of social development—the direction and the course of progress are given in nature. Social and political crises do occur on occasion and appear to set the course of history in another direction, but they are not the primary determinants of history. They occur at key junctures in history to spur on the predetermined natural historical process and, in this way contribute to its progressive development.

What is the character of this natural law of history? Comte tells us that it is the law of the three stages, according to which the various branches of human knowledge, the education and development of the individual, and the evolution of social life invariably pass through three stages of development: the theological, the metaphysical, and the positive. Together, these developments constitute the progress of humanity.

To understand this natural law of history, we need to know at least two important characteristics. We need to know the end point toward which this historical process is naturally tending, and we need to know the motor of history or the mechanism that sustains the process. Both of these Comte derives from human nature, or, more precisely, his theory of human nature.

"Progress," writes Comte, "is only a more complete development of the pre-existing order" (G.V., p. 274). Order is given in nature. Comte assumed that nature cannot be in contradiction with itself, that there is harmony in nature. If this is so then the discordant elements of our personal and social lives must necessarily be temporal and "unnatural." With the actualization of the natural historical process, social discord and personal disunity will come to an end. It is the function of positivism to accelerate this process. Note the following:

Where in the past there was succession, in the future there must be co-existence, for all the social states of the past, though apparently contradictory, answered to so many wants or tendencies of human nature, and as such must be susceptible of harmony. So we verify the complete and exclusive competence of the Positive religion by virtue of its relative character for the ultimate regeneration of Humanity, to which all our aspirations will converge, each having lost the peculiar features which for the time placed it in opposition with the others. (**Pos. Pol.** IV, pp. 10–11)

In the Comtean system, man in a "state of nature" possesses "heterogeneous and often antagonistic tendencies," (G.V., p. 24) and therefore exists in a condition of personal disunity and social disharmony. It is the stated objective of the Religion of Humanity to unite in a permanent synthesis, on both the social and individual levels, the discordant tendencies of our human nature—to "bring the three primary elements of our nature into harmony." (G.V., p. 13) One of the necessary conditions is the subordination of the intellectual and active faculties to the affections. "Unity in our moral nature is . . . impossible, except so far as affection preponderates over intellect and activity" (G.V., p. 16). The other is the necessity of bringing the cerebral functions into harmony with the external world, since the latter is governed by invariable natural laws. "The true path of human progress lies . . . in furnishing external motives for those operations of our intellectual, moral and practical powers, of which the original source was purely internal" (G.V., p. 30). By providing correct knowledge of both human nature and the external order, Positivism will facilitate the natural historical process.

The individual enters Comte's world as a defective creature, naturally endowed with selfish tendencies which are greater in strength and persistence than the more noble social sentiments. "It is the fundamental defect of our nature, that intrinsically these [social] affections are far weaker than the selfish propensities connected with the preservation of our own existence" (G.V., p. 247).

In the course of history, our social sentiments gain ascendancy over our egoistic inclinations, but this is not achieved initially through the exercise of the rational faculties, since the latter in the primitive state simply respond to the demands of affective faculties—selfish or social—and lack the independence and spontaneity required to initiate social change. Rather, cooperative efforts (e.g., marriage), often motivated by selfish desires (e.g., sex), inadvertently stimulate the social sentiments, which in turn consolidate the resulting union, since functions and organs are "developed by constant exercise, and atrophied by prolonged inaction."

The growth of social sentiments, "though spontaneous, may be materially hastened by organized intervention" (**G.V.**, p. 102). Positivism addresses itself to this problem, which stated in terms of Comte's theory of human nature, is as follows: "To enable the three social instincts, with the aid of the five intellectual organs, to gain ascendancy over the impulse resultant from the seven personal propensities, restricting these latter to the necessary limits, so as to concentrate the three active organs on the furtherance of social interests." (**Pos. Pol.** I, pp. 592–93)

In the course of human development, the cerebral functions themselves undergo change; each in its own way passes through three stages in accordance with the fundamental law of progress. Thus, there are in the Comtean scheme of things three major laws of progress, one corresponding to each of the primary elements in the human constitution:

> The three preside, each in its due place, over the contemporaneous movements of the intelligence, the activity, and the feeling of man. The first law consists in the succession of the three states, fictitious, abstract, and positive, through which every understanding passes in all its conceptions without exception. . . . The second is a recognition of an analogous progression in human activity, which in its first stage is Conquest, then Defense, lastly Industry. The third law shows that man's social nature follows the same course; that it finds satisfaction, first, in the Family, then in the State, lastly in the Race, in conformity with the peculiar nature of each of the three sympathetic instincts. (**Pos. Pol.** IV, pp. 156–57)

It is largely under the influence of these laws that man and the social order undergo parallel transformations until they become united into one harmonious whole—the "Great Being."

The Great Being

The Great Being is *"the continuous whole formed by the beings which converge,"* a whole, "constituted by the beings, past, future, and present, which co-operate willingly in perfecting the order of the world" (**Pos. Pol.** IV, p. 27; emphasis in the original). It is simply Humanity—the whole human race as it actualizes itself in history. While Comte speaks of the Great Being as if it were a corporeal entity, it is clear that he

is referring to an ideal "pre-existing order" and its growth and development in the course of history. The Great Being is discernible in history, but it is not equivalent to history itself. We may regard the Great Being as the spiritual ideal toward which the progress of humanity has been and is tending.

Comte writes primarily of the progress of humanity [*l'humanité*] rather than of social evolution. But, in Comte's view, a society constituted according to Positivism is an "objective presentation" of the Great Being. Both the positive society and the Great Being reflect Comte's vision of collective life. And what was that vision?

Following in the footsteps of the French conservatives, de Bonald and de Maistre, Comte presents us with a holistic view of society and collective life. The free, autonomous and unbounded creature of the Enlightenment is, in Comte's view, nothing but an abstraction, and the natural rights of man are but mere metaphysical dogmas, neither of which is capable of supporting a true social order. To Comte, the pure unvitiated reason of the *philosophes* is insufficient for purposes of establishing a durable society and, in the absence of "affection" is meaningless, dispersive, incomplete and anarchic (**Pos. Phil.** II, p. 275ff). The entire Enlightenment period characterized by its metaphysical dogmas is repugnant to Comte, as it was to the French conservatives. In the minds of these thinkers the social chaos that followed the Revolution was a direct result of the ill-conceived anarchic social philosophies of the deluded Enlightenment thinkers—"doctors of the guillotine," Voltaire and Rousseau.

Comte declares that Positivism will "show us the impossibility of understanding any individual or society apart from the whole life of the race." He continues:

> We have but to look each of us at our own life under its physical, intellectual, or moral aspects, to recognize what it is that we owe to the combined action of our predecessors and contemporaries. The man who dares to think himself independent of others, either in feelings, thoughts, and actions, cannot even put the blasphemous conception into words without immediate self-contradiction, since the very language he uses is not his own. . . . [The Positive doctrine] . . . appeals systematically to our social instincts, by constantly impressing upon us that only the Whole is real; that the Parts exist only in abstraction. (**Pos. Pol.** I, pp. 177–78)

Society is a collective entity, "bound by laws of

her own," existing in space and time. Comte likened society to a biological organism with its own internal laws of organization and growth: "We have . . . established a true correspondence between the Statical Analysis of the Social Organism in Sociology and that of the Individual Organism in Biology (**Pos. Pol.** II, p. 239).

Just as a biological system cannot be reduced to its constituent organs, since the whole is qualitatively different from and greater than the sum of its parts, neither can society be reduced to individuals, not even for purposes of analysis. "A *society* . . . can no more be decomposed into *individuals*, than a geometric surface can be resolved into lines, or a line into points" (**Pos. Pol.** II, p. 153). From this point of view, an entity is indivisible except into component parts which are of the same character as the whole. For Comte, the smallest unit of analysis is the family.

In perfect agreement with the conservatives, Comte insists that society is logically and ethically, and in large measure, historically prior to the individual. Society not only provides the "inns and resting places" for the human soul, as Edmund Burke had maintained, but it also completes and makes meaningful our very existence as individuals. In Comte's

words, "no coherence, no dignity have been or are possible for the individual unless in subordination to some larger and composite existence. It is only in dependence on some such existence that we can satisfy our desire to perpetuate this transitory life, for we then link it to an imperishable being" (**Pos. Pol.** IV, p. 22). In the absence of complete subordination to the Great Being, man's "feelings would be ill-regulated, his thoughts incoherent, his actions mere sources of disorder" (**Pos. Pol.** IV, pp. 34–35).

Comte drew his inspiration from the conservatives, and, by likening society to an organism, anticipated the later social organists. Society is viewed as a collective organism comprised of interrelated parts which are united by the *consensus universel*, a characteristic of all systems. In the evolution of society, as in the development of the organism, structures and functions become increasingly differentiated at the same time that they become more harmoniously interrelated, thus enabling the unity to better achieve its common end. However, unlike some organicists, Comte believes that society differs from the biological organism by the fact that the latter is immutable, while the former is amenable to improvement if guided by scientific principles.

2

Herbert Spencer

Introductory Note

Throughout this chapter abbreviations are used to refer to other sections of the text. All references to other published materials appear in abbreviated form in parentheses. The following abbreviations have been used:

Statics   Herbert Spencer, **Social Statics**. New York: Robert Schalkenbach Foundation, 1954.

Principles   Herbert Spencer, **The Principles of Sociology** 3 vols. New York: D. Appleton and Company, 1910.

Barker   Sir Ernest Barker, **Political Thought in England, 1848 to 1914**. London: Oxford University Press, 1928

Carneiro   Robert L Carneiro (ed), **The Evolution of Society: Sections Herbert Spencer's Principles of Sociology**. Chicago: The University of Chicago Press, 1967.

Hofstadter   Richard Hofstadter, **Social Darwinism in American Thought**. Boston: The Beacon Press, 1955.

A Brief Biographical Sketch

Herbert Spencer was born in Derby, England on April 27, 1820. While he was one of nine children, he was the only one to survive infancy. He was a sickly child, and throughout much of his life he suffered from chronic neurasthenia. His middle-class parents were resolute non-conformists and Dissenters who were deeply committed to the values of individualism, liberalism, and egalitarianism in all matters pertaining to religion, society, and politics. Much of

Spencer's later writings reflect the influence of his family background.

His father was a private school teacher of mathematics and science who had very little faith in the teaching enterprise. He favoured self-education and encouraged Herbert to pursue his own studies of science and history. Except for a brief stay of three months in a private school in which his uncle was schoolmaster, Herbert received no formal education. He was self-taught or taught by his father and later his uncle at home. He tended to avoid the traditionally taught subjects and later admitted that he received a first-rate education only in mathematics. At a very early age Herbert focused his attention on general principles and logic and, as a result, developed his faculties of deductive reasoning.

Preferring intellectual freedom to formal education, Spencer chose not to go to university or pursue a university career. He never enrolled in a single course and, even after he had become an accomplished writer, he gave very few lectures. He regarded himself as "unfit" for the academic profession, and at the age of seventeen went to work for the London and Birmingham Railroad, where he displayed his interest in mechanics and eventually acquired the skill required to assume the responsibilities of a chief engineer. After eleven years with the railroad, Spencer resigned his position and accepted the editorship of the **Economist**. Four years later Spencer left the journal and decided to pursue a career as an independent writer. While Spencer never became wealthy, he was able to earn an adequate living as an independent writer, and he spent the remainder of his life pursuing his literary objectives.

Spencer never married, and he had very few close friends. Largely because of ill health, he spent many of his later years in virtual seclusion. He seldom left his home except to attend meetings, read periodicals, and play billiards at a few well known social clubs. In 1882, he visited the United States for a lecture tour, but ill health forced him to cancel many of the scheduled lectures. Despite his chronic illness which reduced his working day to a few hours, Spencer lived to the age of eighty-three. He died on December 8, 1903.

Spencer's Work

Spencer first gained attention for his article, "The Proper Sphere of Government," published in the **Nonconformist** in 1842. In this article Spencer argues that the adaptation of man to his material and social environment is a natural process and should not be interfered with by the actions and policies of government. The central idea of this article is the basis of the doctrine of *laissez faire* and it permeates much of Spencer's evolutionary theories. The year 1850 saw the publication of **Social Statics**, in which Spencer enunciates his First Principle of a system of ethics and outlines a series of natural rights. While this book is generally regarded as a glowing tribute to individualism, it also contains some of Spencer's early thoughts on social development.

Expressing his preference for cardinal principles and broad generalizations over detailed descriptions of phenomena, Spencer conceived of his universal theory of evolution in the decade that followed. The theory was constructed from two fundamental insights: that all matter evolves from a homogeneous to a heterogeneous state, and that the homogeneous state was inherently unstable. As we shall see later, it is this principle that largely informs Spencer's evolutionary theories, and it is the application of this principle to social phenomena that prompted critics to regard Spencer's substantive contributions to sociology as mere exercises of deductive reasoning.

In 1858, Spencer conceived of a grand scheme of applying the evolutionary idea to the fields of biology, psychology, sociology, and ethics, and in 1860 he announced his plan to write a ten-volume treatise synthesizing the cardinal principles of the organic and superorganic theoretical sciences. This later became known as the **Synthetic Philosophy** and was published in successive parts as follows: **First Principles of a New System of Philosophy** (1862); **Principles of Biology** (1864–1867), 2 volumes; **Principles of Psychology** (1870–1872), 2 volumes; **Principles of Sociology** (1876–1896), 3 volumes; **Principles of Ethics** (1879–1893), 2 volumes.

The Study of Sociology, initially intended as an introduction to **Principles of Sociology**, was published as an independent book in 1873.

While Spencer had little inclination to collect data himself, he realized in 1867, well before he began work on **Principles of Sociology**, that he would require a vast amount of ethnographic and historical data to substantiate a theory of social evolution. Thus, he hired a university graduate to extract materials from original sources and arrange them systematically according to a scheme which Spencer devised. Originally published in eight volumes as **Descriptive Sociology**, the data provide the supporting evidence for his generalizations in **Principles of Sociology**.

While few read Spencer today, his work was exceptionally well received during his lifetime in both Europe and America and played a very important role in the development of the social sciences. The influence of Spencer can be found in the works of Emile Durkheim, and, in the United States, Spencer's work may well have been the single most important factor in establishing sociology. As Charles Horton Cooley wrote in 1920: "I imagine that nearly all of us who took up sociology between 1870, say, and 1890, did so at the instigation of Spencer" (cited in Carneiro, p. x). Lester Ward, William Graham Sumner, Franklin Henry Giddings, and Albion Woodbury Small, the "Fathers of American Sociology" were inspired by Spencer, as were the leading figures in the world of business. There was a period in America, from the end of the Civil War to the turn of the century, when no educated person would admit to not having read Spencer.

Spencer and Comte

Spencer went to great lengths to deny his familiarity with Comte (indeed, he denied that anyone had influenced him in developing his theories), but there are a number of similarities between the two men. These could be accidental because both drew on knowledge of the theoretical sciences that was common at the time, and both attempted to synthesize the generally accepted scientific truths into a single, coherent philosophical system. In any event, Spencer claims that he had not read Comte until 1850, and he felt moved to write an article dissociating his work from that of Comte.

Similarities include the following: a) both saw the universe (inorganic, organic, and superorganic) as governed by invariable natural laws that could be understood by man; b) both agreed that the various branches of knowledge comprised an interdependent whole, and therefore were bound by a common set of principles; c) both felt that knowledge of natural laws could be acquired only though the use of positive methods, that science had to be based upon reason and comparison and freed of metaphysical speculation; d) both felt that social phenomena comprise an interdependent whole; e) both developed theories of evolution and progress; and f) both developed typologies of society.

There are also many differences between Spencer and Comte, and only a thorough comparison of their respective works would reveal all of them, but Spencer does identify what he considers to be the major points separating the Synthetic Philosophy from the Positive Philosophy. These are outlined in "Reasons for Dissenting from the Philosophy of M. Comte."

The Evolutionary Theories of Herbert Spencer

Spencer and Social Darwinism

Charles Darwin is generally regarded as the father of evolution, but Herbert Spencer's formulation of a theory of universal evolution clearly antedates the publication of **The Origin of the Species** by at least two years. Darwin and Wallace discovered the principle of natural selection and applied it to the evolution of organic species, whereas Spencer conceptualized the evolutionary process as a universal principle and applied it primarily to the evolution of human societies. Darwin and Spencer had considerable respect for one another, and on at least two occasions Darwin expressed his appreciation of Spencer's contributions to the development of evolutionary theory. It was Spencer who coined the phrase "survival of the fittest," and Darwin, in a letter to his colleague, Alfred Russell Wallace, indicated his preference for this expression of the selective process in nature over that of his own.

Regardless of who is considered to be the father of evolutionary theory, it is clear that as early as 1850 Spencer had some vision of a natural selective process that filtered out the unfit of the species. In **Social Statics** Spencer regards as a fact that "under the natural order of things, society is constantly excreting its unhealthy, imbecile, slow, vacillating, faithless members . . . (p. 289)." In 1852, seven years before the publication of **The Origin of the Species**, Spencer publicly rejected the notion of special creation and proposed an hypothesis of organic evolution. He also came close to recognizing the struggle for existence as a mechanism in the evolutionary pro-

cess. In an article published in **The Westminster Review** that year, Spencer writes:

> For as those prematurely carried off must, in the average of cases, be those in whom the power of self-preservation is the least, it unavoidably follows, that those left behind to continue the race are those in whom the power of self-preservation is the greatest—are the select of their generation. So that, whether the dangers of existence be of the kind produced by excess of fertility, or of any other kind, it is clear that, by the ceaseless exercise of the faculties needed to contend with them successfully, there is ensured a constant progress toward a higher degree of skill, intelligence, and self-regulation. (cited in Carneiro, p. xx)

The concept of universal evolution is systematically applied to human societies in Spencer's article, "Progress: Its Law and Cause," originally published in **The Westminster Review** in 1857.

Influenced by the writings of Thomas Robert Malthus (1766–1834), Spencer adopted the view that the pressure of subsistence upon population would have a beneficial effect on mankind. The struggle for existence, if unimpeded, would lead to progress, since those individuals with superior skills, intelligence, self-control, ability to adapt to technological changes, etc. would survive, while incompetents would fall by the wayside. Since Spencer accepted Lamarck's view that acquired characteristics and successful adaptations are inherited by succeeding generations, he reasoned that the process of natural selection would lead to a better civilization. This same process would also bring about moral perfection, since in Spencer's scheme of things, "all evil results from the non-adaptation of constitution to conditions (**Statics**, p. 54)." Spencer was persuaded that the "ultimate development of the ideal man is logically certain—as certain as any conclusion in which we place the most implicit faith; for instance, that all men will die (**Statics**, p. 59)."

Since evolution is a natural process, it must not be interfered with. Thus, Spencer denounced all forms of State interference in the lives of individuals and opposed such things as public education, state aid, poor laws, sanitation supervision, housing regulations, state protection of the ignorant from medical quacks, state banking, tariffs, and a governmental postal system. These, Spencer argues, would favour the unfit. In Spencer's view, "the whole effort of nature is to get rid of such, to clear the world of them, and make room for better (cited in Hofstadter, p. 41)."

While the notion of the survival of the fittest is the basic tenet of what has become known as Social Darwinism, the idea appears in at least three different forms in Spencer's work (Carneiro, p.xliv). In one of its forms, Social Darwinism refers simply to the natural selective process whereby inferior beings are eliminated from the human race. It follows from this view that the State should do nothing to ameliorate the conditions of those who are deemed to be unfit— the poor, the indigent, the ignorant, and the unhealthy.

In another form of Social Darwinism, the notion of the survival of the fittest is applied to society's economic institutions. The argument is that if individuals and corporations are left free to pursue their own self-interests in economic affairs, the resulting competition will weed out the unfit business enterprises and lead to prosperity and progress. The role of the State is simply to ensure that the terms of freely established contracts are observed and that individuals and corporations not infringe on the rights of others to pursue their self-interests. This is known as the doctrine of laissez-faire, and it had considerable appeal to American entrepreneurs and captains of industry prior to the turn of the present century.

In its third form, the idea of natural selection is applied to whole societies. Spencer argues that through the mechanism of warfare superior forms of social organization endure and flourish, while unfit societies perish. The establishment of the state is largely attributed to success in warfare, and warfare is regarded as one of the most important factors in the creation of large, highly organized, complex societies. In Spencer's view, many features of a nation's social, political, economic, and religious institutions are directly attributable to the creative effects of warfare. It is clear that Spencer had no foreknowledge of the destructive capabilities of nuclear weapons.

The Universal Law of Evolution

Underlying the theory of social evolution which Spencer first presented systematically in 1857 in "Progress: Its Law and Cause" and later more fully developed in the three volumes of **Principles of Sociology** is a cosmic principle which, in Spencer's mind, applied to all matter—inorganic, organic, and superorganic. This is the law of universal evolution, and it is enunciated in **First Principles**.

The law of universal evolution is phrased in abstract terms and is built upon a set of established principles in physics—indestructibility of matter, persistence of force, continuity of motion—and four

corollaries derived from these principles. The law states that: "Evolution is an integration of matter and concomitant dissipation of motion; during which matter passes from a [relatively] indefinite, incoherent homogeneity to a [relatively] definite, coherent heterogeneity; and during which the retained motion undergoes a parallel transformation."

What this means is that all phenomena move from a state in which the parts are essentially alike both in structure and function to a state in which the parts become increasingly differentiated and functionally specific. At times Spencer appears to argue that the homogeneous state of matter is inherently unstable; in which case it would follow that universal evolution is an absolute necessity. However, in the fourth edition of **First Principles**, Spencer claims that the law works only when favouring conditions are present; historically conditions may arise which inhibit and even reverse the evolutionary process. That progress has occurred simply points to the fact that conditions conducive to it have prevailed. The latter understanding of the law is consistent with Spencer's substantive theories of evolution, whereby evolution is explained in terms of mutual adaptation of internal and external factors.

The law of universal evolution may be regarded as a summary statement of Spencer's "Cardinal Principles," which he published in 1884 to distinguish his **Synthetic Philosophy** from the Positive Philosophy of Auguste Comte. In this short essay, Spencer outlines the "leading propositions" which underlie his encyclopedic synthesis of scientific knowledge. From an examination of these principles, we can see that the law of universal evolution is the foundation of Spencerian social and political theory.

The Law of Social Evolution

The Law of Social Evolution is a specific application of the universal law to the evolution of human society. In Part II of Volume I of **Principles of Sociology**, Spencer compares the evolution of society to the growth and development of a biological organism. He summarizes their common features and notes that society:

undergoes continuous growth. As it grows, its parts become unlike: it exhibits increase in structure. The unlike parts simultaneously assume activities of unlike kinds. These activities are not simply different, but their differences are so related as to make one another possible. The reciprocal aid thus given causes mutual dependence of the parts. And the mutually dependent parts, living by and for one another, form an aggregate constituted on the same principle as is an individual organism. (Sp 4.5, p. 59)

Thus, as a society evolves it experiences increasing size, increasing structural and functional differentiation, increasing interdependence of parts, and increasing coherence and integration.

Societies grow in size not simply through natural increases in population, but, more importantly, through the "aggregation and reaggregation" of smaller societies. Coalescence of smaller societies into larger nation-states occurs largely through warfare. Primitive hordes are undifferentiated headless clusters which acquire structure through union with other tribes. The different tribes assume different functions, and an organization of unlike parts begins to form. Structural differentiation continues partly in response to variations in local circumstances but mostly as a consequence of the compounding process. In any event, differentiation proceeds from the general to the specific: "First the broad division between ruling and ruled; then within the ruling part divisions into political, religious, military, and within the ruled part divisions into food-producing classes and handicraftsmen; then within each of these divisions minor ones, and so on (Carneiro, p. 214)." Along with structural differentiation occurs differentiation and specialization of functions. Parts become increasingly unable to perform the functions of other parts and, therefore, become mutually dependent upon one another. The result is increased coherence and integration.

In Spencer's view, the activities of society are organized into systems, initially into two broad systems—the sustaining and the regulating. The sustaining system organizes efforts to provide the necessities of life; these may be regarded as economic or productive activities. As such they are shaped by the character of the inorganic and the organic environment. The regulating system is largely concerned with relations of society with its superorganic environment, essentially with environing societies. Since these are habitually hostile during early stages of development, the regulating system is concerned with matters of offence and defence. Activities governed by this system are primarily military in nature. The extent to which one or the other of these systems predominates determines the character of the society.

As society evolves and becomes increasingly complex in structure, a third system of activities emerges to sustain the activities of the initial two systems. This is the distributing system, and it mobilizes efforts required to transfer goods and services from one sector of society to another. Transportation systems, communication networks, and the like, become increasingly important in the maintenance and survival of society as it grows in size and becomes compounded in structure.

Militant and Industrial Societies

Societies are classified by Spencer in two ways, the first of which is according to their "degrees of composition." Societies are either simple, compound, doubly-compound, or trebly-compound, depending on the extent to which they are internally differentiated and organized. Social evolution begins with simple, undifferentiated societies and continues through the compounding process until it reaches the full-blown complex, modern nation-state. According to this schema, societies are differentiated one from the other in terms of the *degree* of social organization.

Spencer also classifies societies according to the *kinds* of activities that predominate in them. Societies are typed as either militant or industrial, depending on whether their activities are organized primarily for purposes of offence and defence or primarily for the production of goods and services. In the first type, the regulating system prevails, and all efforts, including those of the economic institutions, are mobilized for purposes of survival or expansion. In the industrial type, the sustaining system predominates, and efforts are focused on the productive process, in order to ensure prosperity and material progress.

In reality a society is never entirely one or the other type, since both regulating and sustaining activities are essential to the survival of the social organism. However, one or the other system of activities will predominate and will influence in a very profound way the character and structural features of society. To illustrate these differences, Spencer draws a sharp contrast between these two types of societies, but it is clear that this typology is intended to be used for analytic and comparative, and not purely descriptive purposes. Militant and industrial societies are what Weber would call "ideal types" (Cf. Weber).

Spencer describes the militant type of society as "one in which the army is the nation mobilized while the nation is the quiescent army . . . (**Principles** I, p. 557)." Society, including its institutions, is organized along military lines, even during times of peace. A militant society is characterized by strong centralized control, a hierarchical governing structure with an autocratic head, strict discipline and compulsory compliance among citizens as well as warriors, and the complete subordination of the individual to the State.

An industrial society possesses the following features: authority is decentralized, and functions are regulated by a plurality of governing agencies representing the citizens; there is less need for government as organizations and institutions are free to pursue their individual goals; cooperation is voluntary, and individuals are free to establish contractual relations for their mutual benefit; industry flourishes, and the division of labour is extended naturally; and the State is organized for the benefit of the individuals.

In Spencer's view, early societies tend by and large to be militant. If they are peaceful, they will necessarily develop into a militant type if they are to grow in size and progress. However, in the course of subsequent social evolution, industry is developed and the militant tendencies are attenuated. While a number of conditions can facilitate or inhibit the evolutionary process, conditions such as the entrenchment of caste-like social structures, remnants of earlier historical periods, peculiarities of the physical and organic environment, and the posture of environing societies, the general course of social evolution is to produce the industrial society.

The Mechanism of Human Progress

Spencer maintained that all discrete phenomena—animate or inanimate, individual or aggregate—are propelled by intrinsic forces and are, at the same time, subject to the forces external to them. Thus, they tend to evolve toward a state of mutual adaptation. In the process, both the entity in question and its environment undergo "progressive modifications." This process continues until some predestined state of equilibrium is reached.

The principle of mutual adaptation is applied by Spencer to the evolution of man and society. Spencer imagines man in the dawning of history to be solitary and self-sufficient and subject only to the conditions of organic life. In time he is forced by the pressures of population growth to surrender his solitary existence and to originate the social state, which in turn becomes one of the external conditions to which he is subject. In the course of evolution, the constitution of the individual and the organization of society are transformed until they are brought into accord in an equilibrated state. Spencer imagines this state to be one in which a morally perfect individual lives in harmony with his fellow creatures in a perfectly integrated social system.

Spencerian man is endowed with certain faculties essential to life and conducive to pleasure which, in accordance with the Divine Will, must be constantly exercised to reap fulfillment (**Statics**, pp. 67–68). Deeply rooted in man is a natural impulse which seeks, on the one hand, to maximize individual gratification ("instinct of personal rights" or self-instinct) and, on the other, to recognize the limits and constraints necessary for the like fulfillment of others ("sympathy" or social instinct). In the course of history man experiences evil and misery resulting largely from the "non-adaptation of constitution to conditions," but where "this non-adaptation exists it is continually being diminished by the changing of constitution to suit conditions (**Statics**, p. 57)." The measure of progress is the extent to which the fundamental impulse is actualized, wherein the natural rights of man—liberty, property, speech, etc.—are respected and the social conditions favouring their complete realization occur with greater regularity.

It is clear from the preceding that Spencer provides us with a mechanism to account for ethical and moral progress. Through a process of natural selection and mutual adaptation, the inherent goodness of mankind is actualized and society attains the civilized state. "Regarded thus, civilization no longer appears to be a regular unfolding after a specific plan, but seems rather a development of man's latent capabilities under the action of favorable circumstances; which favorable circumstances, mark, were certain sometime or other to occur (**Statics**, p. 372)."

Individualistic View of Man and Society

Though Spencer did not initially use the term "individualism" to describe his political philosophy and social theory, his anti-Statist posture nevertheless earned him a reputation as a "staunch individualist" and one of the "most extreme defenders of liberalism, individualism, and *laissez faire* (Simon)." It was precisely this individualism that appealed to early American sociologists and endeared him to such ideological protagonists of capitalism and as Andrew Carnegie and Edward Youmans and such industrialists as James J. Hill and John D. Rockefeller (Hofstadter, pp. 31–50).

In the "Introduction" to **Social Statics**, Spencer makes clear his fundamental starting point: "There is no way of coming at a true theory of society but by inquiring into the nature of its component individuals (p. 17)." Spencer argues that it is a fact of nature that the character of an aggregate is a function of the properties of the individual units, and human aggregations are no exceptions. He seems to reject any notion of society as a reality *sui generis*. He writes: "The characteristics exhibited by beings in an associated state cannot arise from the accident of combination, but must be the consequences of certain inherent properties of the beings themselves (Statics, p. 17)." Social and political institutions are but manifestations of "sentiments," "desires," and other innate characteristics "existing in each of us." It is this view of society and its institutions that Durkheim will find necessary to criticize in **The Division of Labor in Society**.

Spencer builds his "true social philosophy" on the premise of individual man. He insists that:

> the first principle of a code for the right ruling of humanity in its state of *multitude* is to be found in humanity in its state of *unitude*; that the moral forces upon which social equilibrium depends are resident in the social atom—man; and that if we would understand the nature of those forces and the laws of that equilibrium we must look for them in the human constitution. (**Statics**, p. 18)

Through this mode of reasoning, Spencer arrives at his First Principle, namely that: "Every man has freedom to do all that he wills, provided he infringes not the equal freedom of any other man." From this principle automatically flows a series of individual natural rights: "life and personal liberty," "use of the earth," "property," "property in ideas," "property in character," "right of exchange," "free speech," "rights of women and children," and the "right to ignore the State."

An individualistic view of man and society is also to be found in Spencer's later works, including his sociological writings. In **The Study of Sociology**, Spencer uses the example of a heap of cannon-shot to demonstrate the general truth—which "evidently holds of societies as of other things"—"that the character of the aggregate is determined by the character of the units (pp. 43–45)." In his major contribution to sociology, **Principles of Sociology**, Spencer accounts for the rise and development of society largely in individualistic terms. He divides the "primary factors of social phenomena" into two sets: extrinsic and intrinsic. The former includes the physical environment, climate, flora, and fauna, but not the "social aggregate." Individual man, or, more precisely, his physical, emotional, and intellectual traits constitute the intrinsic factor. In the initial chapters of Volume I, Spencer assumes a self-sufficient, autonomous individual that is historically and logically prior to society. This pre-social creature responds to the conditions of life—inorganic and organic—and "creates" society—the realm of the super-organic—which then, and only then, becomes a condition of his future existence. In the course of evolution both man and society are transformed. The social theory that accounts for this transformation begins with man himself.

As these examples show, Spencer's social and political theories are informed by an individualistic conception of man and society. But, while this is indeed true, it is at the same time a one-sided interpretation of Spencer's work. Spencer's fame is no less based on his conception of society as an organism. Indeed, it is the latter that has earned Spencer a rightful place in textbooks on sociological theory. In the next section, we examine Spencer's holistic conception of man and society.

The Organic Analogy

To the question, "What is society?" the "staunch individualist" answers: "A society is an organism." And like the biological organism, the social organism is an entity in its own right—"the individuality of the whole as distinguished from the individualities of its parts"—and is subject to its own laws of organization and growth. In a manner not entirely unlike that of Emile Durkheim, Spencer writes: "Hence arises in the social organism, as in the individual organism, a life of the whole quite unlike the lives of the units; though it is a life produced by them (**Sp** 4.5)."

In the early chapters of Part II of Volume I of **Principles of Sociology** (**Sp** 4.5–4.8), Spencer outlines the similarities and differences between a social organism and a biological organism. *Similarities*: a) the biological organism and society differ from inorganic matter in that both undergo growth; b) the increase in size of living organisms is accompanied with increase in structural and functional differentiation (i.e., increased complexity); c) increase in differentiation is accompanied with increased integration and interdependence ("changes in the parts are mutually determined, and the changed actions of the parts are mutually dependent."); d) in both the organism and society the individual parts have some independent existence (when the whole is destroyed the parts will live on for awhile). *Differences*: a) in the biological organism the parts comprise a concrete whole; in the social organism the parts comprise a discrete whole (parts are free to some extent and relatively dispersed); b) in the biological organism consciousness is concentrated in one part of the whole; in the social organism consciousness is diffused throughout the parts; and c) in the biological organism the parts exist for the benefit of the whole; in the social organism, the whole exists for the benefit of the parts.

There is considerable controversy over whether this analogy is to be taken literally or whether it is to be used as a scaffolding or model from which testable hypotheses are to be derived. It is clear that Spencer uses the terminology of organicism. Note the following: "So completely is society organized on the same system as an individual being that we may perceive something more than an analogy between them; the same definitions of life apply to both." But he concludes his discussion of the parallelism between the biological organism and the social organism by stating: "I have used the analogies elaborated, but as a scaffolding to help in building up a coherent body of sociological inductions. Let us take away the scaffolding; the inductions will stand by themselves."

Whether the organic analogy is to be taken literally or regarded as a scaffolding, it is clear that in the discussion noted above Spencer views society as a *system* of functionally interdependent parts. In this conception, society is seen as a whole that cannot be reduced to or derived from the individuals that comprise it. It is this conception that clashes with the individualistic view of man and society outlined in the previous section.

Was Spencer unaware of the difference between these two conceptions of social life? Hardly, since he opens his discussion of the organic analogy with a clear statement of the "controversy between nominalism and realism." Was the organic conception of society a view he held at one point in his career and not another? Not really, for it is visible in both his early works and his later writings. How are we to make sense of this seeming inconsistency?

Sir Ernest Barker, one of the leading authorities on Spencer, points out that Spencer was subject to varied and competing influences and embodied these in his theories. From his early upbringing in the English Radical tradition and from his association with Thomas Hodgskin, Spencer acquired a distaste for collective authority and an ethical preference for the individual; for the German idealist tradition, which he acquired from a reading of Coleridge, Spencer derived the notion of a transcendental life force, whereby nature and society are envisioned as living organisms evolving toward some predestined end. These views are based on diametrically opposed conceptions of man and society, and, according to Barker, Spencer was unable to reconcile them in his writings. In Barker's view, Spencer is unable to overcome a "fundamental confusion," resulting from the "fact that the *a priori* conceptions of individual rights with which he starts do not and cannot accord with the organic and evolutionary conception of the State." Thus Barker describes Spencer's philosophy as an "incongruous mixture of Natural Rights and physiological metaphor" (Barker, p. 71).

Spencer and Functionalism

As Parsons notes in the "Preface" to **The Study of Sociology** Spencer's view of society is close to that of modern day functionalism. Functionalism (or Structural-functionalism) is a theoretical viewpoint which is based on a conception of society as a system of functionally interdependent parts which is or seeks to be in equilibrium. Spencer shares at least three notions with this tradition.

First, Spencer considers society to be a *self-regulating system* comprised of factors which are interrelated and in balance. Changes in one part of the system necessarily have repercussions on other parts; this is followed by a mutual readjustment of the parts so that the equilibrium of the whole is preserved. Second, as we have seen above, Spencer considers societies to be *structurally differentiated*, with each of the parts performing a different function. Spencer also notes that the parts become increasingly unlike one another as societies evolve. Third, Spencer accepts the view that society seeks to be in a state of *equilibrium.* "Equilibration" is a natural tendency of the evolutionary process. It is a movement toward equilibrium, the ultimate end point toward which society is tending. At that point structural differentiation reaches its limit, and a stable, harmonious, perfectly adapted social state is attained. While most functionalists today reject evolutionary theories, they accept the notion that society is a system in equilibrium.

3

Karl Marx

An Intellectual Biography

Karl Marx was born on May 5, 1818 in Trier (Trèves), a German town on the border with Belgium and Luxembourg, and died on March 14, 1883 in London, England. He was classically trained in the German Gymnasium, and he studied law at the universities in Bonn and Berlin. In 1838, however, intoxicated with the philosophy of Hegel[1] Marx discontinued his legal studies (to his father's displeasure) and threw himself instead into the difficult work of mastering the arcane texts of the Hegelian philosophy. (Although Hegel had been dead since 1831, Marx studied under some of the master's most brilliant protégés.) It was this initial encounter with the thought of Hegel, with the highly charged 'dialectical' amalgam of logic and history, which fashioned the foundation upon which Marx was to develop theoretically over the course of the succeeding decades. Time and again, before beginning some complicated project, e.g., the writing of his *magnum opus* Capital, Marx re-read Hegel's **Science of Logic**.

Having submitted his doctoral dissertation to the University in Jena in April 1841 (on the "Difference Between the Democritean and Epicurean Philosophy of Nature"), Marx became centrally involved in the philosophical, political and social debates then current. His 'allies' were young intellectuals, who, like himself, had been touched by the mind of Hegel.

George Wilhelm Friedrich Hegel

Marx's relationship to Hegel was a complicated and ambivalent one. On the whole, he asserted the greatness of Hegel's thought and, in writing **Das Kapital**, reminded his readers that he declared himself to be a "pupil of that mighty thinker" when it was no longer fashionable to do so.[2] Throughout the *corpus* of his work, the positive comments on Hegel significantly outweigh the critical references. In Marx's mature writings we see that he viewed his own method as a *rational* appropriation of Hegel's. On account of this important link between the two thinkers, it is necessary to review those elements of Hegel's thought which appealed to Marx and which he re-worked in the course of his intellectual development.

Hegel and the philosopher Friedrich Wilhelm Joseph Schelling developed different versions of what has come to be known in the history of philosophy as *objective idealism*, which sought to address the critical problems of the *subjective idealism* of Immanuel Kant and Johann Gottlieb Fichte.

Immanuel Kant began his philosophical odyssey with an attempt to overcome the scepticism of the David Hume, who, in his **Enquiry Concerning Human Understanding** demonstrated that the relations of cause and effect in human experience are not an element of objective reality, are not universal and necessary, but are merely a habit of the mind. In his **Critique of Pure Reason**, Kant, asking the question "how is knowledge possible?" drew a distinction between the intuited object (the object as it appears

---

1 Georg Wilhelm Friedrich Hegel (1770–1831) was the last, and arguably the greatest of the German idealist philosophers.

2 "The mystifying side of the Hegelian dialectic I criticized nearly thirty years ago, at a time when it was still the fashion. But just as I was working at the first volume of 'Das Kapital,' it was the good pleasure of the peevish, arrogant, mediocre who now talk large in cultured Germany, to treat Hegel in the same way as the brave Moses Mendelssohn in Lessing's time treated Spinoza, i.e., as a 'dead dog.' I therefore openly avowed myself the pupil of that mighty thinker, and even here and there, in the chapter on the theory of value, coquetted with the modes of expression peculiar to him. The mystification which dialectic suffers in Hegel's hands, by no means prevents him from being the first to present its general form of working in a comprehensive and conscious manner. With him it is standing on its head. It must be turned right side up again, if you would discover the rational kernel in the mystical shell." **Capital**, pp. 19–20.

to us through the organization of the sensory data by the mind) and the object as a "thing-in-itself" which is by definition unknowable. Time and space are simply intuitions of the mind and cause and effect is not a relation of objects, conditions of extra-human reality, but are among the categories of the human mind, the ordering principles of sense perception. This fundamental dualism which drove a wedge between subject and object and ultimately between mind and nature led Kant into a series of antimonies and contradictions. He could not establish the rational character of the universe through his epistemological dualism of subject and object. Nevertheless, Kant held to the notion of a rational constitution of the universe and historical development, but he did so on the basis of faith since such a rational harmony could not be established empirically or otherwise fathomed by the mind.

Hegel attempted to solve the problems associated with this dualism by means of the concepts of the Absolute (which he borrowed from Spinoza via Schelling) and the creative Ego (which he took from Fichte). The starting point for Hegel is neither the individual mind confronting an alien reality, nor a cosmic Mind or Spirit[3] confronting nature. Rather, subject and object, Mind and Nature are differentiations within the same whole. If subject and object confront one another as alien, as in subjective idealism, it is because Mind is alienated within itself, viz., it does not know itself as all of reality. But Mind is not static; it is dynamic and the source of its dynamism is precisely this self-alienation. (In his early works Hegel referred to this as *Entzweihung*, or the rending in two of Mind—in the English translation this appears as *diremption*, from the Latin *diremptio*—to tear). Mind finds this diremption an obstacle to its self-understanding and it does not recognize itself in its alien mode.

Matter, which is an expression of Mind, confronts it as something foreign, external, other i.e., lacking reason. But it is precisely this obstacle to its self-understanding which drives Mind forward and this forward movement is given expression in history. What we view as history and historical progress, Hegel saw as the expression of Mind's growing conscious of self. And since the essence of Mind is

thinking, and since thinking is free, Mind develops insofar as it becomes increasingly conscious of its own freedom. In other words, as Mind overcomes its self-alienation, it becomes more and more conscious of its freedom and this is reflected in human institutions which are but the embodiments of Mind at different stages of its development. At the end of history—which Hegel considers to be the chronicle of Spirit's march through the world—Mind, as the Absolute knows itself as all of reality.

In his **Philosophy of History**,[4] Hegel followed the course of Mind's development as it embodied itself in dominant cultures in different epochs. Since human history represents an embodiment of Mind at the various stages of its development, in overcoming its self-alienation, the different cultures in human history give expression to different degrees of the consciousness of freedom. Ancient Chinese civilization, for example, gave expression to a low degree of consciousness of freedom since only one person, i.e., the emperor, was free and all others were his slaves. Classical antiquity, the civilization of ancient Greece and Rome, on the other hand, represented a higher level of Mind's consciousness of it's freedom, since we now find a whole class of people who are free, even if the majority are in some form or other of servitude. In modern Europe, freedom has been realized universally, but only as a formal matter—a matter of political and legal right. In Hegel's words:

> The Orientals have not attained the knowledge that Mind—man *as such*—is free; and because they do not know this, they are not free. They only know that *one is free.* But on this very account, the freedom of that one is only caprice . . . that *one* is therefore only a Despot, not a free man. The consciousness of freedom first arose among the Greeks, and therefore they were free; but they and the Romans likewise, knew only that *some* are free—not man as such . . . The Greeks, therefore, have slaves; and their whole life and the maintenance of their splendid liberty, was implicated with the institution of slavery . . . The German nations, under the influence of Christianity, were the first to attain the consciousness, that man, as man, is free: that it is the *freedom* of Mind which

---

3 The term which Hegel used in German, *Geist*, has been variously rendered as 'Mind' or 'Spirit' in English. Neither word captures the German accurately. The word 'Mind' refers to a matter of individual psychology and the word 'Spirit' implies something religious. Neither of these meanings is necessarily implied in the German.

4 In the **Philosophy of History** Hegel follows the development of Spirit as it achieves concrete embodiment in different historical epochs. In his **History of Philosophy**, he outlines the process whereby Mind contemplates its own development. Philosophy is the self-reflection of Mind, or, as Hegel expressed it in his **Philosophy of Right**: "philosophy is its own time apprehended in thought."

constitutes its essence. Marcuse, **Reason and Revolution**, p. 235.

Yet Hegel recognized that the substance of freedom was wanting. It was this lack of substantive freedom in modern civil society, viz. the substantive freedom of the class of social labour that Marx addressed in a more concrete fashion as we shall see.

Ludwig Feuerbach

Before we move to consider the relationship between Marx and Hegel further, there is one thinker whose works made an impact upon Marx and his Left-Hegelian contemporaries: Ludwig Feuerbach. In opposition to Hegel, and indeed, to the thrust of modern German philosophy, Feuerbach declared himself to be a materialist and humanist. Subjecting Hegel's philosophy of mind to scrutiny, Feuerbach argued that Hegel had simply translated into high philosophical jargon the conceptualization of reality and history proffered by Christianity. According to Feuerbach, Mind or Spirit is simply an abstract philosophical word for God and the story of Spirit's march through the world is nothing other than the biblical story of the creation. The alienation of Spirit from itself is but the alienation of God and man, Spirit and Nature. Hegel has simply poured the old wine of religion into the new bottle of German idealist philosophy. Instead of God creating man, Feuerbach understands God to be a figment of the human imagination. Thus, theology which presents the creative force in the universe to be that of God is to be replaced by humanism, according to which humanity is the creative force in the world. Human beings have created God because they have not recognized themselves as the great creative power. This failure to recognize themselves in this way stems from the fact that human nature is centred in the species, human being is a species-being (*Gattungswesen*) which stands opposed to each singular individual.[5] This distancing of ourselves from our species nature is the source of our positing a God who represents the alienated power of our species. We must, in order to unite with our own creative source, change our consciousness about how we view the relationship between God and man. If we could come to the realization that we create God because we are disunited from our true nature, then we could reclaim that power and develop ourselves as robustly human. As long as we are enslaved to the imaginary creatures of our minds (i.e., God, Angels, etc.) we will never realize our truly human potential.

One might have expected Marx to have applauded Feuerbach's 'materialistic' savaging of Hegel, all the more so since Marx had suggested in **Capital** that Hegel had stood the dialectic on its head. And yet Marx came down on the side of Hegel writing that "in comparison with Hegel Feuerbach is poor." If we can understand why Marx considered Hegel to be a richer thinker than Feuerbach, we will have come a long way in grasping Marx's own understanding of theory and method.

What was Feuerbach's accomplishment in his critique of Hegel's mysticism, according to Marx? It was simply a matter of replacing one word—"God"—with another word—"Man" (*der Mensch*)[6] But according to Marx both these words are empty abstractions and have the same 'empty' status. That God is an empty abstraction for Marx is clear, but why does "Man" have that same status? It is precisely here that Hegel's superiority to Feuerbach is evident. Hegel understood that human beings differ according to their respective cultures—the ancient Chinese were different from the old Greeks and Romans who were in turn different from modern Europeans. Hegel knew, and Marx followed him in this, that the category "Man" was an abstraction. There is no actual historical concretion of generic human being. There are only communities of people in different times and different places who differ from one another according to their environment, relations to nature, relations to one another, relations to peoples of surrounding societies, etc. It is not unlike language. No one speaks "language" even though every human neonate may have the capacity to speak some language or other. People speak or have spoken, Paleo-Canaanite, Babylonian, ancient Greek, Latin, Swahili, Russian, English, Inuktituk, and various dialects of these. We can, of course, and we do, use the word "language" to describe these phenomena, but we use it as a convenient abstraction and never confuse the abstraction with the concretions.

---

5 This notion of 'species-being' applied to human nature is already foreshadowed by Hegel, a point which is made both by Lukács (1972) and Marcuse (1969).

6 There is no English equivalent for the gender neutral term *Mensch* in German. In classical Greek the term ανθροπο, anthropos, referred to men and women indifferently. French is also lacking in such a non-gender specific term. Human being is too abstract and would be used to translate the German *Menschenwesen* or *menschliches Wesen*. We will use the term "Man" or "men" where the German *Mensch* or *Menschen* is indicated.

The Young or Left-Hegelians

The "Young Hegelians" (or Left Hegelians) considered themselves to be the philosophical champions of a new revolutionary Spirit which was in the process of overturning the relations of an outmoded and decrepit world of institutions, customs, traditions, and authority. In general, they were transfixed by the negative force of the Hegelian dialectic,[7] the movement of overcoming the old in the process of establishing the new. It is a testimony to Hegel's greatness that the radicals on the left and the conservatives on the right both felt at home with the concepts of his philosophy. The former were attracted to the dialectical movement of supersession, the latter to the Hegelian system with its apotheosis of the present; the one to historical overcoming, the other to historical realization, both to the concept of Reason. The battleground between the two schools of Hegelianism was the field of religion. Marx remarks at the beginning of the **German Ideology** that the two wings of Hegelianism were in agreement concerning the centrality of religion; but whereas the conservatives saw in religion the true bonds of humanity, the radicals understood it to be the fetters upon human development.

At this time, Marx began writing and publishing critical articles in the radical newspaper, the **Rheinische Zeitung** (a publishing outlet for the Young Hegelians), and in October 1842 he was made editor of the paper. Shortly thereafter the paper was suppressed by the authorities, even though Marx resigned his post in hopes of staving off the closure. From 1843–1845, the period of his first exile in Brussels and Paris, Marx read an enormous number of books and monographs on philosophy, economics, history, and socialism. He became highly critical of his erstwhile Young Hegelian comrades, although he never forgot his debt to the master.

The Critique of Hegel's Philosophy of Right

In 1843, he made a critical study of Hegel's **Philosophy of Right** (Rechtsphilosophie). In his critique, Marx attacked Hegel's panlogism as an attempt to derive the real process of history from the logical relations among categories. Time and again Marx was to argue that the theory of history (and society) had to bow before real social and political history. Thought and the categories of thought were but historically specific expressions and as such the motor of their development lay in the practical movement of history itself.

The introduction to the **Critique of Hegel's Philosophy of Right** still rings with the poetry of it's revolutionary message. Unlike the fragment of the body of the **Critique** which was not published until after Marx's death, the **Introduction** appeared in 1844 in the **Deutsch-Französische Jahrbücher (German-French Annals)** which Marx edited with Arnold Ruge. The themes which had been taken up in the text appear again in the terse polemical form which characterized much of Marx's writings. The political, legal, religious, and philosophical realms of human existence are expressions of the particular economic relations of civil society (as one actual and possible form of society). It is impossible to understand the development of politics, religion, law, and philosophy by means of political, religious, legal, and philosophical analysis. Rather, in certain forms of society, the relations which constitute that society, the 'law of motion' which sets that society apart from others, assumes a political, religious, legal, and philosophical expression. In 1859, in the preface to his **Introduction to the Critique of Political Economy**, Marx described his 'discovery' in the following words:

> The first labour undertaken to dispel the doubt which plagued me was a critical review of the Hegelian philosophy of right, a labour whose introduction appeared in the **Deutsch-Französische Jahrbücher** published in Paris in 1844. My investigation led to the result that legal relations just as the forms of the state, can be comprehended neither out of themselves nor out of the so-called universal development of the human spirit, but rather are rooted in the material relations of life, the entirety of which Hegel, after the forerunners in England and France of the 18th century, brought together under the name 'civil (bürgerliche) society'. However, the anatomy of this civil society is to be found in the political economy.

The Young Hegelians, with the exception of Feuerbach, were dedicated philosophical idealists who believed that the essential basis of reality, and

---

7 Plato used the term διαλεκτικη επιστημη—dialectical knowledge or truth—to signify the truth which emerged out of the opposition of conflicting points of view. But Hegel viewed the development of the world itself as dialectical. In overcoming the dualism of thought and being, he attempted to show that world historical development was only the outer expression of the development of Mind or Spirit. Social-historical change was thus understood as change of the incarnations of this Mind or Spirit in time and space.

hence, of humanity, was spiritual and that history was the record of the development of the Spirit to its completion. Materiality was considered to be an expression of the inadequacy of the attainment of the Spirit or, in Hegelian terminology, the alienation of Spirit from itself. But because the active factor in history was spiritual, the material obstacles which the Spirit encountered in its path to self-realization were nothing more than the creations of Spirit's own immaturity, or rather an expression of its self-alienation. Seizing on these notions from a reading of Hegel's philosophy, these Young Hegelians obviously believed that it was the growth of Spirit, its forward movement, which occasioned transformations in the material and social world. (We must recall that in the early 1840s Marx was himself part of this critical-philosophical movement. He was attracted to its revolutionary sentiment, to the notion of progress and development, and, above all, to the concept of the advancement of freedom In history.) But in order to arrive at the real process of social and historical development, Marx had to systematically criticize the purely spiritual cast of the theory. We must be very clear about this. Marx's criticism of the idealism of the Hegelian schools was not developed on the basis of a simple philosophical materialism. Marx did not develop a metaphysics which held to the ultimate reality of matter and derivative nature of spirit. Marx's critique of idealist philosophy was not a return to an older form of materialist thought but the development of a position which rejected metaphysical (i.e., absolute and theoretical) premises in favour of a practical-historical starting point: the relations between man and man, and the relations between man and nature, both of which are historically specific. The inseparability and interpenetration of these two modes form the basis of the materialist investigation of society.

The concept of materialism which Marx employs does not begin with the matter-in-motion[8] of the materialists of an earlier epoch, but rather it is founded upon the material relations of man to nature which are everywhere mediated by the material relations in society. Religious criticism, political criticism, philosophical criticism can never be the motor of historical change because they address expressions of a reality whose centre lies elsewhere. Religion, according to Marx, is not in itself substantial. It is an expression of despair, of want, and, at the same time, it registers a protest against those conditions which are found wanting. It is a fantastic representation of a reality which requires fantasy because the demands made on the reality can only be satisfied in a fantastic form within the confines of that reality. The atheistic Young Hegelians are wrong in believing that they can attack religion directly. The demand that religion be abolished by knocking religious ideas out of the heads of individuals is to lend to religion a substantiality which it does not have, according to Marx. The only way to break the *seeming* hold of religious ideas on the human spirit is to eradicate the conditions which give rise to those ideas in the first place. The demand made by the Young Hegelians concerning the giving up of religion (i.e., of the fantastic realization of man) can only be satisfied by the practical elimination of those conditions which require, or give rise to, the fantasy.[9]

Imagine walking into a house in which a pot of stew is cooking on the stove. The first impression you will have of the stew will be conveyed through your sense of smell. You will sense the aroma of the stew before you see it or taste it. No one would confuse the aroma and the stew itself, or the taste with the smell. Religion, for Marx, is very much like the aroma of the world; it is its necessary complement, just as a stew has an aroma as its complement. The Young Hegelians have taken the aroma (religion) far too seriously, mistaken it for the world.

Or, consider the fate of a person languishing in prison, who develops an obsession with the idea of freedom. So obsessed is this prisoner with this fixed idea, that he or she is prevented from being creative at all. If the prisoner had been an artist, then he or she could no longer produce art. To remedy this state of affairs the Young Hegelians approach the cell and exhort the prisoner to knock this fixed idea of freedom out of his or her head and to become creative once more. It is this fixed idea of freedom, this 'false

8 Many materialists of the eighteenth century, for example, believed that material and ideal phenomena could be reduced to, and thus be explained by matter in motion.

9 Marx's critique of the Young Hegelian assault on religion has been viewed as challenge by materialism to idealism. While true, this view misses the deeper point. As Lawrence Krader has pointed out in his learned introduction to **The Ethnological Notebooks of Karl Marx**: "The religious field was then subjected to dialectical critique not because it afforded the occasion for a performance of virtuosity wherein the converted spirit was reconverted into matter, but rather because, by the mystical formulations, a relation between men has been replaced by a relation between things, and a material interest has been substituted by its supernatural representation, or by an abstraction. That interest is the interrelation of the subjective and objective sides of man in a particular social relation, but it has been externalized solely as a hypostasis, its ethereal form, in its religious representation." pp. 22–23.

consciousness' which is enslaving the poor unfortunate who cannot express the creativity with which he or she has been endowed. Marx, on the contrary, suggests that this fixed idea of freedom is a *necessary* expression of the prisoner's incarceration. The only way to eliminate this idea is to open the door and allow the prisoner out. In other words, the idea of freedom only arises as a result of the actual condition of unfreedom and the only way to overcome the idea is to establish freedom as an objective fact.

In the same way, religion is nothing substantial, for Marx. It is a complement of a false reality—a reality of human suffering, weakness and injury—a necessary if illusory haven from this hard reality and, at the same time, a protest against this hard reality.

But if Marx took issue with the pure spiritualism of the Hegelians, he did so on the basis of the discovery of what he took to be the real movement of social history. Everyone knows, if he or she knows nothing else about Marx, that he identified the 'history of all hitherto existing society' as 'the history of class struggles'. If the Hegelian idealists saw the motor force of history as the self-development of Spirit, then for Marx the motor of historical development was to be found in the struggle between social classes, not only over the distribution of the social surplus, but also over the form of class relations themselves. In his introduction to the **Critique of Hegel's Philosophy of Right**, he portrayed the struggle of the modern class of social labour—the proletariat, engaged in the struggle with the exploiting classes—as a struggle not only of one class with another. (Indeed, since all of history is the recorded struggle of classes with other classes, there would be nothing new in this.) For Marx, the modern struggle of the proletariat was directed by a *universal* interest, because the liberation of the class of social labour represented, at the same time, the liberation of all humanity. The victory of the bourgeoisie over the feudal aristocracy was formally a victory of the humankind over tyranny. It was a victory of man in the abstract, as the juridical personality, as citizen, as political man, but not of men and women in the daily world of work. The bourgeois revolution in content was a victory of one class over another, the victory of one form of exploitation over another. But for Marx, the victory of the proletariat represents not only the victory of one class over another, but rather the abolition of all classes and the overcoming of all relations of exploitation. It is important to note that Marx did not assert the revolutionary role of the proletariat as a moral principle to be carried out. Rather, he

believed to have discovered the real revolutionary movement of the proletariat as an actual force in modern history. The revolution for Marx was not a pious wish, as it had been for earlier socialists and communists, but an expression of the class consciousness of the proletariat in its historical struggle with the agents of capital.

The Holy Family and the German Ideology

After having written his **Critique of Hegel's Philosophy of Right** in 1843, Marx collaborated with his newly found friend, Friedrich Engels, in producing two critical works on the Young Hegelian philosophy. The first essay, **The Holy Family or the Critique of the Critical Critique**, initially appeared in 1845 (Marx was responsible for over ninety percent of it). The second, a more substantial piece, **The German Ideology**, was not published in Marx's lifetime. Of the latter work Marx wrote in 1859: "The manuscript . . . had long since arrived at the publishers in Westphalia, when we received news that changed conditions didn't allow its being printed. We left the manuscript to the gnawing criticism of the mice all the more willingly since we had reached our major goal—self-understanding."

In the **Holy Family** Marx took issue with the basic standpoint of the Young Hegelian philosophy, using their literary criticism as a focus for his own critique. Written primarily as an attack on Bruno Bauer and his followers, it focussed on the spiritualism of the Hegelian left, which Bauer had developed in his concept of Self-consciousness as the motor of reality. Bauer and his associates, the critical critics, opposed the movement of Self-consciousness to the existence of mass or matter. Insight into reality could only be had by those who understood the development of Self-consciousness, i.e., by the critical critics themselves. But in order to make the world intelligible, they had to first translate 'mundane' matters into the concepts of critical criticism, i.e., into the concepts of Hegelian logic. Bauer had to transmogrify real empirical relations into logical categories, before he could reveal their 'critical' secrets. Marx consistently opposed this matter of 'critical' logic to the logic of the matter of real relations.

Although the **German Ideology** as a whole was a sweeping critique of the leading Young Hegelians (including Bruno Bauer and Max Stirner—né Johann Kaspar Schmidt) and the True Socialists (e.g., Karl Grün), the first chapter was devoted to the critique of the theories of Ludwig Feuerbach. Marx and Engels had both come under the influence of Feuerbach's philosophy shortly before the writing of the **German Ideology**. Although Marx expressed the opinion that Feuerbach was "poorer" than Hegel, as we have seen, the former did provide an original materialist critique of Hegel's spiritualism or idealism. Indeed, Feuerbach had cogently argued that man was the creator of Spirit, or religion. To the spiritualism of the Hegelians, Feuerbach counter posed a philosophic humanism. For Feuerbach; "Consciousness of God is self-consciousness, knowledge of God is self-knowledge." In a view which comes close to that expressed by Emile Durkheim some fifty years later, Feuerbach argued that religion was an illusion which was caused by the antithesis of human nature, in general, and the individual. Religion, therefore, is the alienation of man from himself, from his own essence. From his **Essence of Christianity**, Feuerbach continues:

> Religion is the disuniting of man from himself; he sets God before him as the antitheses of himself. God is not what man is—man is not what God is. God is the infinite, man the finite being; God is perfect, man imperfect; God eternal, man temporal; God almighty, man weak; God holy, man sinful. God and man are extremes: God is the absolutely positive, the sum of all realities; man the absolutely negative, comprehending all negations.

But in religion man contemplates his own latent nature. Hence it must be shown that this antithesis, this differencing of God and man, with which religion begins, is a differencing of man with his own nature.

But the human essence, the species-being of mankind is an anthropological given for Feuerbach. Marx's criticism of Feuerbach's 'materialism' was directed at: (1) the purely theoretical understanding of the human essence and of reality; (2) the ahistorical conception of the human essence which stands at the centre of Feuerbach's religious criticism; (3) the indifference of the human essence to differing forms of society; and (4) the contemplative and passive implications of Feuerbach's philosophy.

But the real significance of the first chapter of the **German Ideology** for sociological thought is broader than the critical comments directed at Feuerbach. For Marx does not remain content with advancing critical abstractions to counter those of Feuerbach. Instead, he attempts to develop a concrete historical portrayal of the dynamics of social evolution and revolution. Feuerbach conceived of history as the realization of the human essence of Man in the abstract. In this he did not differ in any substantial

way from the idealist Young Hegelians. Marx believed that when Feuerbach considered history he was no materialist. The starting point for Marx—and it was a principle which he tenaciously adhered to in all of his writings—was the relations, conditions, and actions of real individuals which were *always historically specific*. There is for Marx no inherent human essence which is 'realized' or 'suppressed' in history. For Marx, there is no human nature as such, save as a poor abstraction. Rather, real men and women differ from one another in history as their mode of production differs. The mode of production is the economic formation or foundation of society, and it is constituted by the historically specific relations between the producers and by the historically specific relations between man and nature mediated by the former social relation. In the **German Ideology**, Marx investigated the relations of production, reproduction, division of labour, opposition of town and countryside, forms of property, consciousness, language, alienation, communism, the state, and civil society. In the same chapter, Marx briefly deals with the world-historical presuppositions of "Communism" for it cannot be a localized development without falling back into "the same old nonsense." This "Communism" of Marx was not an ideal which he and his colleagues hoped to realize by appeals to this or that group. Rather, Marx firmly believed that he had detected in modern society the movement and tendencies which were bringing "communism" into being. Marx distinguished himself from other socialists precisely on this point. The Utopians in France and the True Socialists in Germany conceived of the principles of socialism or communism in an entirely ethical or philosophical way, as ideals which people of good will should attempt to realize. Marx firmly asserted that "communism" was not born of a theoretical or moral wish, but was the real movement of the history of real class-individuals driven by practical wants and conditions. He stated:

> They (i.e., the True Socialists) detach the communist system, critical and polemical writings from the real movement, of which they are but the expression, and force them into an arbitrary connection with German philosophy. They detach the consciousness of certain historically conditioned spheres of life from these spheres and evaluate it in terms of true, absolute, i.e., German philosophical consciousness. With perfect consistency they transform the relations of these particular individuals into relations of 'Man.' In so doing they have

abandoned the realm of real history and returned to the realm of ideology, and since they are ignorant of the real connection, they can without difficulty fabricate some fantastic relationship with the help of the 'absolute' or some other ideological method.

It is important always to be conscious of the extreme respect which Marx showed for the historically specific conditions and relations of life, and his consistent and sustained criticism of speculative thinking concerning society and its development.

Although the **German Ideology** was never published in Marx's lifetime (it was first published in its entirety in 1932), it represents a great forward movement in the development of his distinctive analysis of modern society. He continued to subject speculative social science to radical criticism in the latter half of the decade of the 1840s. At the same time, he intensified his own study of political economy, and extended his contacts with groups of socialist workers in a number of European countries. (Marx was living in Brussels for the most part during this period.)

Pierre-Joseph Proudhon and The Poverty of Philosophy

The ink of the **German Ideology** was barely dry before Marx took up his pen once again to write a bitter, polemical pamphlet attacking a work of Pierre-Joseph Proudhon, one of the fathers of modern anarchist thought. Proudhon's two-volume work, **Système des contradictions économiques ou la philosophie de la misère**, was to be a critical examination of the workings of political economy. Proudhon sent Marx a copy of the book asking for criticism, a request which Marx answered by publishing his **Misère de la philosophie** in 1847. Although Marx's critique is rich and complex, the central point concerns the confusion exhibited by Proudhon concerning ideas and things, or more properly, between logical categories and real historical relations. Proceeding in Hegelian fashion, Proudhon has erected a set of logical categories and has made historical institutions, conditions and relations into so many incarnations of these ideas or categories. Hence, Proudhon substituted for real history the fantastic history of ideas and categories of thought.

For Marx, the categories of the mind, which are by no means eternal—that is, common to all men at all times in all cultures—are expressions of the conditions in which they arise and to which they are related. In **Poverty of Philosophy,** Marx emphasized this point in the following passage:

> Economic categories are only the theoretical expressions, the abstractions of the social relations of production. Proudhon, holding these things upside down like a true philosopher, sees in actual relations nothing but the incarnation of these principles, of these categories, which were slumbering—so M. Proudhon the philosopher tells us—in the bosom of the 'impersonal reason of humanity'.
>
> M. Proudhon the economist understands very well that men make cloth, linen or silk materials in definite relations of production. But what he has not understood is that these definite social relations are just as much produced by men as linen, flax, etc. Social relations are closely bound up with productive forces. In acquiring new productive forces men change their mode of production; and in changing their mode of production, in changing the way of earning their living, they change all their social relations. The hand-mill gives you society with the feudal lord; the steam mill, society with the industrial capitalist.
>
> The same men who establish their social relations in conformity with their material productivity, produce also principles, ideas and categories, in conformity with their social relations.
>
> Thus these ideas, these categories, are as little eternal as the relations they express. They are historical and transitory products. (pp. 95–96)

But Marx not only criticizes Proudhon's theory, he also attempts to explain why Proudhon defends this particular point of view. This does not mean that Marx is interested in Proudhon's psychological make-up—this would be an important question for those who were interested in *why* this particular individual Proudhon held to these views—but rather he looks for the social interest (i.e., the class interest) which these views express and seek to advance. Proudhon was a radical and criticized existing society. At the same time, he wanted to 'preserve' the 'good side' of social institutions and relations. Marx observes:

> From head to foot M. Proudhon is the philosopher and economist of the petty bourgeoisie. In an advanced society the petty bourgeois is necessarily from his very position a socialist on the one side and an economist on the other; that is to say, he is dazed by the magnificence of the big bourgeoisie and has sympathy for the sufferings of the people. He is at once both bourgeois and man of

the people. Deep down in his heart he flatters himself that he is impartial and has found the right equilibrium, which claims to be something different from mediocrity. A petty bourgeois of this type glorifies contradiction because contradiction is the basis of his existence. He is himself nothing but social contradiction in action. He must justify in theory what he is in practice, and M. Proudhon has the merit of being the scientific interpreter of the French petty bourgeoisie—a genuine merit because the petty bourgeoisie will form an integral part of all the impending social revolutions. (p. 167)

The attempt to substitute the history of supposedly eternal categories for real, profane history thus represents the attempt by the petty bourgeoisie to have their cake and eat it too, according to Marx. In this way, one can be radical and reactionary at the same time. The little shopkeeper is opposed to big capital (his creditors and suppliers), but he still idealizes buying and selling (albeit on a smaller scale) as the truly human and eternal relations of social life.

The Manifesto of the Communist Party

Marx's views on society and social change were given summary expression in the **Manifesto of the Communist Party**. Shortly before the outbreak of the revolution of 1848, Marx and Engels had written this fiery document on behalf of the Communist League of which they were members. The **Manifesto** was a political statement conceived from within the practical struggles of associations of socialists which were active in Europe at the time. It should not be judged as a weighty, scholarly work. It is to be understood as its supporters understood it, i.e., as a weapon in the struggle between the classes. As such, it contained stirring slogans for the revolutionary class which were meant to bolster courage and induce confidence. At the same time, the **Manifesto** was clearly meant to be more than self-aggrandizing bravado, for, even though the subjective appeal to the revolutionary will and consciousness is manifest, the analysis which undergirds the demands and goals of the movement contained profound thoughts on society and history.

Compare the following passages from the **Communist Manifesto** with the earlier ideas of the **Poverty of Philosophy**, the **German Ideology**, the **Holy Family**, and the **Critique of Hegel's Philosophy of Right**:

All the preceding classes that got the upper hand, sought to fortify their already acquired status by subjecting society at large to their conditions of appropriation. The proletarians cannot become masters of the productive forces of society, except by abolishing their own previous mode of appropriation, and thereby every other previous mode of appropriation as well. They have nothing of their own to secure and to fortify; their mission is to destroy all previous securities for, and insurances of, individual property.

All previous historical movements were movements of minorities. The proletarian movement is the self-conscious, independent movement of the immense majority. The proletariat, the lowest stratum of our present society, cannot stir, cannot raise itself up, without the whole superincumbent strata of official society being sprung into the air.

The theoretical conclusions of the Communists are in no way based on ideas or principles that have been invented, or discovered, by this or that would-be universal reformer.

They merely express, in general terms, actual relations springing from an existing class struggle, from a historical movement going on under our very eyes. (Emphasis added)

The Critique of Political Economy

As we have seen, Marx and Engels were both active in the revolutionary movement of 1848 in Germany and elsewhere in Europe (the socialists with whom they were most closely associated conceived of the revolution as primarily international in scope). During this stormy period they founded the **Neue Rheinische Zeitung (New Rhenish Paper)** to provide the revolutionary movement with up-to-date social and political analyses of current events. In 1847 Marx delivered a number of lectures at the German Workers' Society in Brussels concerning the economic and social relations of modern society. The content of these lectures appeared in a series of leading articles in the **Neue Rheinische Zeitung** in 1849. At a later date they were collated and issued in pamphlet form by Friedrich Engels under the title of **Wage Labour and Capital**. In this pamphlet Marx attempted to analyse the economic relations which gave rise to the political struggles occurring in Europe at the time. For the first time Marx tried to lay bare the fundamental relations, the law of movement of modern society. We recall that Marx eschewed the question of society as such, society in general. Although we can understand the concept 'society', it is only a concept, i.e., the product of a mental operation having no specific empirical referent. Empirically, there are only various societies which exist in time and space. Many of these societies are organized on similar principles, and we can group them accordingly. But what distinguished fundamental principles from secondary ones? In other words, how are we to identify the specific laws of motion of different societies? According to Marx the fundamental relations which underlie human life are, as we have seen, twofold: man's relation to nature and man's relation to man (or social relations). There can be no human life without the relation to nature *and* the relation in society. They are not the same, but they must always be taken together. All other relations are derived from these two. The nexus of the two fundamental relations is the historically specific way in which people produce their livelihood. This mode of production is the economic formation of society (it is not the whole of society, but only its economic foundation), and it is constituted by the specific human relations to nature (raw materials, climate, tools, technology, energy sources, science, skill, etc.—in short, the *forces* of production, and the social division of labour, specialization of task, exchange, social classes, distribution, consumption, exploitation, freedom and bondage of labour, etc.—in short, the *relations* of production). A hard and fast line cannot be drawn between the forces and relations of production because the organization of labour, which is a social relation, is, in Marx's view, a most powerful productive force. The forces and relations of production interpenetrate, for the relation of man to nature is never direct (insofar as he or she is human) but always mediated by the relations in society. However, the most basic relation of man to nature and of man in society is the relation of labour. We can then begin to distinguish between different modes of production on the basis of the different forms of social labour. Our concern at the moment is the form of social labour which lies at the foundation of the capitalist mode of production. Wage labour is the dominant form in the modern world. In **Wage Labour and Capital**, Marx specifies the relation of wage labour to capital, its counterpart. Wage labour is formally free labour. The labourer enters into contract with a capitalist (the personification or owner of capital) and agrees to sell the latter a specified quantity of labour capacity for which he or she receives a wage in recompense. The wage is the price of the labour capacity which is purchased in this way. Since Marx follows the assumption of the classical political economists that commodities are exchanged at their values, the value of the labour capacity which is sold to the capitalist, and the value of the commodities (or money) received by the seller of the labour capacity or labour power are equal. The value of the labour capacity which the worker alienates is determined by the value of the commodities which must be consumed in order to replenish the strength of the labourer expended in the process of labouring for the contracted period and to provide for his or her offspring who represent a new source of labour power for capital. The interest of the wage labourer is thus in the reproduction of his or her life and of the lives of their family members. But what is the interest of capital? Before we can answer this question, we must first ask about the nature of capital. This is precisely the point at which Marx takes issue with the economists and with our common sense:

> Capital consists of raw materials, instruments of labour and means of subsistence of all kinds, which are utilised in order to produce new raw materials, new instruments of labour and new means of subsistence. All these component parts of capital are creations of labour, products of labour, accumulated labour. Accumulated labour which serves as a means of new production is capital.
>
> So say the economists.
>
> What is a Negro slave? A man of the black race. The one explanation is as good as the other.
>
> A Negro is a Negro. He only becomes a slave in certain relations. A cotton-spinning jenny is a machine for spinning cotton. It becomes capital only in certain relations. Torn from these relationships, it is no more capital than gold in itself is money or sugar the price of sugar.

Capital is thus not a thing, according to Marx, but a *social relation of production in the form of a thing*. It is in the interest of wage labour to maintain life in the first instance and then to seek a higher standard of living. It is in the interest of capital (or rather of the capitalist since capital as a thingly form has no subjectivity or will except that of the capitalist) not only to reproduce itself but continually to augment itself, to add to its value. It is absurd for a capitalist to invest $100,000 and receive $100,000 in return. The essence of capital is to continually produce more value, to increase itself. But there is no way known to science (natural and social) whereby *things* can reproduce and augment themselves. And yet, in Marx's view, the entire modern world rests upon this power of capital to create more capital. How is this contradiction to be resolved?

The power of capital is not related to its *physical form* but to its *social substance*. The power of capital is the power over living labour. It is the power of past, objectified, accumulated labour over the living labourers. This social power is wielded by the class of those who speak and act for capital, i.e., the capitalist class. But how does capital wield this power over living labour? Let us consider the relation between capital and wage labour more closely. It is true that the worker contracts with the capitalist for the sale of his or her labour power for a wage and that this wage is equal to the value of the commodities which replenish the labour expended in the process of production. In this way, the capacity to labour is a commodity like any other. Yet, the labour which is expended in the process of production creates *more value* (objectified in the value of the commodities which emerge out of the production process) than the value of the labour power which is expended in the labour process. In other words, the labourer labours part of the time for himself or herself (to reproduce the physical strength which is sapped in the process of labour) and part of the time for the capitalist, for which the labourer receives no recompense. If we consider the end result of the process of production to be a certain amount of a commodity which belongs entirely to the capitalist, then we can divide this quantity in the following way: (1) one part whose value represents the value of the raw materials, machinery, fuel, etc., which was used up in the process of production; (2) one part whose value represents the value of the labour power expended in the process of production and which returns to the labourer in the form of wages; and (3) one part whose value represents the extra or surplus value created by the labour (not labour power) of the worker during the process of production. If we consider this relation between labourer and capitalist not as an individual one but as a relation between two social classes, then the total social value created anew in the process of production consists of the value of the commodities which are consumed by the class of social labour as a whole and the surplus value which accrues to all other social strata. This surplus value is in turn divided among the capitalists, landlords, state, church, etc., in the form of profit, rent, taxes, tithes, etc., respectively.

For Marx, capital is the dominant social relation in modern society. It is the domination of things over

their creators, of the past over the present, of the dead over the living. Marx adds:

> How, then does any amount of commodities, of exchange value, become capital?
>
> By maintaining and multiplying itself as an independent social power, that is, as the power of a portion of society, by means of its exchange for direct, living labour power.
>
> It is only the domination of accumulated, past, materialized labour over direct, living labour that turns accumulated labour into capital.
>
> Capital does not consist in accumulated labour serving living labour as a means for new production. It consists in living labour serving accumulated labour as a means for maintaining and multiplying the exchange value of the latter.

This relation of wage labour and capital is the basis of the law of motion of society in which the capitalist mode of production dominates. Marx had already worked out the basis of his understanding of modern society by 1849. (Engels correctly points out in the introduction to the pamphlet that Marx had not yet drawn the crucial distinction between labour and labour power. Yet, even though this distinction had not yet been made, the basic relation of exploitation had been grasped and the nature of capital as a historically specific social relation masquerading in the form of things had been laid bare.)

After the defeat of the revolution and the closing of the **Neue Rheinische Zeitung** by the authorities, Marx emigrated to England where he helped establish the **Neue Rheinische Revue** to continue the political journalism which had engaged him in Germany. There was a large colony of German emigrés in London with whom Marx was in contact; the **Revue** was one means of providing the analysis of social and political questions to a large number of readers most efficiently. The **Revue**, however, enjoyed only a brief existence. It had become clear to Marx that the revolutionary ferment in Europe was over and that a period of reaction was setting in. In the last issue of the **Revue**, Marx proclaimed that the secret of the defeat of the revolution in Europe could be found in the analysis of conflicting economic conditions and relations.

Although Marx had been engaged in the study of the works of classical political economy (from about 1843), it was only during the period of his London exile that he began a systematic and disciplined review of the theory and a profound critique of it, a critique which eventually culminated in the writing and publication of his *magnum opus*, **Das Kapital** in 1867. During his early London period, however, Marx depended upon the material support of his close friend and collaborator, Engels. Beginning in 1851, Marx made regular contributions to the **New York Daily Tribune**, a quasi-Fourierist and pro-abolitionist newspaper published in the United States by Horace Greeley. Marx also contributed to Chartist newspapers and journals. In his articles, he tackled the political, economic, and social questions of the day, and the analytic work which he undertook for his journalistic writings fed into his detailed examination of economic theory. He drew upon this store of knowledge in his later writings. (For example, the theory of the Asiatic mode of production, in particular, and that of historical periodization, in general, was largely developed during this period of his life, even though they were significantly revised over the course of the ensuing decades as his knowledge of historical and anthropological sources deepened.) It was during this period as well that Marx wrote and published his famous study of the defeat of the French revolution of 1848, **The Eighteenth Brumaire of Louis Bonaparte.**

Between 1857 and 1859, Marx concentrated his efforts on writing a propaedeutic to his systematic critique of political economy. The **Contributions to a Critique of Political Economy** (1859) represents just a fraction of the manuscript material which he wrote during that period. About half of these notebooks were first published in 1939 and 1941 under the title **Grundrisse der Kritik der politischen ökonomie (Sketches of the Critique of Political Economy)**. (An English translation entitled **The Grundrisse** first appeared in 1972.) The notebooks which comprise the **Grundrisse** contain preliminary formulations of matters which make an appearance in **Capital** and the **Theories of Surplus-Value**; there is, in addition, a number of areas covered which are not explored in subsequent works.

Although the **Grundrisse** was not published in its pristine form in Marx's lifetime, a short work on the **Critique of Political Economy** did appear in 1859. In it we find the first mature exposition of the theory of value which was to be the framework within which Marx's theory of society and history was to be cast. We have already had occasion to consider aspects of this theory of value in light of the substance of the pamphlet **Wage Labour and Capital**. This theory of value, adopted from the great exponents of the classical school of political economy, is the key to understanding Marx's entire project. The

theory of value is not a theory of economics directly. It is not concerned with questions of markets, prices, inflation, etc., i.e., with the *phenomena* of economic life. It is concerned above all with the historically specific relations which give rise to the specific phenomena of economic life. As a theory of social relations it comes under the purview of sociology. The language of value is a kind of hieroglyphic which allows Marx to write about determinate social relations in a highly condensed, yet extremely efficient form. We shall have occasion to review the highlights of the theory of value when we come to consider the first chapter of **Capital**.

During the first half of the 1860s, Marx wrote thousands of pages on the history and critique of political economy. Although he had developed a number of schemes for organizing and publishing his works, he lived only to see the realization of a small part of his efforts. The only book to appear in his lifetime (after the **Critique of Political Economy**) was the first volume of **Capital**. After Marx's death, volumes II and III of **Capital** were edited and published by Engels based on Marx's rough, and in some cases, very rough notes. The **Theories of Surplus-Value** which, for the most part were composed during the first part of the 1860's, were transcribed and edited by Karl Kautsky, a leading socialist intellectual in Germany at the turn of the century. There are thousands of pages of Marx's writings which have yet to be transcribed. They are locked away in the archives at the International Institute for Social History in Amsterdam.

Capital

Until very recently, sociologists have ignored **Capital**, Marx's *magnum opus*, on grounds that it is a work which is relevant to students of economics, but not to students of sociology. Sociologists, it was argued, should concentrate upon the sociological works of Marx, such as **The German Ideology** or **The Communist Manifesto**. The theory of value which lies at the heart of **Capital** was understood by sociologists as an economic theory which expressed the laws of the capitalist economy and sought to explain the nuts and bolts of capitalism, e.g., markets, prices, profits, competition, etc., in terms of the essential law of value which controlled them. But the law of value is not a law of nature; it is a law of society which is authored neither by God nor by nature, but by human beings. There is a tradition in Western thought reaching back to Socrates, which draws the distinction between the laws which we make and thus can change, and those which we do not make, and over which we have no control. If we think of any sport, baseball or hockey, for example, we can readily see that the rules of the game are made by people and can be changed by them. There is no intrinsic or natural reason why first base must be 90 feet from home plate or why the blue line is blue instead of black or brown. The law which governs the 'rising of the sun' every morning is not the same kind of law as the law which governs baseball or hockey. (We should note, however, that the line which divides the laws which we make from those which we do not is not fixed but moveable. As we gain insight into the laws of nature and come to 'dominate' them, we can bring under our control that which was formerly beyond the pale of our means.) But further, the laws of baseball are specific to the game of baseball. It would be absurd to play baseball according to the rules of hockey. Similarly, the law of social value consists of the 'rules' of a particular society. Just as pre-civil forms of human association operated on the basis of different 'rules' or laws, so too will the society, which follows it, operate on the basis of different rules or laws. (Of course, just what the content of those new rules will be cannot be foretold in advance, just as the rules of a game, which has yet to be invented, cannot be known beforehand.) Although this analogy may be helpful to understand certain aspects of the nature of the law of value, it breaks down in a number of ways. In the first place, society is a necessary or essential part of human life, whereas no game exists on the basis of this kind of necessity. We can agree to abolish baseball but we cannot agree to abolish society.

Second, it is immediately apparent that the rules of a game are provisional, a matter of convention which can be changed and, indeed, which have been changed. The rules which govern society *appear* to be fixed by nature, to be a second nature which exist by dint of some iron necessity over which we can exercise no control. Disruptions in these rules, e.g., wars, revolutions, crises of all kinds, are only seen as temporary suspensions of the rules; yet, in the end, it is argued, they reassert themselves and reestablish their domination. If there were societies in history which operated according to different rules, then they were 'immature' stages of the development of the 'final' rules of the 'game' by which we now play and from which there can be no deviation even if we desire change. It is this position that Marx directly challenges.

Third, the rules of a sport are set down consciously, objectively and are agreed upon by those involved (players, umpires and spectators). Changes in the rules are made by consensus. Yet, the fundamental rules or principles of society are not generally formed in this way. The great changes in the form and content of society to this point have occurred 'behind the backs' of the members of those societies. Just as the rules which control the movement, the process of social interaction, appear to be 'natural', i.e., beyond our control; so too does social change appear to be a matter of 'providence', the hand of God, etc.

In his presentation of the law of value in the first chapter of **Capital**, Marx not only seeks to lay bare the law of motion of capitalist society, but he attempts to show why the law of motion of capitalist society—i.e., the fully developed law of value—appears to the members of that society to be a law of nature over which they have no control. Emile Durkheim argued that the law which governs the development of society is the same law which governs development in nature. Just as we give ourselves over to the laws of nature, so too must we give ourselves over to the laws of society. Hence, Durkheim argued, the transition from the society founded upon mechanical solidarity to the one founded upon organic solidarity is a natural process to which we must submit. But for Marx, this transition involving the growth of the division of social labour was not natural but social, the two being distinguished in the way we have just outlined. It is men and women who have posited the change and who fought for it, and against it, throughout history. The fact that they have not always been conscious of the changes which they have brought about or that the consequences of their actions were unrelated to their intentions does not mean that some other agency is responsible. Yet, the time has come, says Marx, for men and women to begin to make their own history *consciously*. In order to do this, they must seize hold of that alienated social power which appears as the power of nature and bring their own social forces under their conscious control. Man will no longer serve the machine (capital) but the machine will serve man.

The law of value is the expression of social relations which is specific to historically determinate forms of society. The law of value did not dominate those societies which we have been called primitive or simple; the law of value will not be the law of motion of a future society, at least not in its present form. The law of social value is the law of motion of capitalist society, and, in a less systematic way, of all societies which are called *civil*. Civil society is the society which is constituted by the relations of exchange, of social classes and of the state. The law of value is created with the separation of the unit of production and consumption when men begin to work for one another, when the exchange relation eats into the heart of social production; in short, the law of value is born with the creation of the exchange relation and the *production of commodities*.

In all forms of human association, primitive as well as modern, men must labour to create the products which are necessary to maintain life. But only in those societies in which the law of value asserts itself do these products become commodities. The commodity is a mysterious thing because it is a unity of two components, one visible, the other 'invisible'. The visible component, according to Marx, is the natural property of the product of labour—colour, texture, consistency, coarseness, malleability, conductibility, density, penetrability, etc. The visible or sensuous component is the natural characteristic of the commodity; it has this in common with the products of labour found in non-commodity producing societies. The invisible or supersensuous component of the commodity is *wholly social*; it is *real*, not fictitious. In commodity producing societies, individuals do not labour collectively for the communal satisfaction of their wants; they labour independently, privately, and then exchange the products of their labour with others who have laboured in the same fashion. The social relations of these individuals do not assert themselves directly as relations of individuals at work in the common production and reproduction of their lives, but as a social relation between the products of their labour. Because the exchange relation binds the individuals—not directly but through the products of their labours—the social power of the individuals of that society appears not as the collective power of the labourers, but as the power of the products of their labour. The value of commodities is the expression of the social character of the labour which produces them and is measured by amount of labour time socially necessary on average required to produce the commodity. Value being a wholly social relation cannot be seen or detected in any way by the senses. Yet, the value substance has a *formal* expression. The form of value is *exchange value* which is manifested in the act of exchange. If five beds are exchanged for one house, then the exchange value of the five beds is one house. This simply tells us that the amount of social substance, i.e., value, which is embodied in five beds is the same amount

which is embodied in one house. The *value* of the five beds is now expressed in the *use-value* or body of the one house. We cannot 'see' value, but we can see its tracks in the exchange value of commodities. But because the social character of the commodity is hidden by its material or physical form, and because the social labour of individuals appears as private labour, the illusion arises that the value of a commodity is *by nature* a property of its physical qualities. Just as a commodity is heavy, brittle, colourless, etc., so too does it possess value. Hence, the character of the labour, i.e., social labour which fashions commodities, appears not as a quality of the social individuals engaged in social production (albeit privately in form), but as a quality of the products of labour themselves. This Marx describes as the *fetishism of commodities* whereby the products of human labour come to exercise an independent power over their producers as their alienated social power. This can be most forcefully seen in the case of gold. Gold is a commodity like any other. It has a use-value and a value. But because of its qualities and because of a long historical development, it has come to serve as a universal equivalent in exchange. Hence, by habit, we express the value of all kinds of commodities in the bodily form of gold. Hence, gold appears to be by its very nature the very incarnation of wealth. But any commodity can theoretically serve as the universal equivalent. The power of gold stems only from its traditional role as such in the history of commodity-producing society. The physical properties of gold have been taken as the source of its power. In fact, it is only because gold has traditionally become the universal equivalent (i.e., that it has become the commodity whose physical properties commonly express the value of all other commodities in society) that it appears to have this strange power over men. But, Marx argues, until the social producers band together to re-capture their alienated social power through the exercise of the rational control over the production process, the fetishism which is attached to commodities will continue to exist. It cannot be the state or some other agency of society which does this *for* the producers, for the alienation of their social power will not be overcome thereby.

The differences between a non-commodity and a commodity producing society can be outlined diagrammatically. Figure 1 shows the configuration of production relations in a non-commodity producing society, say a village community in which the associated producers constitute both the unit of production and the unit of consumption. The members of this

Figure 1

Commodity Producing Society

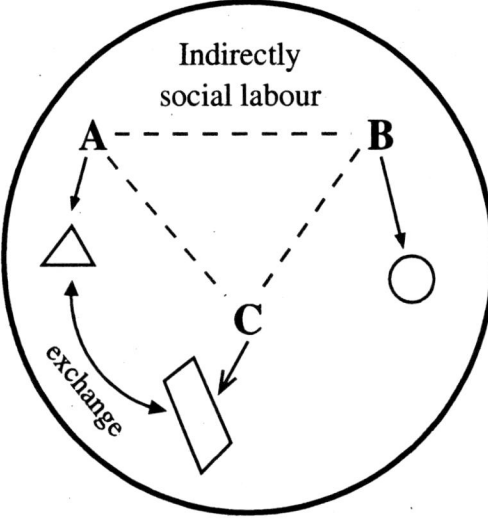

Non–commodity Producing Society

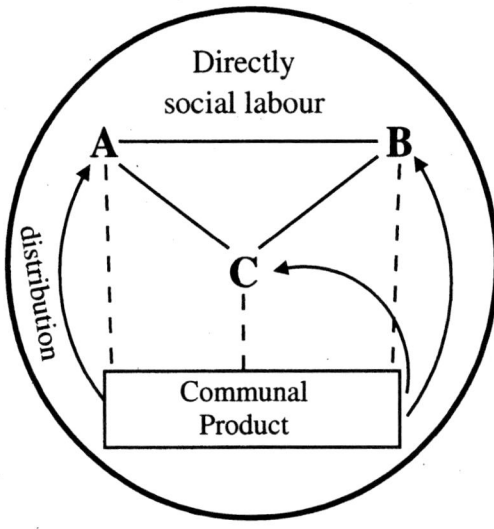

village community participate in a division of labour indicated by the different letters which locate the various individuals (A, B, C). "A" may be a hunter, "B" a gatherer of roots and berries, "C" may weave baskets, and so on. However, even though each member of this commune may be engaged in a different type of labour, it is clear to each of them that their own labour represents but a portion of the total labour of the community. The success of one's labour signifies a benefit to all. That these members of the village community labour for one another is a fact known to them before, during and after they labour. It is clear to them that their labour is directly communal in character. It is also clear to each of them that what they produce are the objects which will satisfy their

wants. The communal or social character of labour is expressed as a *directly human relation between the producers themselves*. The products of their various labours constitutes the common product which is then shared among the various members of the community.

It is otherwise in the society of commodity production. Here we find people producing privately, independently of one another. They may not know one another and only come into contact with one another when they take the products of their labour to market. This they must do, for each requires the products of the others' labours in order to live. Even though the character of their labour is private in form, the fact that each ultimately consumes the product of the others' labour shows that their labour is social in its substance. In other words, these 'independent' producers are labouring for one other. However, this relation does not achieve a directly human expression in commodity producing society. The expression which it does achieve is that between the products of labour in the act of exchange. In other words, the fact that these commodity producers are labouring for one another, i.e., that their labour is social, is expressed not directly between themselves, but between the products of their labour. It is only because the social relations between the producers are expressed as relations between the products of labour in the act of exchange that the products are values. This inversion of the human and the thingly is a necessary consequence of commodity production and can only be overcome by the establishment of directly social relations of labour.

To this point we have discussed the relations of value, exchange value and use-value. But there is a further dimension to the theory of value which is crucial for our understanding of Marx's concept of civil society, in general, and the capitalist mode of production, in particular. Civil society is not only the society in which exchange predominates, but it is also the society in which social classes have been formed. In general, we can speak of the class of producers who produce all the value in society (and all the wealth) and a class of non-producers who do not produce value but who, nevertheless, live from part of the value produced by the class of producers. The class of producers, or the class of social labour as a whole, thus produces the value which is embodied in those commodities which are necessary for the production and reproduction of itself as a class and a surplus-value which is embodied in those commodities which accrue to the class of non-producers. In the capitalist mode of production, the surplus-value appears in the form of profit, interest, rent, and taxes. The basis of surplus-value production in the capitalist mode of production is the exploitation of labour by capital. Capital, as we have seen, is a social relation in thingly form. These things are the products of past labour. The labour of the past comes to stand over and above the living present labour in the capital relation, the dead augmenting itself at the expense of the living. But capital, the thingly form of a social relation requires a consciousness, a will, a subjectivity, for things cannot act on their own. The capitalist thus appears as the personification of capital, capital endowed with consciousness and will, in Marx's words. Capitalists are in this sense *agents* of capital. By virtue of their agency, the surplus-value falls to them. For a capitalist to remain a capitalist, however, he or she cannot unproductively consume the surplus-value which is harvested, for the laws of the capitalist economy demand a continual transformation of surplus-value back into capital so more surplus-value can be pressed out of living labour. Capital appears to be the self-valorization of value where value augments itself as though it were a power *sui generis*. This is the fetishism of capital where things speak and act, and men listen and react.

The labourer confronts the capitalist in the market place as an equal, viz. both are buyers and sellers of commodities. The labourer must sell a portion of his or her labour power to the capitalist in order to convert it into food and other necessaries of life. The capitalist, on the other hand, requires the labour capacity in order to set the process of production into motion. When the exchange between the labourer and the capitalist takes place the labourer must accompany the capitalist to the site of production since the labour capacity which has been contracted for is not separable from the living labourer. At the site of production the labourer exercises his or her labour capacity as the time of labour stipulated in the agreement of sale with the capitalist. Let us assume that the capitalist has agreed to pay the labourer the full value of his or her labour power for 10 hours. Let the price of the labour capacity under given market conditions be $X. These $X represent the market price of those commodities which the labourer is required to buy in order to replenish what he or she expended in the process of production during the course of the labour. But if the labour gets back everything that he or she expended in the course of labouring, then two questions arise: 1) how is the labourer exploited? 2) what is the source of the capi-

talist's profit? According to Marx the labourer receives the full value of his or her labour capacity, but he or she does not receive the full value of what the labourer has added to the raw materials in the course of production. In other words, labour is capable of producing more value than is required to maintain the living labourer. Figure 2 makes Marx's point clearly.

Figure 2
The Labouring Day

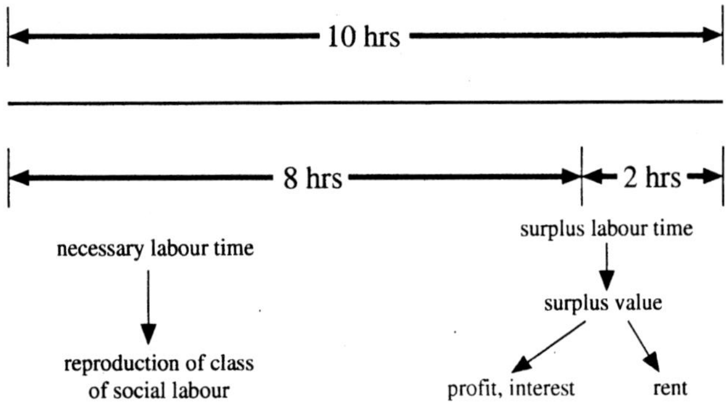

The necessary labour time represents that portion of the labouring day which the labourers are required to work to maintain their standard of living even if there were no capitalists. However, the surplus labour time represents that portion of the working day in which the value produced accrues to the capitalist in the form of surplus value. This surplus value is then converted by the capitalist into profit, interest, rent and taxes. In this way the surplus value produced by the labourer provides the source of livelihood for all the non-producing classes in society.

The law of value has its roots in the relations of exchange and of the social classes, as we have outlined above. Although the development of the relations of exchange do not necessarily lead to the opposition of social classes, i.e., to the relations of surplus-value, historically the development of exchange and surplus proceeded together. Whatever the road taken beyond the capitalist mode of production, it must overcome the relations of exchange and surplus-value. This is not a theoretical but a practical matter. Marx comments: "The philosophers have only interpreted the world in various ways, the point, however is to change it."

In 1864, Marx took part in founding the International Workingman's Association, the so-called First International. The I.W.A. was a kind of coordinating organization for working-class groups in a variety of industrial, capitalist countries. Marx was a leading figure in the I.W.A. until its demise in 1876. (After

1873, it was racked by such disaffection and dissension that it ceased to play an important role in the working-class movement.) The International conceived itself to be the organization of the working class in its struggle against capital; it was a struggle which knew no national borders, no country, no flag. Capitalist production itself created the world market and the world-historical conditions for the struggle between living labour (the class of wage-labourers) and the thingly form of the objectified, past, dead labour (capital) and its personification in the capitalist class. During the 1870s Marx continued to refine his critique of the political economy, revising the first edition of volume I of **Capital** and preparing drafts of volumes II and III. In addition, he keenly followed the developing socialist parties in Europe, especially those in France and in his native Germany. His **Critique of the Gotha Programme** was a response to the direction which the socialists in Germany had taken at one of their party congresses. Marx subjected the party programme to a thorough review, demonstrated its weakness, and offered principled criticism.

At the close of the 1870s, Marx rekindled his interest in anthropology evidenced in his systematic reading and excerpting from major anthropological works of his day. He was concerned with the question of social evolution, the transformation of society from one stage to another. Earlier, Marx had identified four modes of production or economic formations of society which had different laws of motion by which they were governed. By applying the concepts which he developed in his analysis of the laws of motion of capitalist society to the earlier conditions, he attempted to penetrate them as well. If we consider the capitalist mode of production to be a jigsaw puzzle in which all the pieces fit together, then the earlier modes of production can be seen as the same puzzle with many of the pieces still missing. Because we have already seen the way the whole puzzle hangs together, we can understand the partial puzzle using this as the key. His anthropological studies seem to have been directed toward an understanding of the Asiatic mode of production which Marx believed to be the first mode of production of civil society. However, Marx died in 1883 before he had time to complete whatever new projects he was planning.

Karl Marx: An Assessment

It would be an impossible task to assess the impact of Karl Marx upon world history let alone social thought given the vicissitudes of Marxism and indeed of world history over the course of the last century. A sea change has surely occurred since the fall of communism in Eastern Europe. Here we limit this brief assessment to the history of sociological theory.

Prof. Irving Zeitlin has suggested that the entire history of the development of sociological theory can be understood as having been driven by a debate with Marx's ghost. The two major figures in the history of sociological theory which followed the death of Marx were Emile Durkheim and Max Weber. Durkheim offers us a view of society which is practically the mirror opposite of that of Marx. For if Marx proclaimed that the history of all hitherto existing society is the history of class struggles, then Durkheim champions the view that that history is the history of the evolution of the forms of order. Weber has sometimes been called the 'bourgeois' Marx in that he rejected both the Hegelian framework of Marx's method and relativized the concepts of class and power. His return to a Kantian framework methodologically led to a pluralism which corresponded well to his notion of sociology as a probabilistic science but his theory of a growing rationalism in the West remains ambiguous except as general orientation. Simmel took sociology in a formal direction methodologically again on the basis of a Kantian epistemological orientation. Pareto explicitly criticized Marx in his work *Les systèmes socialistes* for his utopian view that the struggle between the proletariat and the bourgeoisie would lead to the end of the class struggle. In Europe Marxist intellectuals generally worked outside of sociology although they had some influence upon some sympathetic few within the field. Karl Mannheim, in helping to establish the foundation of the Sociology of Knowledge was influenced by the writings of both Karl Korsch and Georg Lukàcs, although his own brand of *gnosiosociology* was considered by most Marxists to be a bourgeois competitor.

In the United States the early American sociologists were greatly influenced by the neo-Hegelian movement of the late nineteenth century. In particular the development of the social psychology of Charles Horton Cooley and George Herbert Mead was enriched by the writings of the Harvard Hegelian scholar Josiah Royce and by the pragmatists John Dewey and William James during the Hegelian phase of their own intellectual development. Yet neither Cooley nor Mead seemed to have been influenced by contemporary Marxist writings. Thorstein Veblen was one of the few that worked creatively with some aspects of Marx's theory, although he was certainly closer in temperament and sympathy to the anarcho-syndicalists than to the Marxists.

During the 1930s a new generation of sociologists came into their own and, during the height of the depression, sought to enrich sociology with their Marxism and temper their Marxism with their sociology. Lewis Feuer, S.M. Lipset, Dan Bell, Philip Selznick and others had been attracted to Marxism during this period, although they all made the move 'from socialism to sociology' in subsequent years and attained leading positions within the discipline. It was not until the watershed of the 1960s that Marx's works were to become of central concern to large numbers of sociologists. It is beyond the scope of this current writing to analyze the reasons for the meteoric rise of Marxist theory within sociology during this volatile decade but it was surely linked to the Cold War, the coming of age of the largest generation of middle class youth in history, the civil rights movement in the United States and the agitation against the War in Southeast Asia. At the same time one does well to recall that the development of Marxist theory during and after this decade was very often incompatible with the method and theory of Marx's own writings and represented a significant revision or departure from them. This was especially true of the concept of historical agency which, in Marx's writings, and among the traditional Marxist parties, had meant the proletariat, understood as the blue-collar working class. Some have argued that this burst of Marxist activity within sociology represented a flowering of Marxist scholarship which had something important to say about significant new social realities. By aligning Marxism with Feminism, Existentialism, Phenomenology, Psychoanalysis and by focussing on new issues such as ecology, racism, sexism, etc. many felt that Marxism had become relevant again after a long period of stagnation. Others felt that this kind of eclecticism represented nothing more than widespread confusion and the indulgence of a large student generation. Sydney Hook, a 1930s Marxist turned pragmatist, caught something of the flavour of this when he wrote:

> The oddest syntheses result. I have known professors and graduate students, suddenly stirred into a passion of social protest by some current evil, who have convinced themselves shortly after reading Marx that he was *au fond* a phenomenologist, an existentialist, a positivist, a Spinozist, a Kantian, a Freudian, a Bergsonian, an anticipator of Samuel Alexander (all they had in common were their ethnic origin and their beards!)—and, of course, an Hegelian. There are some Catholic writers who rather cautiously suggest that, despite Marx's

atheism, Aristotle and Aquinas would not have disowned him. Some Protestants, and not merely pro-Soviet figures like Karl Barth and Niemöller, declare that Marx is essentially a more religious man than many of his religious critics. **Revolution, Reform and Social Justice**, pp. 7–8

Today Marxism represents a subdued force within a larger focus on cultural studies with a distinctively post-modernist bent. The writings of Marx are all but forgotten as literary criticism pulls the neo-Marxisms of the last three decades further away from their historical sources. The fall of Communism in Eastern Europe in the late 1980s may have signalled the beginning of the end of the Marxist influence within current sociological theory.

Karl Marx's Writings

Below are listed the titles of English translations of Marx's major works, as well as some minor ones. A general bibliography follows with references to citations in the foregoing chapter.

Capital, 3 vols. Moscow: Progress Publishers, 1968.

"The Critique of Hegel's Philosophy of Right: Introduction." In **Collected Works of Karl Marx and Friedrich Engels,,** vol. 3. London: Lawrence and Wishart, 1975.

The Critique of Political Economy. New York: International Publishers, 1968.

"The Critique of the Gotha Programme." In **Karl Marx and Friedrich Engels: Selected Works,** vol. 3. Moscow: Progress Publishers, 1969.

The Eighteenth Brumaire of Louis Bonaparte. New York: International Publishers, 1969.

The Ethnological Notebooks of Karl Marx, edited by Lawrence Krader. Amsterdam: Van Gorcum, 1972.

The German Ideology. Moscow: Progress Publishers, 1968.

The Grundrisse. London: Penguin, 1972.

"The Holy Family." In **Collected Works of Karl Marx and Friedrich Engels,,** vol. 4. New York: International Publishers, 1975.

"The Manifesto of the Communist Party." In **Karl Marx and Friedrich Engels: Selected Works,** vol. 1. Moscow: Progress Publishers, 1969.

The Poverty of Philosophy. Moscow: Progress, 1966.

The Theories on Surplus Value, 3 vols. Moscow: Progress Publishers, 1968.

"Wage Labour and Capital," In **Karl Marx and Friedrich Engels: Selected Works,** vol. 1. Moscow: Progress Publishers, 1969.

Other Works

Feuerbach, L. **The Essence of Christianity.** New York: Harper and Row, 1957.

Hegel, G.W.F. **The History of Philosophy**

_____ **The Phenomenology of Mind**. London: Allen and Unwin, 1968.

_____ **Lectures on the Philosophy of History** [1837]

_____ **Elements of the Philosophy of Right** [1820]

_____ **The Science of Logic**. London: Allen and Unwin, 1972.

Korsch, Karl. **Karl Marx**. New York: Russell and Russell, 1964.

_____ **Marxism and Philosophy**. London: New Left Books, 1970.

Lukács, Georg. **History and Class Consciousness**. London: Merlin, 1972.

_____ **The Young Hegel**. London: Merlin, 1976

Mehring, Franz. **Karl Marx**. London: Allen and Unwin, 1966

Rubin, I. **Essays on Marx's Theory of Value**. Montreal: Black Rose Books, 1975.

Rosdolsky, Roman. **The Making of Marx's Capital**. London: Pluto Press, 1977.

4

Max Weber

Life and Work

It can be argued that only Karl Marx and Sigmund Freud have had a greater impact on twentieth century social thought than has the sociologist Max Weber. Certainly no one has had a greater effect on sociology itself. Indeed, Weber's hold on the imaginations of sociologists is today as great as, perhaps greater than, it has ever been in the past. Despite the complexities and ambiguities of his arguments, the playfulness and sense of irony in his writing style, and the vicissitudes of translation, all of which have led to confusion and misunderstanding, Max Weber is considered by many to be the greatest sociologist of all time. How is it that someone from the second generation of sociology, a man who, after all, died about 75 years ago, should continue to have such significance for sociologists today?

Our hope is to introduce students to the richness, breadth, and depth of Weber's understanding of social life in this chapter. Our approach will be to provide a biographical sketch of Weber, an exposition of the main points in his interpretive sociology, and a list of the major works by and about him. This should be read in combination with the readings from Weber's own writing. To appreciate Weber's significance properly, and to understand his ideas fully, one would need to relate them to those of other second-generation sociologists and *fin-de-siècle* thinkers, such as Simmel, Tönnies, Durkheim, Pareto, Sorel, Croce, Gramsci, Bergson, Dilthey, Jung, and Freud. One would also need to consider in detail the influence on him of German Idealism (Windelband, Rickert, Dilthey), of German Historicism (Roscher, Knies, Schmoller, Brentano, Wagner), and of specific thinkers such as Nietzsche, Marx, Michels, Simmel, and Tönnies. Further, one would need to relate his arguments to his social context, and particularly to the great and eventful socioeconomic and political change which he experienced and observed around him. Perhaps some of our readers will be moved to develop such a fuller understanding after having considered our exposition.

Biographical Sketch

Max Weber was born on April 21, 1864 in Erfurt, the eldest of the seven children of Helene Fallenstein and Max Weber.

His father was a lawyer and magistrate from a Protestant family of well-to-do industrialists. Max Weber Sr. was a successful politician; first a municipal councillor, he later sat in the *Diet* of Prussia, and eventually was a National Liberal member in the German *Reichstag*. The National Liberal Party essentially represented the interests of the large manufacturers in Germany. Weber's close observations of that party began very early in his life, as the family home was often crowded with politicians (as well as businessmen, artists, and academics like Mommsen and Dilthey). Weber became quite disillusioned with his father and his political associates, mainly because in his view they had abdicated their political responsibilities in the vacuum left by Chancellor Bismarck's death, and had allowed the Prussian civil service to come to dominate German political life. Weber's disillusionment with the compromising centrism of the National Liberals, as well as his fear of the anti-democratic right and his qualms concerning the hypocritical[1] Social Democrats on the left, influenced his views on bureaucracy, capitalism, and of course politics.

Weber's father was also an important source for much of the inner tension he experienced throughout his life. Max Weber Sr. was apparently a hedonistic,

---

1 As we argue in more detail later, Weber was unhappy about the Social Democratic Party's tendency to internal oligarchy and external quietism despite its radical and democratic rhetoric.

self-satisfied, shallow, and hypocritical man who, perhaps compensating for his relative impotence at work, took to bullying people at home, particularly Weber's mother. Helene Fallenstein was a shy, withdrawn, extremely pious, and altruistic Christian, too prone in Weber's view to "turning the other cheek." She and her sister, Ida Baumgarten, were followers of the New England "Divine" William Ellery Channing. Their religiosity had a significant impact on Weber's interest in religion and his high regard for Calvinist virtues, despite his self-acknowledged inability to accept any religious world-view himself. Weber lived for a time with his Aunt Ida and Uncle Herman, who were in effect second parents to him. His aunt had a highly developed social conscience and was much more forthright and active than was his mother, putting into practice what both sisters believed. Herman Baumgarten, an 1848 type liberal[2] who, unlike Weber's father, had never reconciled himself to the Bismarck regime, had a significant influence on young Max, both politically and intellectually. Weber was also engaged, for six years, to the Baumgarten's daughter Emmy.

The Webers moved from Erfurt to Berlin when young Max was 5. By the time he was 13 he had already given evidence of intellectual genius, having written clever letters citing people like Homer and Virgil and precocious essays on German and Roman history. In 1882, Weber, following in his father's footsteps, began to study law at Heidelberg, drink heavily, get involved in duels, and indulge in other typical student pursuits of the day. It was in 1883–84 that he became close to the Baumgartens while living in Straßburg in connection with military duties. From 1885–86, Weber was back in Berlin preparing for his law examinations. From 1887–88, he lived again in Straßburg as well as in Posen, falling in love with his cousin Emmy and joining the Union for Social Policy, a group of academics with whom he was to be associated for many years. In 1889, Weber received his doctorate in law, *magna cum laude*. His thesis was on commercial enterprises in the middle ages.

During this period of his life, Weber had

extremely intense yet highly organized work habits. He was a driven yet methodical scholar. In 1890, he began a series of studies of East Elbian farm workers for the Union for Social Policy. In 1891, he completed his *Habilitation* thesis thus qualifying for a university teaching post on Roman agrarian history. His first teaching job was at Berlin in 1892. At the same time, Weber continued practicing law, and completed his military service.

Weber became engaged in 1892 to another cousin, Marianne Schnitger, whom he "stole" from a close friend and married in 1893 after having broken off his engagement with the sickly Emmy. His uncle and mentor, Herman Baumgarten, died in 1893.

Weber joined the nationalist Pan-German Union and lectured on "the Polish question"[3] in 1893. At that time he was being considered for teaching posts at Berlin (in commercial law) and Freiburg (in economics), accepting the latter in 1894. In that same year, he reported to the Evangelical Social Congress on the studies of farm workers begun some four years earlier. His inaugural address at Freiburg, "The National State and Economic Policy," had quite an impact. Largely because of it, Weber succeeded Knies in political science at Heidelberg in 1896, after travelling to Great Britain in late 1895.

The Weber home in Heidelberg eventually became a famous Sunday afternoon gathering place for such thinkers as Troeltsch (who lived with the Webers for a time), Lukàcs, Michels, Sombart, Bloch, George, Windelband, Rickert, and Jaspers. Already by 1896, Weber's reputation as a man of independent views, political realism, enormous intellect, and encyclopaedic knowledge in such areas as economic, legal, cultural, military, and political history; philosophy; archeology; ethnography; and linguistics was well

---

2 Some of Herman Baumgarten's generation remained inspired by the liberal ideas and sentiments of the short-lived but significant revolution which had spread across continental Europe in 1848. This revolution emerged in the wake of reaction by increasingly miserable peasants, decreasingly influential artisans, and considerably frustrated factory workers against the emerging dominance of the urban/industrial middle class. Liberal thinkers like Herman Baumgarten refused to compromise their principles by accepting the *status quo*, including the way in which party politics worked in Germany after Bismarck, choosing instead to criticize the trends of the day.

3 Weber was concerned about the implications of the importing of Polish migrant workers by the Junker owners of large estates in East Elbia. They did so as part of an effort to move towards a capitalist approach to agriculture so as to compete effectively with Russian and American grain growers. One consequence was the movement westward of large numbers of German peasants formerly permanently resident in the territory, and thus the likely emergence there of a Polish ethnic majority, albeit one which could be deported if it should appear desirable to those in power. As a late nineteenth century discussant of what is now called the "guest worker" phenomenon in Germany, Weber was concerned that the self-interested actions of one particular group, the Junkers, could threaten the well-being of Germany as a whole. We shall enumerate here neither the particulars of Weber's concerns nor his specific policy recommendations. What is important to recognize is that Weber saw this rural crisis as a matter of national economic *policy*. Thus, the issue needed to be addressed by politicians, rather than leaving unchecked a group trying to solve its own economic problems without regard to the consequences for the nation.

established. He was physically and temperamentally impressive as well, and was a "charismatic" lecturer.

In 1897, a series of events occurred which dramatically interrupted Weber's personal and intellectual life. A month or so after he had thrown his father out of the house over a row they had had concerning his father's bad treatment of his mother, Weber's father died of a stroke. This, along perhaps with Weber's feverish work habits, his possibly unconsummated marriage, his broken engagement and "stealing" of Marianne from a friend, and/or other unknown factors which may have caused him inner conflict and tension, contributed in some way to a drastic mental breakdown suffered by Weber. This breakdown led to severe melancholia, with only brief relapses, for a period of about five years. During this period Weber found he was unable to write very much, or lecture at all. He resigned from the Pan-German Union and ceased teaching, tried again, resigned again. He travelled through the Alps, various parts of Italy, Corsica, Switzerland, and the Riviera.

By 1902, Weber was back at Heidelberg, and began his writings on methodology, the first part of which was completed in 1903. He resigned his teaching post, travelled in Italy, Holland, and Belgium, and began his study of the Protestant Ethic. He also became coeditor of the **Archiv für Sozialwissenschaft und Sozialpolitik**, with Sombart and Jaffé. In 1904, Weber was invited to lecture at some scholarly meetings connected with the St. Louis World's Fair. This was the first time he had lectured in six and a half years. Weber's experiences while in the United States for three months influenced his conception of capitalism, Protestantism, bureaucracy, and democracy. The trip also signalled his return to an active intellectual, political, and social life. The first and second parts of Weber's first version of **The Protestant Ethic and the Spirit of Capitalism** were published in 1904 and 1905. In 1905, he taught himself Russian so that he could comment on the First Russian Revolution. In 1906, he attended a convention of the Social Democratic Party. In 1907, he criticized the Social Democrats (as well as the Kaiser) at a conference of the Union for Social Policy. He also began to do an empirical study of factory workers. In 1908, Weber participated in the National Liberal Party convention, and caused quite a stir by forcefully arguing with someone opposed to parliamentarism. Also, in 1908 he openly criticized the practice of using political criteria in the making of university appointments.

In 1909, Weber wrote a major essay on ancient economic history. In 1910, he cofounded the German

Sociological Association with Simmel and Tönnies and began to work on his *magnum opus*, **Economy and Society**. When the First World War began, Weber was too old to fight, so he took a post as an administrator of nine military hospitals. His brother Karl died in action in 1915. Weber became even more politically active, writing letters and polemical essays on political matters and strategies of war. He also continued to help and counsel friends with personal problems. In 1915, he began to work on his sociology of religion, and studies on Confucianism, Taoism, Buddhism, and Hinduism were published in 1916. In 1917, **Ancient Judaism** came out, and Weber gave the first of his celebrated Munich lectures to students, "Science as a Vocation."

In 1917–18, he wrote a series of newspaper articles on the need for parliamentary and civil service reform which almost caused him to be tried for high treason. Weber actually *joined* a political party, a new one called the German Democratic Party. He lost the nomination to be a candidate for that party, although he had been touted as a potential minister or ambassador. In 1917, Weber gave another famous lecture, this time to some Austrian naval officers, on "Socialism." In 1919, he delivered "Politics as a Vocation" in Munich, where he accepted a teaching post. He took an executive position with the German Democratic Party, participated at Versailles in the drafting of the German reply to the victorious allies' memorandum on war guilt, contributed to the writing of the new constitution and thus to the Weimar reconstruction, tried to persuade General Ludendorff to surrender, and engaged in numerous other political activities. His mother died in 1919.

In 1919–20, Weber lectured extensively on economic history. In 1920, Weber's sister Lili committed suicide and Max and Marianne made plans to adopt her four children. Weber angered some rightist students by advocating "rational democracy," and the first part of **Economy and Society** went to press in 1920, so he was still politically and intellectually active. Weber died of pneumonia on June 14, 1920. His last words reportedly were "The Truth is the Truth."

We see in all of the above a man who was very much engaged in the world, except for the five year period of his illness. His sociological writings reflect that experience, and when appropriate we shall point out important instances of this when discussing Weber's arguments. There is of course a danger in relating someone's sociology to his biography, or to his social context for that matter. We have not introduced Weber this way so as to "reduce" his ideas to his uneasy relationship with his father, his close relationships with his mother, his aunt, or his uncle, his trip to St. Louis, and the like. However, we do believe that knowing these particulars of Weber's biography will help students to understand how he became sensitized to certain issues, and to some extent why he analyzed them the way he did. Certainly the broad point can be made that Weber's active and rather anguished life helps us to understand his being torn in his work between various oppositions, such as those between bureaucracy and democracy, the ethic of ultimate disposition and the ethic of responsibility, rational and non-rational social action, and science and politics. Having made that point, we also recognize that what he wrote about these matters needs to be examined on its own merits rather than in terms of possible roots in certain specific personal experiences or his general psychic torment.[4]

As we said earlier, the intellectual influences on Weber should also be recognized. We have chosen to confine our comments on this pretty much to our expository section.

Let us now consider Weber's sociological ideas.

Weber's Conception of Social Science

In order to explain the "purpose" of social science for Weber, it is necessary first to touch on a common misunderstanding of part of what is conventionally discussed as Weber's "methodology," viz., his notion of "value neutrality."

Despite Weber's obvious political involvements, his clear commitment to certain values, and his strong ambivalence towards bureaucracy, some commentators argue that he advocated a scholarship completely devoid of values, except perhaps for the value of knowing itself. They believe that Weber was trying to develop a social science purged of any bias, a "value free" or "value neutral" sociology. From this point of view, such contaminants as religious conviction, political commitment, nationalism, statism, or racism

should not interfere with objective social analysis. Weber's alleged search for a neutral, scientific sociology informed by what Nietzsche wittily called the "dogma of immaculate perception" has been applauded by some, while others have seen it as dangerous because of its "sociology for sale" implications that social science could be used in the service of any interests and the individual sociologist was free to act opportunistically. The longstanding debate within sociology over the relationship between "facts" and "values," which debate flourished particularly during the years of the Viet Nam War, led sociologists on all sides of that controversy to misapprehend and misrepresent Weber's own views on this matter. His own views are of course our present concern.

Weber's arguments about "relatedness to value" and "value neutrality" need to be understood in the context of his conception of "science as a vocation." "Relatedness to value" is a term Weber adopted from the neo-Kantian Heinrich Rickert. In a nutshell, the argument is that what we choose to study, what questions we ask about it, and hence to a certain degree what answers we get to our questions, are related to our values. The way we conceptualize the world is influenced by what is (historically and culturally) significant to us. Out of the vast flux of human experience, which we cannot hope to understand fully, we select, according to our value orientation, in order to gain partial knowledge. As researchers, we are aware that we have selected, and we know that our knowledge is partial, and that is precisely why research is unending. These ideas are all present in the following passage from Weber:

> The cultural problems which move men form themselves ever anew and in different colours, and the boundaries of that area in the infinite stream of concrete events which acquires meaning and significance for us ... are constantly subject to change. The intellectual context from which it is viewed and scientifically analyzed shift. The points of departure of the cultural sciences remain changeable throughout the limitless future as long as a Chinese ossification of intellectual life does not render mankind incapable of setting new questions to the eternally inexhaustible flow of life.
> (The Methodology of the Social Sciences, p. 84)

Given that what we're interested in, what we choose to analyze, and what questions we raise about it are related to our values, are we not henceforward bound to pursue our research in as objective a manner as possible? Weber's answer to that question is

---

4 For this reason, we have not included in this biographical sketch very much about the fascinating intellectual and emotional relationship between Max and Marianne Weber. However, we would like to note that Marianne Weber, herself a feminist scholar and legislator, edited much of **Economy and Society** and wrote Max Weber's biography after his death. Indeed, much of what we know about Max Weber's relationship with his mother, his subsequent interest in religion, and his breakdown is derived from Marianne Weber's biography. Also, Marianne was clearly a source of significant emotional support for Weber during his breakdown periods, although her understandable reticence to discuss such matters directly in the biography and her unfortunately having destroyed Weber's autopathography (his own account of his illness) in 1945 has frustrated Weber analysts.

found not only in his purely "methodological" writings of the early 1900's, but also on those occasions when he prefaced or ended some clearly value-laden remarks with cautions about their nonscientific character and, in most mature form, in his celebrated Munich lectures of 1917 and 1919, "Politics as a Vocation" and "Science as a Vocation."

Precisely because individuals—even those who argued that this should be done—found it difficult to keep analysis and polemics separated, Weber sometimes proposed an institutional and pragmatic rather than a personal solution to this problem. One of Weber's concrete concerns was the unbridled passion for bureaucratization exhibited by Schmoller and others within the Union for Social Policy, an organization to which Weber belonged, and which consisted largely of economists and civil servants committed to the monarchic welfare state. He suggested in 1910 that a new organization, the German Sociological Association, be organized so as to confine itself to scholarly discussion, leaving partisan ones to other organizations, if not other people. In 1912, he tried to organize such a segregation within the Union for Social Policy itself. Both attempts were unsuccessful.

Weber was also concerned to gain autonomy for the liberal university from state interference. He fought against the use of political criteria advocated by colleagues, bureaucrats, and politicians, for appointment to university positions, just as he argued and acted against the "zoological nationalism" (racism) of some students and colleagues who argued for ethnic and religious criteria for making academic appointments.[5] However, sometimes Weber seemed to be recommending the suicide of self-repression over the homicide of external suppression of statements of political value-judgment. For example, he argued that the university should be open to all political and philosophical viewpoints, as long as professors were productive scholars who made honest arguments rather than just propagandists.

Actually, Weber argued both ways on the question of the open espousal of political values in the classroom. On the one hand, he did distinguish between speechmaking and lecturing, between preaching values and stating values. Like his uncle, he was particularly

disturbed, for example, by the historian Treitschke's glorification of the Hohenzollerns, the Prussian monarchy. On the other hand, he preferred dramatic to bland lecturers, because students could more easily perceive and "discount" the values in the presentations of the former. So, although he saw danger in the pseudo-objectivity of dull presentations, he also feared the formation of personality cults in the classroom, because this might result in a decline in students' taste for and ability to perform sober, empirical analyses. This latter concern was related to the circumstance that, in Weber's day, even students able to "resist" persuasive oratory so as to maintain critical, independent judgment would have found it difficult to "talk back" in the lecture hall. Weber was also concerned that scholars should try to eschew parochialism and suspend moral reactions to issues. Like J. S. Mill, he argued that scholars should seek out facts "inconvenient" to their own value-positions, just as they should face students with facts that contradict their assumptions about the world. Weber's reasons for this argument hinge on his notion that the purpose of social science is to provide clarity, which makes clear choices between values—the political vocation—possible.

The vocation of science by which Weber meant all scholarship (humanities, social sciences, and natural sciences) involved sober, rational enlightenment, rooted in the Socratean ethos of intellectual integrity. Scholars should face the world matter-of-factly and with intellectual honesty. The critical contribution of social science so conceived was to provide clarity concerning the relationship between means and ends, and the consequences of choosing particular means. Although the determination of ends was not itself part of the scientific vocation, the latter could reveal the ultimate values involved in a situation, so that rational choices could be made by the autonomous, responsible individual. Such decisions would not be easy, but the revelation by social science of all foreseeable consequences would help individuals decide what to do.

It should be clear from all of this that Weber was recommending neither moral indifference nor cynical opportunism when he discussed value-neutrality. A scholarship devoid of passion was to be feared as much as pure partisanship. In avoiding the fanaticism of absolute commitment, sociology should beware adopting the opportunism of no commitment. Caught between these two poles, Weber proposed that our hearts should remain alive while our heads stay clear.

---

5 Thus, for example, Weber actively supported his friends Simmel and Michels in their efforts to obtain academic positions in the face of discrimination against them on ethnic/religious and political grounds, respectively. Simmel's father was Jewish, although he had converted to Christianity much as Marx's father had, and Michels was a socialist, albeit a very much disaffected one.

The Conceptual and Methodological Foundations of Weber's Sociology

The key to understanding the conceptual and methodological foundations of Weber's sociology is to appreciate the centrality of the notion of "meaning" for him and other "interpretive" sociologists.

In contrast to what we might broadly call "positivistic" social science, "interpretive" sociology (and Weber is a very significant example of this approach) concentrates on the meaning that social action has for the actor. Interpretive sociologists focus on how people act and interact with one another on the basis of the meanings that situations have for them. Such meanings *may* become widely shared meanings, and this results in patterns of interaction, patterns which may persist for very long periods of time. Thus, interpretive sociologists agree with those taking a more positivistic approach that relatively persistent patterns of interaction exist, but for them it is most significant that these patterns emerge from a more basic process of meaningful interaction. In other words, the social "reality" focussed on by positivistic social scientists is socially constructed and socially maintained, and it is the processes of social construction and maintenance which need to be investigated, according to interpretive sociologists.

Now, what *methodological* implications would such a focus have? Since *meaning* has such a central place in their conception of social life, interpretive sociologists see their main task as *grasping meaning*.

As we shall see, grasping the meanings in terms of which people are interacting, and grasping the shifts in meaning that develop as social interaction proceeds, lie behind every concept that Weber developed and every methodological argument that he made. His insistence on the necessity of focussing on meaning continues to exert a profound influence on sociology today.

To get a sense of Weber's basic concepts and his fundamental methodological approach, let us consider the implications of a single sentence taken from the part of the didactic treatise **Economy and Society** which was written towards the end of his life and which serves as a summary of his fundamental concepts.[6] "Sociology . . . is a science concerning itself with the interpretive understanding of social action and thereby with a causal explanation of its course and consequences" (**Economy and Society**, p. 4). What does Weber mean by "social action," and what is the relationship between "interpretive understanding" and "causal explanation?"

In the two sentences which follow the one quoted above, Weber distinguishes "behaviour," "action," and "social action."

We shall speak of "action" insofar as the acting individual attaches a subjective meaning to his behaviour be it overt or covert, omission or acquiescence. Action is "social" insofar as its subjective meaning takes account of the behaviour of others and is thereby oriented in its course.

"Behaviour" is human activity which is unreflective; for example, it may be based on instinct, emotion, or custom for example, or it may be merely reactive imitation.[7] "Action" on the other hand is behaviour to which an intended subjective meaning is attached, and *"social action"* involves intersubjectivity, that is it is action which is oriented to or takes account of the presumed meaning of the activity (behaviour, action, or social action) of others.

Precisely because only activity which involves subjective meaning can be *understood*, action (Weber says social action) is the *core* of sociology's subject matter. He does not wish to argue by this either that social action is all that sociologists examine or that it is more important than behaviour. It simply constitutes the central interest of the sort of social science that Weber was trying to develop, one in which we are attempting to grasp with some certainty the meaning of activity.

Weber distinguishes four ideal *types* of social action.[8] Two of these types are "rational," and two "non-rational."

The non-rational types of social action, which Weber acknowledges (*Ibid.*, p. 25) both lie on the borderline between behaviour and action, are *traditional* and *affectual*. These two types of non-rational social

---

6 Our readers should be aware that the conceptual *Summa*, Part One of **Economy and Society**, tends generally to be drier, more abstract, and more conceptual than the descriptively rich and concrete Part Two, which was actually written earlier. Apart from the differences in style between Parts One and Two, there are some significant conceptual disparities which would be con-

fusing if you were to read comparable selections from Part Two. For example, the typology of social action developed in the earlier Part Two was much more complex than that outlined in the later Part One.

7 Historian philosophers like R. G. Collingwood and social philosophers such as Alfred Schütz have similarly emphasized the significance of intentionality and reflectivity in defining the subject matter of the social sciences. Also, readers may note later certain apparent parallels between Weber's distinction between "behaviour" and "social action" and George Herbert Mead's distinction between "biosocial interaction" and "symbolic interaction." There are some important differences as well, which will be clear after a careful reading of the Mead chapter.

8 Weber's meaning for the term "ideal type" is explained below.

action are in a sense residual categories for Weber; he focussed his analysis on *rational* social action.

This does not mean to say that Weber believed rational actions outweigh or are more important than non-rational actions; it is simply that in his view rational social action is more susceptible to social-scientific analysis, for the same reasons as he argued social action and not behaviour should lie at the centre of the sociologist's attention.

A rational act, according to Weber, is one in which all the elements of the act, both the means and the ends, are critically examined by the social actor. Such an act is based on a clear understanding, *from the individual actor's point of view,*[9] of the meaning of ends within the context of other ends, as well as of the relations between means and ends, possible byproducts of the means chosen, and so forth. The distinction between the two *types* of rational social action value-rational and purposefully rational (or instrumentally rational) action is buried in the definition of rational social action itself. Value-rational action corresponds to what Weber elsewhere called the "ethic of ultimate disposition" ("Politics as a Vocation," p. 122), where the actor is guided by an unconditional espousal of some (religious or political) value, not considering other possible ends, and not critically examining the appropriateness, likely effectiveness, or possible unintended consequences of the means chosen to attain the unquestioned end. Although value-rational social action is "rational" in comparison with affectual and traditional social action, in that the relation between means and ends is considered, it is not as rational as purposefully rational social action. The latter corresponds precisely to the definition of rational action given above, account being taken of conflicting ends, various alternative means, and potential consequences which might contradict the actor's intentions. Purposefully rational social action is informed by what Weber called the "ethic of responsibility," in which a person must anticipate the foreseeable results of his or her actions.[10]

Perhaps our readers can already see the connection between Weber's notion of rational social action and the clarificatory role of social science (as a "vocation") in helping individuals make decisions. This theme will be addressed later on, when we discuss "Politics as a Vocation."

The distinction between value-rational and purposefully rational social action is only one among a number of overlapping and crosscutting distinctions which Weber made in discussing rationality and rationalization, which latter important themes are discussed at some length later. For the moment, it is sufficient to see them as two of the four types of social action[11] which, along with his distinction between behaviour, action, and social action, constitute Weber's fundamental building block concepts. On this foundation, Weber constructed[12] whole series of other concepts, such as "social relationship," "communal relationship," "associative relationship," "open relationship," "closed relationship," "organization," "voluntary organization," "compulsory organization," and his entire political sociology, which we shall discuss in detail later.

If these are Weber's basic concepts, then what is his fundamental methodological approach? What is the relationship between "interpretive understanding" and "causal explanation," the two terms found in the single sentence which we quoted earlier?

The relationship between "understanding" (*Verstehen*) and "explanation" (*Erklären*) lies at the heart of Weber's methodological writings. His ideas on this question were informed by a longstanding debate within German intellectual circles a debate which continues even today concerning the appropriate methodology for the "cultural sciences," the disciplines which deal with human behaviour. Although Weber accepted the distinction drawn by Wilhelm Dilthey between these two methods, he did *not* view them as independent and antagonistic; he tried to develop a social science which *combines* the methods of explanation and understanding. Although Weber argued strongly for the *interpretation* of social action, he was still searching for objective knowledge, as is signalled by the sentence with which we began. Thus, he sought what he called "explanatory understanding" (*erklärendes Verstehen*).

---

9 This is in contrast to, for example, the distinction drawn by Vilfredo Pareto between nonlogical and logical conduct, the latter being essentially action viewed as "rational" from the point of view of the external, "scientific" observer. See the discussion of this in the chapter on Pareto.

10 The two ethics are discussed in more detail below.

11 Elsewhere, Weber distinguished, on the basis of the degree of rationality, persistence, and legal compulsion involved, five types of social action.

12 Readers should not be misled into inferring from this statement that Weber's conceptual apparatus was either constructed by him, or outlined for his readers, in such a clearcut and orderly way; although certainly he made an effort in what is known as Part One to do so, we have still had to simplify and clarify his ideas in our presentation of them.

The method of *Verstehen* is not itself subjective; rather, it takes as its subject matter the subjective interpretations that people make. As Weber argued, for example, to analyze land distribution practices in the Roman Empire we need to be aware of the trigonometric "mistakes" of Roman surveyors. To analyze the social action of the Lubbavitcher *chassidim*, Irving Oil Limited, or the Reform Party of Canada, we need to begin at least with the ways in which those particular social actors view the world.

Unlike natural science then, sociology can (indeed must) take into account what its subjects are thinking, what their intentions are, what motivates them, and the like.[13] This is accomplished by putting ourselves in their place, by attempting to see the world from their point of view. This method can be used to understand history and as we shall see many of Weber's major contributions were in the area of historical sociology because the sociologist can attempt to reconstruct situations as they would have appeared to the actors in them. In his view, the choices that actors make are governed by their perceptions of the situations in which they find themselves. The sociologist makes sense of an act, whether current or historical, by seeing it in its wider context of meaning, by fitting the act in some "understandable sequence of motivation" (**Economy and Society**, p. 9). Thus, the sociological observer comes up with what is essentially a "plausible hypothesis" which is "meaning fully adequate." Sociological interpretation of this sort serves then as an hypothesis, which subsequently needs to be shown to be "causally adequate": ". . . verification of subjective interpretation by comparison with the concrete course of events is, as in the case of all hypotheses, indispensable." (*Ibid.*, p. 10).

On the one hand, hypotheses developed through the question-generating procedure of *Verstehen* need to be empirically assessed. On the other hand, any causal explanation is deficient unless the process described can be meaningfully understood.

A correct causal interpretation of typical action means that the process which is claimed to be typical is shown to be both adequately grasped on the level of meaning and at the same time the interpretation is to some degree causally adequate. If adequacy in respect to meaning is lacking, then no matter how high the degree of uniformity and how precisely its probability càn be numerically determined, it is still

an incomprehensible statistical probability. On the other hand, even the most perfect adequacy on the level of meaning has causal significance from a sociological point of view only insofar as there is some kind of proof for the existence of a probability that action in fact normally takes the course which has been held to be meaningful. For this there must be some degree of determinable frequency of approximation to an average or a pure type.

In this way, Weber argued against those (the positivists) who proposed a unitary scientific method, who believed in other words that natural-scientific methods (explanation) could and should be applied to the subject matter of the cultural sciences. Meaning is critical to the subject matter of sociology as Weber conceived it, so mere "explanation" is not enough. On the other hand, Weber also rejected the arguments of those who believed that using *Verstehen* precluded causal explanation derived from comparison and generalization. Weber saw explanation and understanding as complementary, not opposed, methods. (*Ibid.*, p. 12).

We need now to consider two further aspects of Weber's *verstehende* methodology, the notions of the "imaginary experiment" and the "ideal type," which clarify the relationship between "interpretive understanding" and "causal explanation."

> Often, unfortunately, there is available only the uncertain procedure of the "imaginary experiment" which consists in thinking away certain elements of a chain of motivation and working out the course of action which would then probably ensue, thus arriving at a causal judgment. *Ibid.*, p. 10)

When discussing the "imaginary experiment" idea, Weber cites historian Eduard Meyer's attempt to assess the significance of the Battle of Marathon (491 B.C.) for the future of Greek culture. An historian interested in this question is in effect isolating one of several possible causal factors in the development of Greek political life, and is considering whether the course of Greek history would have been significantly different if that factor had been absent.

Meyer asked what might have happened if the Persians had won at Marathon? In so doing, he was hypothetically eliminating (or altering) one factor in a situation concerning which he had tentatively raised the question of causality. He then hypothetically constructed, through "scientifically trained fantasy," what would likely have been the course of events (what Weber called the "objective possibil-

---

13 This fundamental insight goes back at least to Giambattista Vico (1688–1744).

ity") under these altered conditions. Given the knowledge about Persian colonial practices that has been accumulated, e.g., the way the Persians treated the Jews, or the way they dealt with the native peoples in the Northern part of the Indian subcontinent, it is likely that the hypothetically victorious Persians would have tried to rule the conquered Greeks in part by manipulating their religion to create a theocracy rooted in the mysteries and the oracles indigenous to Greece. Since the historian's speculation leads to this "objective possibility" because of the knowledge of Greek culture and Persian policies which existed at that time, it is not an arbitrary concoction on the historian's part.

The next step for our historian is to compare what might have happened (the "objective possibility") with what did in fact happen. The Athenians won the Battle of Marathon, an independent and democratic Greece flourished, and its culture emphasized scientific, philosophical, and humanist values (e.g., the development of a free mind and spirit).

What conclusions might be drawn from such a comparison? Insofar as the "objective possibility" and what actually happened differ, the difference may be imputed to the factors eliminated (or altered). So, the Greek victory at Marathon, it is concluded, was *a* significant factor in the development of such parts of Greek culture as humanism. It was "a" significant factor, not the sole factor; Weber did not believe in single factor causality. Nor would he have argued that the hypothetical course of events issuing from a Persian victory would have been an inevitability. Weber had a *probabilistic* notion of causality. Note that he discusses not "causal necessity" but "causal adequacy," the latter existing when the probability of an objective possibility is judged to be high.

This sort of "imaginary experiment" is about the best that social science can come up with, according to Weber. Often, even this level of argument is not possible:

> In very many cases of historical interpretation which seem highly plausible . . . there is not even a possibility of the order of verification which was feasible in this case. Where this is true the interpretation must necessarily remain a hypothesis. (*Ibid.*, p. 11)

In other words, in such cases, meaningfully adequate statements must remain hypotheses.

The last methodological idea of Weber's that we shall consider at this time is the notion of "ideal type." We have been using this idea already, without defining it. For example, in passages in Part One of **Economy and Society**, Weber referred to the importance of "an average or a pure type" (*Ibid.*, p. 12) and to "ideally constructed pure types" (*Ibid.*, p. 20) for the development of causally adequate out of meaningfully adequate statements. The fullest discussion of what he meant by "ideal type" is found in his 1904 methodological writings.

One of the sources of misery for sociology students is that sociologists seldom use a term or concept in the same way that "regular" people do. As if that were not bad enough, different sociologists may well use the *same* concept in quite distinct ways. Also, as Weber himself noted:

> the abstract character of the concepts of sociology is responsible for the fact that, compared with actual historical reality, they are relatively lacking in fullness of content. To compensate for this disadvantage, sociological analysis can offer a greater precision of concepts. This precision is obtained by striving for the highest possible degree of adequacy on the level of meaning. (*Ibid.*)

Ideal types are precisely specified, clearly defined concepts. They are analytical constructs which are used as intellectual tools:

> An ideal type is formed by the one-sided *accentuation* of one or more points of view and by the synthesis of a great many diffuse, discrete, more or less present and occasionally absent *concrete individual* phenomena, which are arranged according to those one-sidedly emphasized viewpoints into a unified *analytical* construct (*Gedankenbild*). In its conceptual purity, this mental construct (*Gedankenbild*) cannot be found empirically anywhere in reality. **The Methodology of the Social Sciences**, p. 90).

Ideal types, those you have already encountered (e.g., the four types of social action) and those you will read about later (e.g., the three types of authority, modern bureaucracy, capitalism, the Protestant Ethic, church, sect) are clearly defined. An ideal type is made coherent and unambiguous by emphasizing the characteristic and unique features of the phenomenon in question, by exaggerating certain features to the point that nowhere would there exist any actual, "real" example of it in its pure form.[14] Having

---

14 Weber argued that it was not possible to describe in all its qualities the phenomenon down to its smallest details, precisely because of his neo-Kantian view that we can but partially grasp,

such a logically pure, meaningful, congruent, consistent concept, which is constructed out of empirical experience but has no actual empirical counterpart because it is an exaggeration, facilitates the sort of social analysis Weber advocates. Thus, constructing ideal types which is only possible in the social sciences which can use Verstehen is an integral part of the sociologist's attempt to develop causal explanations.

Weber himself realized that the word "ideal" could lead to the misunderstanding that he meant the phenomena in question were moral or ethical ideals. Against this, he argued that

> an ideal type . . . has no connection at all with value judgments, and it has nothing to do with any type of perfection other than a purely logical one. There are ideal types of brothels as well as of religions. . . . (Ibid., pp. 98–99)

One other possible misunderstanding which we would like to forestall is signalled by Weber's argument that "historical research faces the task of determining in each individual case, the extent to which this ideal construct approximates to or diverges from reality. . . ." (Ibid., p. 90). Weber is arguing here that one should compare reality not to one ideal type, but rather to various ideal types. A particular sociopolitical structure might be compared to the ideal types of "charismatic authority," "traditional authority," and "rational-legal authority." A given organization could be examined in terms of the ideal types of "patrimonial administration" and "modern bureaucracy." A specific religious group might be analyzed in terms of its approximation to the ideal types of "church" and "sect."

So, for Weber, ideal types were means to an end, intellectual tools with heuristic (hypothesis-generating) value. Having ideal types makes it possible to construct (meaningfully adequate) hypotheses which can be assessed for their causal adequacy or to develop a meaningfully adequate understanding of clearly established empirical regularities. Ideal types are neither "true" nor "false"; they should rather be regarded as more or less useful means to the end of causal explanation. They allow us, if they are useful, to construct hypotheses, employing our imagination, our knowledge, and our

methodological training, as Meyer did when analyzing the Athenian victory at Marathon, or as Weber did when assessing the historical significance of the Protestant Ethic (discussed below).

Weber believed that, despite our starting point being related to value, despite our method being Verstehen, and despite our relying on mental constructs called ideal types, objective knowledge is in principle possible in the social sciences. Why? Social science has available to it the "imaginary experiment," a method which takes advantage of our being able to use interpretive understanding in order to reach causal explanations of the course and effects of social action.

Weber's basic concepts and ideas about methodology are not, and have not been, exempt from criticism for their ambiguities, logical inconsistencies, and so forth. We have not dealt with these problems in our discussion, opting instead to present Weber's ideas as clearly as possible.

Weber's Empirical and Historical Sociology

Now that our readers have a better sense of Weber's conception of social science, his "building block" concepts, and his fundamental methodological approach, we can move on to consider what Carl Mayer called his empirical and historical sociology.[15] We shall begin with "rationalization," the pervasive theme which dominates Weber's empirical work.

Rationalization

"Rationalization" seems, at first blush, to refer to some kind of world historical process which like Hegel's "cunning of reason" or Adam Smith's "hidden hand of the marketplace" operates independently of human volition. Such an argument would contra-

---

by selection, part of the vast flux of human experience, as discussed earlier. Nor did he accept the scholastic method of positing an ideal "essence" which lies behind an empirical phenomenon. Instead, he advocated a third course, building meaningful constructs out of empirical materials.

15 In discussing **Economy and Society** in a course on Max Weber which he gave at the New School for Social Research in the late 1960s, Carl Mayer made a distinction between Weber's formal system of sociological categories (which we have already discussed), the application of these categories to substantive fields of social life (e.g., the polity, the economy, religion, and law), and the attempt to illustrate these developed categories by giving historical flesh and muscle to the conceptual bones. We have chosen to collapse the second and third of these themes in our review of Weber's entire work. At this point, we would like to acknowledge the general influence of Carl Mayer's understanding of the work of Max Weber on the development of our own exposition of Weber's thought. Likewise, it should be noted that our interest in and understanding of specific aspects of Weber's thought have been stimulated by such disparate influences as Joseph Bensman, Peter L. Berger, Benjamin Nelson, Emil Oestereicher, and Trent Schroyer, all members of the Graduate Faculty of the New School for Social Research in the late 1960s, as well as by the important contributions of Guenther Roth.

dict the voluntarism and the methodological individualism which inform Weber's basic concepts, as outlined by us earlier. Let us first indicate the sorts of phenomena Weber meant by rationalization, and then we will discuss how this seemingly "systemic," mystical, and abstract force was in fact the consequence of the social action of specific groups of people who attached a particular kind of meaning to their activities in various spheres of life.

Consider, for example, the differences between a Gregorian chant and a polyphonic Requiem; between a simple hut and the Cathedral at Reims; or between the cash basis of accounting and double entry bookkeeping. Finally, compare these two statements of law:

(1) And he that killeth any man shall surely be put to death. And he that killeth a beast shall make it good; beast for beast . . . breach for breach, eye for eye, tooth for tooth. (**Leviticus**)

(2) 11.01 Subject to clauses 11.02 and 11.03, neither the Employer, the Union, nor any employee shall discriminate against any employee on the basis of race; colour; religion; national origin; ancestry; place of origin; age; physical disability; marital status; sex; sexual orientation; creed; citizenship; ethnic origin; political affiliation, belief, or practice; family relationship; membership or lawful activity in the Union; previous or impending exclusion from the bargaining unit; clerical or lay status; language; or mental handicap.

11.02 The provisions of Clause 11.01 do not apply to the operation of the terms or conditions of any pension or insurance plan.

11.03 The provisions of Clause 11.01 concerning physical disability, mental handicap, or language do not apply when such a disability results in an employee not being able to meet his/her professional responsibilities to the Employer in a satisfactory manner. (**Collective Agreement between Mount Allison University and the Mount Allison Faculty Association, 1995–1998**)

What do all these examples have in common at an abstract level, apart from their obvious differences in content? Each example partially illustrates the widening influence of rational social action as defined earlier. This is essentially what Weber meant by the term rationalization.[16] Rationalization is a *process* which

Weber claimed occurred in virtually every sphere of life. In the political sphere, Weber distinguished three ideal types of authority, charismatic, traditional, and rational-legal. He argued that European societies of his day most closely approximated the latter. In the sphere of administration, Weber compared the patrimonial administration in earlier Europe to the increasingly dominant organizational form called modern bureaucracy. As will become clear later in this chapter, Weber's analysis of modern bureaucracy as the type of administrative apparatus typically found in societies characterized by rational-legal authority is a major component of his sociology of politics. In the legal sphere, Weber traced the movement from material law to formal law, and the struggle between what he called "formal" and "substantive" rationality within the law.[17] In the economic sphere, Weber contrasted capitalism ("the pursuit of profit by means of continuing rational, capitalistic enterprise")[18] with other, less rational forms of economy. As part of that argument, Weber put great emphasis on the development of double-entry bookkeeping in 1492 by the Italian monk-mathematician Paccioli.

In music, Weber discussed for example the development of a system of notation, of chromatics and enharmonics, of polyphony based on the fifth, of counterpoint, and of even temperament (as in Bach's "Well-Tempered Clavier"). In art, Weber singled out the notion of spatial perspective, and he emphasized the significance in architecture of the Gothic Arch. A technological change that he stressed was the invention of printing and hence a more widely available literature. Key developments were the rational proofs of Greek geometry (e.g., those of Euclid) and the experimental method of modern science (as advocated, for

---

16 Weber's discussion of rationalization was so complex that commentators differ widely in their explanations of the meaning of

the concept. Commentators have identified ten or more meanings that Weber had for the term, which he conceptualized on at least three levels of abstraction, which he viewed in an ambivalent and dichotomous fashion, and which he discussed in terms of many spheres of social life. We cannot review each of the meanings here. As we have suggested, for our purposes, rationalization can be defined as the widening influence of rational social action in various spheres of social life.

17 This distinction corresponds roughly to that between what some people call the "letter" and the "spirit" of the law. Formally rational law refers to the system of theoretical law guided by legal logic without taking into account extra-juridical considerations, whereas "substantively rational" law may take into account such formally irrelevant, "extraneous" considerations as religious, ethical, economic, or political values. Our general point is that, for Weber, although there was a marked shift in Western Europe towards formal law, within the law there were certain anti-formal tendencies, which were substantively rational as well as non-rational.

18 "The Origins of Industrial Capitalism" (originally called "Author's Introduction"), p. 333.

example, by Francis Bacon). In religion, Weber saw the emergence of the belief in one God and the related notion of individual responsibility as keys to rationalization in the West. Indeed, it was ancient Israel's monotheism and the rational law of the Roman Empire which Weber identified as the most significant roots of the rationalization process in Western Europe.

Unfortunately, Weber's discussion of rationalization was very complex and somewhat ambiguous, so there has been quite a bit of confusion and misunderstanding on the part of his readers on this issue. To some extent this has been due to his discussing rationalization with respect to so many social spheres, which he was able to do because of his encyclopaedic knowledge. Very few of his contemporaries had such general knowledge, and virtually no one in this age of specialization has, so the very breadth of his discussion of rationalization may be one source of confusion. Another is that Weber discussed rationalization on at least three *levels* of abstraction.[19] Furthermore, Weber had a dichotomous conception of rationality; at the highest level of abstraction this is represented by the difference between what we might call "emancipatory Reason" and "technical Reason,"[20] between an increasing and clearer understanding by people in general of the conditions under which they live on the one hand and the increasing calculation of and control over the forces of the physical and social world on the other. To compound matters even further, Weber was *ambivalent* about rationalization,[21] partly because in his view "technical Reason" can come into *conflict* with "emancipatory Reason." For example, Weber points out ("Science as a Vocation," p. 139) that so-called "primitive" people knew far more about their tools and their environment than the early twentieth century ordinary Germans did. He went on to argue that "enlightenment" and "progress" do not necessarily accompany rationalization. Weber's ambivalence about rationalization had other sources as well. Our main point here is that his seemingly positive evaluation of rationalization at some points in his writing,[22] and the clear qualms

that he expressed about it at other points in his work, have led some to interpret his ambivalence as logical contradiction.

A final source of confusion is related to Weber's view that rationalization should not be equated with progress. Quite often, Weber is interpreted as pessimistically arguing that rationalization was an inevitable, irresistible, and irreversible sociostructural process which would lead to a mechanistic society in which people would be mere "cogs" in the system. We shall deal with this misunderstanding in our discussion of Weber's views on bureaucracy.

In sum, Weber's discussion of rationalization is somewhat confusing. It is however his fundamental concept, the single most important argument that he made in his empirical/historical sociology. The opening sentence of his introduction to his comparative **Sociology of Religion** gives an indication of the historical sweep of his argument:

> It is both inevitable and right that someone who is himself the offspring of modern European civilization should approach problems in world history with the following question in mind: through what concatenation of circumstances did it come about that precisely, and only, in the Western world certain cultural phenomena emerged which, as at least we like to think, represent a direction of development of universal significance and validity. ("The Origins of Industrial Capitalism in Europe," p. 331)

After reviewing some of the particulars of rationalization in Western music, architecture, science, and so forth, he states:

> For, in all the cases mentioned, what is obviously at issue is the nature of a specific type of "rationalism" peculiar to Western civilization.... Thus, the primary task is to recognize the special character of Western rationalism in general, and of modern Western rationalism in particular, and to explain its origins. (*Ibid.*, pp. 339–40)

Weber's studies (many of them incomplete) of Ancient Israel, Islam, early Christianity, the Protestant Ethic, Hinduism, Buddhism, Confucianism, and Taoism, as well as his general work on the social-psychological implications of religious belief, were all concerned to explain why rationalization developed specifically in Western Europe. This body of work

---

19 We shall not, however, discuss these different levels in any detail here.

20 This distinction is one that many Enlightenment and post-Enlightenment Thinkers have recognized.

21 Weber was in point of fact ambivalent about many aspects of social life, as will become clear in our discussions of his views on bureaucracy, for example.

22 Examples are the arguments that capitalism is the most productive type of economy and that modern bureaucracy has technical superiority over other forms of social organization. These

---

two arguments are reviewed below, in the sections on Weber's sociology of religion and sociology of politics, respectively.

was in effect a series of rather elaborate "imaginary experiments."[23]

Weber's Sociology of Religion

Although Weber professed to be "religiously unmusical" unlike his mother and his aunt he nevertheless devoted a great deal of time to the sociological analysis of religion. Weber's sociology of religion involved a consideration of the institutional aspects of religion, a focus on the social-psychological functions of religious beliefs for the individual, and an analysis of the role of religion in social-structural change. We shall discuss some of the more important issues that he addressed within each of these areas.

The best-known of Weber's analyses of the role of religion in social change is certainly **The Protestant Ethic and The Spirit of Capitalism**. This should be seen as but a part of his much larger body of work comparing the various world-religions. The significance of the Protestant Ethic thesis has been overplayed, partly because it was the first work of Weber's translated into English, partly because it *seemed* to be largely a critique of the so-called "Marxist" analysis of religion, and for certain other reasons which we shall not discuss here. Although the Protestant Ethic argument has been overemphasized, it does illustrate perhaps better than any of his other writings what Weber meant by the "imaginary experiment."

Weber had the same intense interest in, and the same basic understanding of, capitalism as had Karl Marx before him. A relatively small part of the population ("the bourgeoisie") controlled the forces of production, and labour was performed by "formally free" workers (the "proletariat") who sold their labour power to that small group. Both the proletariat and the bourgeoisie, the two major social classes of capitalist society, first emerged as significant historical actors in the great cities of late feudal Europe. The capitalist system was an expansive and dynamic one, in that, as a matter of principle, the capital accumulated in productive enterprises was reinvested, either to expand existing operations or to develop new ones. The relatively high productivity of capitalist enterprises was rooted in rationalist[24] values and methodical,

disciplined organizational practices (the factory system) calling for maximum efficiency. This new form of economy was very much distinct from that found in feudal Europe, and at first it was peculiar to relatively few Western European societies. Weber was interested in determining why it emerged, and why it emerged where it did. *One* factor that he isolated as possibly significant was a new way of religious thinking a particular variant of Calvinism which he ended up concluding to be *an* important factor contributing to the rise of capitalism.[25]

The major way in which Weber made this argument was to establish that there was an intellectual congruence between "the Protestant Ethic" and "the Spirit of Capitalism." This was not intended by Calvin:

> the cultural consequences of the Reformation were to a great extent, perhaps in the particular aspects with which we are dealing predominantly, unforeseen and even unwished for results of the labours of the reformers. They were often far removed from or even in contradiction to all that they themselves thought to attain. (**Prot. Ethic**, p. 90)

Indeed, Calvin would have been quite horrified by capitalism. The congruence existed because an unconscious "twisting" of his teachings paradoxically[26] implied certain economic activities.

What were the essential features of Calvin's teachings on which Weber centred his attention? First, God was seen as absolute, transcendent, mysterious, and incomprehensible. He created the world and He rules it. Each individual, furthermore, has been "predestined" by God to salvation or damnation. Salvation cannot be *achieved* via one's "works," or by confession, penance, or the dispensation of "indulgences." Salvation comes only through divine grace. Whether we are saved or not, it is our duty to work for the glory of God, to create His kingdom on earth, by pursuing our vocation or "calling" in a rational, methodical, and disciplined fashion. Earthly

---

23 Also, as we shall see, much of Weber's political sociology was rooted in the notion of rationalization as well.

24 So, the Protestant Ethic Thesis is part of Weber's analysis of rationalization. For example, Weber linked the rational-legal type of authority and the rational form of administration called modern bureaucracy to capitalism.

25 In other works, Weber discussed other structural and cultural factors leading to capitalism. These included the development of autonomous cities, the emergence of the bourgeoisie and of a "free" labour market, and the existence of a money economy, rational law, rational-legal authority, and bureaucracy.

26 The posited relationship between these religious and economic ideas is an example of what Weber called "unintended consequences." This latter is one way in which irony plays a role in sociological analysis.

concerns, things of the flesh, belong to the order of sin and death, and should be spurned.

Perhaps our readers can already see certain economic implications of these ideas which would be compatible with capitalism as it was described earlier. For example, the encouragement of hard work no matter what one's "calling," an idea which originated with Luther but was altered by Calvin, is consistent with the rationalist values emphasizing efficiency which lay behind the peculiar productivity of capitalism. In this way, the acquisition of profit was encouraged. Also, the admonition against enjoying "things of the flesh" discouraged consumption, and perhaps encouraged the reinvestment of profit so central to the expansiveness of capitalism.

Weber went even further than this in his analysis. Elsewhere, for example when discussing prophecy and charisma, Weber argued that the teachings of a particular religious leader and what that leader is taken to have been arguing by various followers are not necessarily the same. In his analysis of the Protestant Ethic, Weber distinguishes between Calvin's teachings, the preaching of Calvinist ministers, the writings of Puritan "divines," and what ordinary Calvinist followers may have come to believe.

> We are naturally not concerned with the question of what was theoretically and officially taught in the ethical compendia of the time. . . . We are interested rather in something entirely different: the influence of those psychological sanctions which, originating in religious belief and the practice of religion, gave a direction to practical conduct and held the individual to it. (*Ibid.*, p. 97)

Weber developed a sense of what Calvin's followers came to believe by using the method of *Verstehen*. We suggest that you our readers do the same, by mentally putting yourself in the place of someone who deeply believed in the above version of Calvin's teaching.

How would you act, if you viewed the world in this way? Weber concluded that many people would find the dark uncertainty of predestination, and the "inner loneliness" implied by it, to be psychologically intolerable. Calvinists could not rely on the confessional or the priest for the assurance of grace, nor did they have the Lutheran notion of "*inward* grace." Thus, Calvinists may have been led to seek *signs* of their salvation in their worldly success. Economic success came to be seen as demonstrating "election." By this social-psychological process, Weber argued, some individual Calvinists may have become driven

to work in a systematic and planned way in order to overcome the anxiety resulting from their uncertainty about their eternal destiny. Such acquisitive self-denial, quite antithetical to Calvin's teachings, reduced their psychological uncertainty and paradoxically encouraged capitalist economic activity. The development of capitalist institutions was therefore reinforced by the appearance of certain psychological dispositions encouraged by a particular religious world-view. One might say that this world-view was a necessary, but not a sufficient, cause[27] of the break with tradition that capitalism represented.

Charisma and prophecy are also important concepts in Weber's analysis of the relationship between religion and social change, particularly with respect to the impact of ideas on social action and social structure.

For Weber, a prophet is a person who proclaims a religious doctrine or reveals a Divine Command. The prophet usually has charismatic authority which rests on trust in the supposedly extraordinary qualities of the person and a belief on the part of the followers in the legitimacy of the orders that the leader has given or revealed to them. Prophets, of whatever type,[28] try to make the world more meaningful and to influence people's conduct so as to increase the likelihood of their salvation. Prophets vary in their degree of success in finding followers, in challenging priestly traditions, and so forth. To the degree that they *are* successful, prophets can have a tremendous influence on the course of history. Charismatic individuals, including military and political as well as religious leaders, can be quite revolutionary forces in history. The enthusiasm of charismatic movements may challenge tradition, may dissolve class and status barriers, and so forth. "Charismatic outbursts" can be quite disruptive of settled traditional authority or of rational-legal authority.

Weber does argue that charismatic situations including religious prophecy tend eventually to become routinized, either in the direction of traditionalism or (more often) rational-legal authority, depending on the nature of the movement's organiza-

---

27 To be clear, Weber's **Protestant Ethic** really only raises the possibility of causality; the study was only one, and an early one, of a whole series of "imaginary experiments" dealing with the rationalization of Western Europe.

28 Weber distinguished ethical prophecy, prevalent in Ancient Israel, from exemplary prophecy, prevalent in India. He also distinguished Greek and Hebrew prophecy in terms of their implications for action: Greek prophecy tended to foretell an inevitable future (*moira* or "fate") whereas the prophets of Ancient Israel foretold the future in order to forestall or alter it.

tion and especially on economic conditions. However, in his analyses of charisma and prophecy he reminds us that religious belief is not always and everywhere a conservative force in history, notwithstanding the Marxist bromide concerning religion being "the opiate of the people."

We have barely touched on Weber's notions of prophecy, charisma, and the routinization of charisma. However, we have said enough to indicate that, however shortlived charismatic disruptions of the social order might be, their impact on the social structure can be considerable. Thus, Weber's writings on charisma and prophecy, like his essay on the Protestant ethic, show some of the ways ideas can influence social action and social structure.[29]

We would like now to consider some of Weber's ideas concerning the social-psychological functions of religious belief for the individual. We have already briefly encountered two of his arguments in this regard in our earlier discussion of the reduction of uncertainty aspect of the Protestant Ethic thesis and the creation of meaning involved in prophecy.

We argued earlier that Weber insisted on the need for understanding the meaning that social action has for the actor. Religion is one way in which situations come to be seen as meaningful by social actors. We can see this in for example Weber's concepts of *theodicy* and *elective affinity*.

"Theodicy" comes from the Greek words for "God" and "justice." It is a theological term first used by Leibnitz in 1710, and refers to religious writings, doctrines, or theories which attempt to explain, vindicate, or justify the ways of God in the face of the existence of suffering, injustice, and evil. Theodicies come into play when people ask perplexing specific questions like, "Why does God allow little children to starve to death in Ethiopia?" "Where was God at Auschwitz?" or, more generally, "If God is all-powerful and all-good, then how is it that the innocent and the virtuous suffer?" Weber argued that such questions are more likely to arise in societies in which there is a high level of rationalization and ones in which ethical monotheism prevails. They are also more likely to be raised at points in an individual's biography when s/he is confronted with seemingly senseless experiences, such as the death of a young child. The nature of the answers to such questions varies. Sometimes, for example, it is argued that although God is omnipotent and benevo-

lent, for His own reasons He endowed humans with free will, and it is to the latter that the world's defects should be attributed. Questions concerning divine justice thus become turned into accusations of human sin, as in the Book of Job. The young and innocent die, the righteous suffer, and the wicked prosper, but this is explained as part of the Divine Plan.

Weber identified several *types* of theodicy, which vary in their degree of explicitness, rationality, plausibility, and so forth.[30] He discussed certain *specific* theodicies, including Zoroastrian dualism, the Hindu notion of *karma*, and the Puritan belief in predestination. More abstractly, he distinguished negative theodicies, in which, for example, the poor might find meaning in their weakness and poverty, from positive ones, in which the rich might find meaning in their power and wealth. In the latter situation, such religious explanations might serve to rationalize, justify, or assuage guilt concerning relative privilege and, in the former, theodicies may serve to legitimate, make tolerable, or explain away relative deprivation. In both situations, differential advantages are made more meaningful for the individual by religious doctrines. Theodicies help people make sense of what might otherwise appear to them to be a senseless world. They enable people to see equity in injustice, parity in inequality, and order in chaos.

"Elective affinity" (*Wahlverwandtschaft*), a term Weber took from the German poet/dramatist Goethe, who had himself borrowed it from chemistry, is a concept which can easily be misunderstood. It is important to discuss because it is the key to understanding Weber's argument concerning the relationship between (religious) ideas and social position. It also serves to clarify further Weber's writings on prophecy and the Protestant Ethic.

The "sociology of knowledge," a small but significant and controversy ridden sub-discipline within sociology, focuses on the relationship between ideas and social location. Weber's writings on religion form an important part of that sub-discipline. His discussion of the relationship between social position, interests, and ideas explains the apparent "affinity" between certain groups and certain ideas, which have somehow "found" one another, by showing how certain *ideas help people to make sense of their experiences* in their particular life-situations. Note that here again Weber is talking about how religion helps people to see their situation as meaningful.

---

29 The meaning-creation functions of religious ideas (including those of the prophets) will be discussed below, and in the section on Weber's political sociology we will say a bit more about charismatic authority.

30 Some of these variations are discussed in Peter L. Berger, **The Sacred Canopy** (1967), pp. 53 ff.

An analogy might be helpful. Think of the prophet as a "sower" of various "seeds" (religious ideas). Those "seeds" need to germinate and grow in some "soil," *viz.*, within certain social groups. Some groups are more receptive to certain ideas than to other ideas, and some groups are more receptive to certain ideas than are other groups. Different soils and different seeds are particularly well-suited to one another. However, the concept of "elective affinity" is not meant to suggest some kind of automatic "fitting together" of certain groups and particular ideas. Weber suggests that the ideas of prophets are selectively emphasized and reinterpreted[31] by people in various social strata such that they develop an "affinity" with their "interests," which latter come out of their day-to-day experience. Concretely, he discusses the varieties of Christianity which exist among aristocrats, the military, civil servants, intellectuals, merchants, artisans, peasants, the modern proletariat, and so forth. For example, the traditional "magical" beliefs and practices exhibited in the Christianity of peasants are contrasted with the more "formalistic" tendencies in the religion of bureaucratic officeholders and the essentially "practical" rationalism of merchants and artisans within the urban bourgeoisie. Members of these social groups have "elected" certain ideas from the Christian tradition which have an affinity to their particular "interests," that is which help them to make sense of their day-to-day experiences.[32]

To be clear, Weber did argue that social strata vary in their degree of religiosity and their degree of sensitivity to prophecy, whether it be exemplary or ethical. More importantly, he also clearly argued that there is no neat one-to-one relationship between particular ideas and specific social groups, and that there is sometimes tension between one's "interests" and one's "ideas." *Most* importantly, Weber makes a distinction between the possible social or psychic sources of the content of particular ideas on the one hand and those social groups which may eventually take up those ideas on the other. For example, Weber argued that the modern proletariat might under certain social circumstances become influenced by salvation religions which were themselves typically "produced" originally by higher status intellectuals. This careful, complex argument differentiates Weber from certain Marxists (if not Marx himself), who argued that certain ideas "reflect" or "express" the interests of particular social groups (classes).[33] It also differentiates Weber from Nietzsche, who tended to "reduce" people's ideas to their psychic needs.[34]

In our discussion of "theodicy" and "elective affinity," we have suggested that for Weber religion is concerned with finding ultimate meaning, something which humans innately need.

> Behind [these varieties of belief] . . . always lies a stand towards something in the actual world which is experienced as specifically "senseless." Thus, the demand has been implied: that the world order in its totality is, could, and should somehow be a meaningful "cosmos." (**The Social Psychology of the World Religions,**" p. 281)

Religion is for Weber the way in which people attempt to deal rationally with a life that is essentially irrational. Some have concluded from this that Weber has provided us with a conservative view of religion as helping people "adjust" to their environment. However, we must remember that he also discussed how religion helps people transcend and even *change* their natural, social, intellectual, political, and economic environments. This latter is indeed the focus of much of Weber's sociology of religion, as can be seen in our discussions of the Protestant Ethic thesis, charisma, and prophecy.

We shall conclude our cursory look at Weber's

---

31 Note the parallel between this argument that believers tend to selectively emphasize and reinterpret certain aspects of a religious doctrine according to their "interests" and Weber's neo-Kantian methodological argument that social analysts necessarily select, according to their value orientations, what they study and what questions they ask about what they choose to study. Note also that in his Protestant Ethic thesis Weber argued that Calvinists unwittingly selected and reinterpreted certain aspects of Calvin's teachings to help them make sense of their experience.

32 In his sociology of religion Weber puts less stress than many others did on ideas as legitimations or justifications for power or privilege, emphasizing instead the meaning-creating functions of religion. However, as we shall see, in his political sociology the legitimating functions of ideas are given considerable emphasis.

33 The relationship between many of Marx and Weber's ideas has been the focus of attention of countless commentators, who often refer to the issue just mentioned as a debate between the allegedly "idealist" Weber and the supposedly "materialist" Marx. We could add to that issue the contrasts between Marx and Weber's arguments concerning the origins of capitalism, already alluded to in our review of the Protestant Ethic thesis. We could also add the different understandings that Marx and Weber had of the concept of "class," as well as the greater significance accorded "status groups" in Weber's sociology.

34 Weber acknowledged both Marx and Nietzsche as major social thinkers who significantly influenced him. One of Nietzsche's ideas which Weber found useful was *ressentiment*, which refers to repressed envy and hatred among the socially disadvantaged. Weber argued that the resentment often felt and the imaginary compensation sometimes developed by the "negatively privileged" can be one significant factor (among others) in the shaping of religious beliefs.

sociology of religion by explaining one distinction that he made in his analysis of religious institutions, and by noting some of the other themes in his sociology of religion which we have not addressed.

Weber borrowed the distinction between "church" and "sect" from his contemporary, the German theologian and philosopher Ernst Troeltsch. He discussed the sociological aspects of this distinction so convincingly that for many years this was one of the two main themes in his sociology of religion for which he was remembered, the other being of course the Protestant Ethic thesis.[35] For this reason we would like to review the distinction briefly.

"Hierocratic" institutions are ones which are ruled by religious dignitaries who enforce order on members "through psychic coercion by distributing or denying religious benefits" (**Economy and Society**, p. 54). A church is a "compulsory" hierocratic organization. A church can be said to exist when the group has eliminated all nonreligious distinctions (such as ethnic differences) and thus claims to be all-embracing and "universal"; when the religious beliefs and practices of the group along with commentaries on them have become rationalized, are set down in writing, and are systematically taught to members; when there exists a professional priesthood, with a distinctive lifestyle, specific duties, salaries, and so forth; and when membership is "automatic,"[36] in the sense that one is "born into" a church, and its benefits are offered to everyone, regardless of "religious qualifications." Churches tend to be conservative in that they support the social structure and culture of the wider society.

"Sects," on the other hand, tend to *reject* the larger society, and have a perfectionist ideology. A sect has usually broken away from a church, and sets itself apart from the outside world, seeing itself as special and unique. (The word is derived from the expression *sectem sequi*, which means to follow a particular course of conduct.) Sects are joined voluntarily by those who have usually as adults met certain tests of religious qualification set by members of the sect. Sects tend to be smaller than churches, and have much more intense religious and social interaction among their members. One might say that they are closer to the object of worship, as well as to one another, than are members of churches. Sects also emphasize "freedom of conscience," and attempt to be apolitical, in the sense of not forging alliances with the politically powerful, as churches sometimes do. Sects practice lay preaching, and do not have a professional, bureaucratic priesthood. They may have clerical officials, but administration is in principle by the congregation; officials are seen as servants of the congregation.

Weber's distinction between "church" and "sect," and variations within each ideal type, have been the focus of much discussion among sociologists interested in religion. We have introduced you to that distinction so as to give you an example of Weber's institutional analysis of religion. We have also discussed, in greater detail, Weber's analysis of the role of religion in social change as well as his ideas concerning the social-psychological functions of religious belief for the individual. We have necessarily had to omit any consideration of certain other important aspects of Weber's sociology of religion. These include his discussion of the differences between magic and religion; the relationship between religious ethics and taboo; the types of religious ethic; the ethical dilemmas posed by the use of coercion; the relationship between various kinds of religious ethics and economic orientations; the influence of religious ethics on non-economic social spheres (such as politics and art); the practice of usury; the differences between prophets and priests; the rationalization of conduct through exemplary and ethical prophecy; "asceticism" and "mysticism," the two generalized and systematic ways in which people try to solve the problem of radical salvation, *viz.*, resolve the tension between their urge to "perfection" and what is possible in this world; the crosscutting distinction between innerworldly and otherworldly orientations; and his focus on innerworldly asceticism (e.g., the Protestant Ethic) as the most significant religious force for social change.

As this partial list is meant to suggest, Weber's sociology of religion involved much more than we have been able to cover. What we have discussed and what we have not forms a very significant body of work.

Weber's Sociology of Politics

Although Weber was concerned about "partisanship" interfering with "scholarship," and although he was reluctant to become actively involved in party politics himself, politics was a central substantive interest pur-

---

35 Indeed one commentator has remarked that the church-sect theme became a "sociological obsession" which led to much sterile and unproductive discussion, especially when efforts were made to apply it to non-Christian societies. Some productive discussions and elaborations of the typology can be found in Berger (1954) and Wilson (1961; 1963).

36 This is related to Weber's distinction, referred to earlier, between compulsory and voluntary organizations.

sued in his empirical sociology.[37] We propose to outline the major arguments that Weber made in this area.

We begin with definitions of four important concepts in Weber's political sociology. "Power" is
defined by Weber as the probability that an actor can
impose his or her own will on the behaviour of other
actors. "Domination" is defined as the probability
that a specific command (or all commands) from a
particular source will be obeyed by a certain group of
persons. In other words, domination refers to institutionalized patterns of power relations. "Authority"
is defined as *legitimate* domination, that is domination
not based on coercion, habit, calculation of economic
advantage, or the like, but domination which has the
characteristic of legitimacy.[38] Weber defined "legitimacy" formally as the quality of a social order which
gives it the character of a norm in relation to which
we social actors develop a sense of moral obligation.
This quality of a society is not inherent "objectively"
within the society but is always imputed or ascribed
to it by social actors. The leader gives orders, and the
followers obey them, because both the leaders and
(especially) the followers *believe* that this domination
is legitimate.[39] Thus, "legitimacy" has to do with the
"meaning" [40] that the leaders and the followers
attach to their relationship; authority is domination
that can successfully claim legitimacy for itself.[41]

Weber identified three ideal types of authority,
traditional, rational-legal, and charismatic. These types
vary in terms of the grounds on which people obey,
the mode in which authority is exercised, and the
nature of the staff which administers the social order.
We shall summarize his argument in a paradigm, or
side-by-side comparison, organized in terms of the
three elements of authority (see Figure 1).

---

37 It may be no accident that religion and politics, the two subjects
to which Weber seemed continually drawn "despite himself,"
were each areas of life which were particularly significant for one
or the other of his parents. His mother's life was centred on religion, his father's on politics.

38 "Legitimacy" is another one of Weber's key and pervasive
themes. Like rationalization, it occurs again and again, in different forms and at different levels of abstraction, throughout
his writing.

39 Of course, if the leader were consistently to fail to meet the criteria in terms of which his or her authority is defined s/he
might jeopardize the legitimacy of the domination and thereby
forfeit the authority.

40 There's that word again!

41 Weber clearly identified two other sources of order besides the
belief in legitimacy; he identified regularities which are derived
from custom and those based on self-interest. Still, legitimate
domination or authority was for him the theoretically most
interesting source of order, and it had the greatest practical significance because in his view it provided the most stable kind of
regularity.

Some words of explanation and caution concerning this paradigm are necessary. Presenting Weber's
typology in the schematic way that we have runs the
risk of leading readers to the misunderstanding that
such societies actually exist in concrete reality. These
types should be understood as ideal types, as
explained earlier. In particular, readers should
remember that ideal types rarely, perhaps never, have
actual empirical counterparts, but are rather heuristic
devices constructed so as to develop meaningfully
and causally adequate statements. Our readers
should also recall that any given empirical phenomenon needs to be compared to various ideal
types, not just one. Thus, the Germany of Weber's
day had traditional, rational-legal, *and* charismatic
features, each of which he discussed to some degree
(for example in his "Parliament and Government in a
Reconstructed Germany").

You will note that in our paradigm the "nature of
the administrative apparatus" for rational-legal
authority is described with the rather cryptic statement, "the staff is a *modern bureaucracy*." The origin,
nature, and significance of modern bureaucracy is one
of Weber's best-known themes although interestingly
it is perhaps one of his least original arguments so we
would like to consider it in some detail.

First, what is "modern bureaucracy?" The word
"modern" is important to note because Weber's concept of bureaucracy transcends his specific analysis of
the typical staff found in rational-legal orders. At various points in his work, Weber discusses "pre-mod-
ern" bureaucracies, such as those found in Ancient
China, Ancient Egypt, the Byzantine Empire, and the
later Roman Empire. Specifically modern bureaucracy
most closely approximates the ideal-typical "monocratic" (one-ruler) bureaucracy for which Weber
identified ten defining characteristics, which are actually characteristics of the appointment and functions
of the personnel of modern bureaucracy.

These characteristics may be summarized as follows. A bureaucracy consists of a number of positions
("offices") which are organized both vertically and hor-
izontally. The vertical arrangement involves a hierarchy of authority within the organization, which
implies strict and systematic discipline and control in
the conduct of one's office. The horizontal arrangement relates to the division of labour among those
with approximately the same degree of authority: each
office has designated to it a limited "sphere of competence." The bureaucrat is selected and appointed (not
elected) to a position on the basis of technical qualifications, as established by examination, certification, or

Figure 1
ideal-type of authority

	traditional authority	rational-legal authority	charismatic authority

a) *who is obeyed and on what grounds do people obey?*	– rests on a belief in the sanctity of the order and the right of those giving commands to have them carried out
	– obedience is due to the traditional order because it has come down through the ages and is right, good, holy, etc.
	– obedience is also due to those who carry out this order
		– based on a belief in the legality of established norms and therefore a belief in the right of those who give orders to do so
		– obedience is here due impersonal norms, which are deemed to have been legally established/enacted and are therefore seen as legitimate
		– obedience extends to persons in certain offices, but only by virtue of their holding those offices and only within the scope of authority of a given office
			– rests on trust in the presumably extra-ordinary qualities of a person and a belief in the legitimacy of the (divine) orders given or "revealed" by him
			  – military leader
			  – political leader
			  – religious leader

b) *mode in which authority is exercised*	– the system of norms is seen as having always existed
	– the norms are concrete and personal, not impersonal or formal (as in rational-legal authority)
	– the focus is on social status (not office), so a good deal of undefined power is left to those with traditional status
	  – Patriarchalism
	  – Patrimonialism
	  – Gerontocracy
	  – Feudalism of Benefices
	  – Feudalism of Fiefs
	– each of these sub-types is discussed in detail
		– the order consists of a body of general and universal rules impartially applicable to all concerned
		– authority is restricted to the individual's "sphere of competence" as it is defined for the office he holds; there is then a clear-cut separation of the individual's office and his private sphere of action
			– while traditional and rational-legal authority are forms of everyday, routine control of social action, charismatic authority is the direct opposite
			– laws are neither "received" nor "established," but are rather "revealed" by the leader: "It is written, but I say unto you. . . ."
			– laws are valid *only* as long as the particular leader continues to be recognized as genuine by his followers

c) *nature of the administrative apparatus*	*For example:* – in the case of patriarchalism, there is in a strict sense no staff; rather, the ruler has a group of elders with whom he consults about important matters but over whom he does not have full command – in patrimonialism, the chief has a staff—entirely in his hands—which is recruited from relatives, clients and strangers who become totally dependent on him. This staff is superficially similar to modern bureaucracy, except that the selection of staff members is wholly arbitrary; and their authority is diffused, personal, and arbitrary – in feudalism, authority is shared more or less equally by the lords and those carrying out the organizational aspects of the political order. In contrast to patrimonialism, the staff is relatively independent economically, militarily and politically. The relationship between staff and lord is reinforced by contract and the principle of "honour."	– the staff is a *modern bureaucracy* (see detailed discussion in the text)	– strictly speaking, there is no "staff"; there are rather "disciples," who live in a communistic relationship with their leader – if a staff exists, this is a sign of the "routinization of charisma"

both. An office is held on a contractual basis, and the bureaucrat is obliged to obey only with respect to his or her delimited official duties. Otherwise, the bureaucrat is "personally free." The official does not own "the means of administration," nor can s/he "appropriate" the position. The circumstances under which a bureaucrat's appointment may be terminated are specified, and the official is free to resign. The bureaucrat is paid a salary according to a scale determined largely by rank, responsibility, and (sometimes) the requirements of social status. Typically, the bureaucrat also enjoys the right to a pension. The office is viewed as the only, or at least the main, occupation of the officeholder. Holding office constitutes a career, involving promotion due to seniority, achievement, or both. Promotion depends on the judgements of those higher in the hierarchy.[42]

In what we have called the "first" essay, Weber provides us with a richly detailed and concrete description and analysis of modern bureaucracy and how it differs from other forms of administration, particularly patrimonial administration. A major theme which ties all the empirical detail together is the notion of "rationality." Rational-legal authority and modern bureaucracy are seen by Weber as the political and administrative manifestations of "rationalization," as we indicated earlier. When you peruse the excerpt from Weber's first essay that we have included in our readings, you will see recurring such words and phrases as: fixed, ordered, regular, regulated, stable, delimited, methodical, continuous, firmly ordered, thorough, expert, exhaustive, firmly (and generally) prescribed, objective, specific, free from all personal considerations, secure, mechanical,

and so forth. Each of these terms falls into the general nexus of rationality, as we discussed it earlier.

Weber's enumeration of the characteristics of modern bureaucracy dominated sociological discussions of organization and bureaucracy for many years. This is doubly ironic, both because this was probably Weber's least original contribution to the literature on bureaucracy[43] and because this contribution was generally misunderstood as presenting a rational or formal "model." Individual organizations were then compared to this model by researchers doing case studies in the growing sub-discipline of organizational sociology. Weber's so-called "model" of bureaucracy was really a presentation of an ideal type, constructed to represent the *culturally significant* aspects of modern bureaucracy; this phenomenon he argued, was becoming more and more general, and more and more significant, with the rationalization of social life generally, which was the source of the *cultural uniqueness* of western Europe.

Weber also discussed the preconditions, as well as the consequences, of modern bureaucracy. The preconditions included the development of a money economy and, eventually, public finance; the creation of standing armies; the emergence of the modern state, modern democracy, and the mass political party; the increasing requirements for "order and protection," as well as the administration of social welfare measures; and growth of "the specifically modern means of communications," such as the telegraph, railroads, public roads, and waterways. Each of these factors required, or was associated with, bureaucratization. Weber also argued that modern bureaucracy had certain technical advantages[44] over other forms of administration; this helps account for bureaucracy's increasing prevalence, although Weber clearly argues that technical superiority is not enough. The social and political conditions just indicated needed to be present so that the obstacles to the emergence of this technical superiority could be overcome.

Note the emphasis that Weber gave to modern

---

42 See **Economy and Society**, pp. 220–221. Although there are scattered references to modern bureaucracy throughout Weber's writings and some important points are made in such places as "The Origins of Industrial Capitalism in Europe," the stirring closing pages of **The Protestant Ethic and the Spirit of Capitalism**, his report on his wartime experiences as a hospital administrator, and the various addresses "On Bureaucratization," "Politics as a Vocation," "Science as a Vocation" and "Socialism" Weber most systematically discussed modern bureaucracy in three essays. The earliest was written between 1911 and 1913 and revised in 1918; the second was written between 1918 and 1920; the third was actually a series of 1917–1918 newspaper articles later revised, enlarged, and published as a single piece. Each of these essays is found in the *variorum* edition of *Economy and Society*. They vary in intent and level of abstraction. The first essay is more concrete and historical than is the generally more abstract and conceptual second one, while the third is a somewhat polemical look at the situation in Germany at the time. The details provided above are derived from the second essay, and concern "monocratic bureaucracy." Elsewhere, Weber discussed "collegial bureaucracy" and "administration by notables." The major contrast made, most explicitly in the first essay mentioned above, was with patrimonial administration.

43 Weber has essentially provided us with a somewhat reconceptualized analysis of a substantive phenomenon already very well described in German administrative theory generally, and particularly in certain writings of Karl Marx, Robert Michels, and (especially) Gustav Schmoller.

44 Weber did not however ignore entirely, as some students of organization have suggested, either the "dysfunctions" of bureaucracy or the "technical advantages" of informal organization within formal structures. Further, Weber's seeming "enthusiasm" for efficient organization was usually tempered by qualifying phrases and often balanced with reservations concerning the dehumanizing implications of bureaucracy. We shall discuss this further below.

democracy as one of the preconditions for modern bureaucracy. He also examined the implications for democracy of bureaucracy, as part of his analysis of the various consequences of bureaucracy. The paradoxical relationship between bureaucracy and democracy was a major theme in Weber's sociology of politics.

We now need to clarify the various meanings Weber gave to the term "democracy." We are not here concerned with the development of democracy in the ancient and medieval worlds to which Weber did devote some attention except insofar as it helps us to understand his position on *modern* democracy. In this respect, Weber argued that democratization has always been based on militarization and money power; that democracy was first established non-legitimately (through charismatic usurpation); that soon requiring an efficient administration it became routinized in either a traditional or rational direction (in either case producing a multiplication of offices); and that democratization does not lead to the disappearance of domination, because the latter is interdependent with administration. Although medieval and modern (but not ancient) democracy exhibited a tendency forwards "the equalization of classes and removal of unfreedom" (**General Economic History**, p. 330), democratization does not normally lead to the realization of the principle of self-determination.

Rousseau's notion of the citizenry directly expressing its desires was, Weber believed, applicable in his time only to Switzerland, a few American townships, some universities, and other small, local, homogeneous, and private associations. The idea of the direct rule of the *demos* needed to be replaced by Montesquieu's notion of representative government. Many of the characteristics of democratic self-government and immediate democratic administration were inappropriate in the age of bureaucracy. Certain of them, e.g., the principles of recall and referendum could be used in a limited way in modern, "passive," parliamentary, mass, indirect democracy. "Direct" democracy was inherently unstable, and "pure" democracy is a marginal case

> where the group grows beyond a certain size or where the administrative function becomes too difficult to be satisfactorily taken care of by anyone whom rotation, the lot, or election may happen to designate. The conditions of administration of mass structures are radically different from those obtaining in small associations resting upon neighbourly or personal relationships. As soon as mass administration is involved, the meaning of democracy changes so radically that it no longer

makes sense for the sociologist to ascribe to the term the same meaning.... (**Economy and Society**, p. 951)

Weber considered the "mixed type" of constitutional/parliamentary yet plebiscitary democracy to be the only viable democratic form in industrialized mass society.

For Weber, modern democracy and modern bureaucracy were in certain ways mutually supportive, and in other ways mutually antagonistic. They were mutually supportive in that both are opposed in principle to the plutocratic privileges found in feudal and patrimonial administration by notables. Both bureaucracy and democracy attempt to limit the arbitrary exercise of the ruler's will through legal guarantees against the arbitrariness associated with intervention from above, "the personal discretion flowing from the 'grace' of the old patrimonial domination" (**Economy and Society**, pp. 979–80). The demand for "equality before the law" found in both bureaucracy and democracy is satisfied by the "formal and rational 'objectivity' of administration" (*Ibid.*, p. 979). This demand is both "personal," in that it rejects privilege, and "functional," in that it rejects *ad hoc* decision making. A further compatibility between bureaucracy and modern democracy is their common attitude towards specialized examinations, which involve the selection of the qualified from all strata rather than selection based on ascriptive status. Further, the advent of mass democracy encouraged the bureaucratization of political technique and the rise of mass political parties.

If these are the ways in which bureaucracy and democracy were compatible according to Weber, in what senses did he see them as antagonistic? Weber saw bureaucracy as an expansive, permanent, and indispensable feature of modern life. He also saw it as potentially threatening the possibility of democratic decision making *within* organizations, the possibility of the *external* control of civil service bureaucracies by democratically constituted parliaments, as well as the possibility of individual *freedom*. We say "potentially threatening" because Weber also identified democratic counter-tendencies to the expansiveness, the permanence, and the power of bureaucracy which could significantly temper its effects.

We indicated earlier that Weber was theoretically open to and actually concretely discussed the very issues which many later organization theorists accused him of ignoring. One such issue concerns the so-called "means-ends reversal,"[45] the tendency for the personnel in a bureaucratic organization to become so wrapped up in the means (administration) that they lose sight of, and perhaps actually subvert, the ends or goals of the organization. The means in effect become ends in themselves. Weber did discuss this, at several levels. We shall concentrate on the institutional level.[46] We can see Weber's discussion of the means-ends reversal at the institutional level in his analysis of the problem of *oligarchy* (which brings us back to democracy, or rather its negation). Weber's work on oligarchy has been overlooked. His friend Robert Michels's writings on this topic are much better known,[47] and had a significant influence on subsequent American organizational sociology. Weber and Michels agreed that political parties in mass democracies had undergone rapid bureaucratization, with the following consequences. Youth organizations, schools for officials and speakers, and a party press were created; party finances were rationalized, through the introduction of rational budgeting, the regular collection of dues, the organization of fund-raising, and the cementing of ties with friendly economic interests; there emerged full-time party officials, distinct from the party leadership and the rank-and-file; and strict party discipline, including the elimination of freedom of decision by parliamentary deputies, was developed.

Two brief quotations will give you the flavour of Weber's analysis:

> Naturally power actually rests in the hands of those who, within the organization, handle the work continuously. . . . "Politics as a Vocation," p. 103)

> [T]he participation of the rank and file is limited to assistance and voting during the elections, which take place at relatively long intervals, and to the discussion of resolutions, the outcome of which is always largely controlled by the leaders.[48] (**Economy and Society**, p. 1445)

Weber and Michels further agreed that the German

labour movement could not provide a radically different social organization, that neither it nor the Social Democrats posed a revolutionary threat, that the leaders of those organizations had increasingly become more conservative, that the organizations were tending to become ends in themselves, and that in so doing they were indeed violating the very principles (ends) which they claimed to be pursuing. But Weber and Michels *disagreed* in their basic premises about and evaluations of these organizational phenomena. In contrast to Michels's absolutized generalization of an "iron law of oligarchy," Weber insisted that bureaucracy and democracy were not completely incompatible. Alternatives were possible. The bureaucratization of political parties did lessen radical ideology, but it also had positive consequences. For example, discipline and routine made more likely the possibility of party machines devoting themselves realistically to party and national problems, minimizing the dangers of demagoguery, and providing leaders with the organizational skills they would find necessary once attaining high office. In Weber's view, the bureaucratization of political parties was not a fundamental obstacle to representative government (modern democracy), as long as certain safeguards were built into parliamentary democracy.

Weber was actually ambivalent about the Social Democratic organizational "betrayal" of its ideals. This is not the place to discuss this fully, but we wish to make two important points. First, both Weber and Michels argued that the Social Democrats were more tightly organized, centralized, and disciplined than were the bourgeois parties, perhaps precisely because of their more radical aims and the greater hostility of their environment. Second, in his evaluation of the growing conservatism of the Social Democrats, Weber vacillated between the ethics of responsibility and ultimate disposition. Thus, he understood this phenomenon as an organizational *dilemma*, although he had, in Roth's words, "little sympathy for the Social Democratic dualism of radical rhetoric and moderate practice."[49]

The consequences of internal oligarchy include means ends reversal; in the case of the Social Democrats, the more oligarchical they became the more they were betraying their democratic ideals. Thus, "pure" bureaucracy can subvert its own ends. Weber implicitly addressed another aspect of the issue of internal democracy in his discussion of infor-

---

45 Some terms used to connote the same phenomenon are bureaucratism ritualism, the autonomy of means, and the displacement of goals.

46 At another level, Weber related the means-ends reversal phenomenon to the two ethics (the ethic of ultimate disposition and the ethic of responsibility) and to the substitution of formally for substantively rational social action.

47 Weber and Michels were both influenced by the ideas of a Polish thinker named Ostrogorski.

48 This quotation is from what we have called the "third" essay on bureaucracy, "Parliament and Government in a Reconstructed Germany."

---

49 Guenther Roth, **The Social Democrats in Imperial Germany** (Totawa, N. J.: Bedminster Press, 1963), p. 254.

mal organization, which he is reputed to have ignored. In at least two substantive analyses Weber shows that he recognized that informal organization within a formal structure may either promote or retard organizational ends. In a 1909 speech[50] to the Union for Social Policy Weber discussed both the possible recalcitrance of subordinates within organizations and the probable angry reactions of superordinates to such resistance by those below them. Thus, Weber was aware that bureaucracies did not always display the quality of impersonality and impartiality ("*sine ire ac studio*," with neither anger nor passion) which he had included in his ideal type. Also, Weber provided an exceptionally detailed account of his experiences for one year during World War I as a volunteer in German military hospitals, which account he expressly framed in terms of the transition from a volunteer, amateur, necessarily loose and improvised administration to the professional, civil-service, bureaucratic administration which replaced it. Weber took great pains to stress the advantages as well as the disadvantages of both forms of administration.

In his "third" essay on bureaucracy, Weber outlined his concerns about the relationship between the civil service in Germany and its nominal political rulers, the parliament, thus turning to the paradoxical *external* relationship between bureaucracy and democracy. Here the problem was not so much that means became ends in themselves, or that informal-organizational means sometimes better led to given ends than did formal-organizational ones. Instead, he focused on the tendency of bureaucrats themselves to *define* organizational ends, that is to usurp political leadership, and to prefer an ignorant and powerless parliament. Weber's concern about the possibility (he denied its inevitability) of state bureaucracy operating independently of its political controllers was discussed not only as a general problem, but also through a concrete analysis and set of recommendations with respect to the problematic relationship between the civil service and the parliament in the Germany of his day.

Weber's general question was briefly raised in his remarks on the permanence of bureaucracy in the first essay. The conditions under which bureaucracy came to be controlled by its nominal ruler(s), and the conditions under which it came to escape that con-

trol, were briefly discussed in that essay. Thus, on the one hand:

> The power position of a fully developed bureaucracy is always great, under normal conditions overpowering. The political "master" always finds himself, vis-à-vis the trained official, in the position of a dilettante facing the expert. This holds whether the "master," whom the bureaucracy serves, is the "people" equipped with the weapons of legislative initiative, referendum, and the right to remove officials; or a parliament elected on a more aristocratic or more democratic basis and equipped with the right or the *de facto* power to vote a lack of confidence; or an aristocratic collegiate body, legally or actually based on self-recruitment; or a popularly elected president or an "absolute" or "constitutional" hereditary monarch. **Economy and Society**, pp. 991–992).

On the other hand:

> It must also remain an open question whether the *power* of bureaucracy is increasing in the modern states in which it is spreading. The fact that bureaucratic organization is technically the most highly developed power instrument in the hands of its controller does not determine the weight that bureaucracy as such is capable of procuring for its own opinions in a particular social structure.... Whether the power of bureaucracy as such increases cannot be decided *a priori*. (*Ibid.*, p. 991)

Each individual historical case needs to be examined on its own merits. He did discuss in detail one historical case, post-Bismarkian Germany.

For Weber, the pathologies of German political life were rooted in the legacy of Bismarck, whose rule had left a nation with dependent political thinking, impotent party leaders, and a powerless parliament, all ceding rule to the state bureaucracy. Weber argued that irresponsibility and ineffectiveness in crisis, as well as behind the scenes influence being wielded by big capitalists, were all increased when bureaucrats controlled the administration of the state bureaucracy.

One crucial aspect of Bismarck's legacy was what Weber called the "negative politics" practiced in weak parliaments such as in Germany:

> as long as a parliament can support the complaints of the citizens against the administration only by rejecting appropriations and other legislation or by introducing unenforcable (*sic*) motions, it is excluded from positive participation in the *direction* of political affairs. (*Ibid.*, p. 1408).

---

50 "Max Weber on Bureaucratization in 1909," in J. P. Mayer, **Max Weber and German Politics**, 2nd. ed. (London: Faber and Faber, 1956), Appendix I.

This kind of parliament was reduced to mere speech-making and reacting to bureaucratic directives. Instead of principled power struggles over substantive issues by leaders, self-interest and influence-peddling came to dominate parliamentary life. Under these conditions, people with the necessary political inclinations and talents were unlikely to subject themselves to the selection by competition of elections, and "leaders capable of guiding the nation" (*Ibid.*, p. 1410) could not then emerge.

"Parliament's first task is the supervision of . . . policy-makers . . . Politicians must be the countervailing force against bureaucratic domination." (*Ibid.*, p. 1417). For Weber, the way to reverse both the dominance of bureaucrats and the negative politics of a weak parliament and unsatisfactory politicians was the promotion of the positive politics of a strong working parliament best exemplified in the British system and the encouragement of the proper bureaucratic and political vocations.

The professional ethic of the genuine bureaucratic official requires that s/he impartially, devotedly, competently, judiciously, and decisively perform administrative work (means), not determine ends. The bureaucrat's impartiality, devotion, competence, judgement, and decisiveness are always within the rules and towards the goals set by superiors. One's duty is to indicate any disagreement with specific rules or ends, but nevertheless to follow the orders of higher authority.

If impartiality, duty, and subordination are the watchwords of the bureaucrat, then partisanship, responsibility, and proportion summarize the professional ethic of the political leader. Politicians are required to determine ends rather than execute orders. Such determination of ends involves the partisanship found in electoral and parliamentary struggles. The politician is expected to act independently, and to personally accept responsibility for his or her positions and for whatever compromises s/he might have to make. Responsibility could not be passed on to higher authority; rather than like the bureaucrat sacrificing his or her judgment to that of others, s/he was required instead to disavow (through resignation if necessary) any actions which ran counter to his or her position. This partisanship and individual responsibility needed however to be combined with a sense of proportion:

What kind of a man must one be if he is to be allowed to put his hand on the wheel of history?

One can say that three preeminent qualities are decisive for the politician: passion, a feeling of

responsibility, and a sense of proportion. ("Politics as a Vocation," p. 115).

The nobility of political engagement within and against such historical processes as bureaucratization is evident in this description of the ideal political leader. This raises the question of how the political and bureaucratic vocations so recommended, and the parliamentary reconstruction and control of bureaucracy so advocated, were related for Weber to his understanding of the kind of democracy which was possible in the modern world.

In the modern state, a free parliament, combined with (bureaucratic) political parties and leaders elected by the people to govern them, was the only feasible solution to the problem of civil-service rule. While not ideally democratic, this was the best that could be gained in modern, mass, rationalized society. It formed the middle ground between the twin dangers of "mass irrationality" and "bureaucratic tyranny." Weber was concerned to oppose *Caesarism*, a system of absolute government by one ruler (as in the Roman Empire of Julius Caesar), which he saw as the potential outcome of direct, plebiscitary democracy. He was also opposed to *bureaucratic rule*, which resulted from the ultimate inability of active mass democracy to control the civil service. The solution contained elements of Caesarism, but it was a constitutional and English brand of Caesarism, presupposing also a reconstructed parliament. The dangers of demagoguery were to be controlled or neutralized by constitutional democracy. Charismatic leadership would be combined with a rational-legal constitutional framework, including an efficient bureaucracy and an effective parliament. Here we see Weber clearly and forcefully arguing for a "mixed type."

Weber viewed this difficult vocational and institutional reconstruction as a means to certain more important ends, *viz.*, the "vital interests of the nation" (*Ibid.*, p. 1383). The classical conception of democracy, with politicians being directly responsible to the electorate, did not interest him precisely because in his view it was impossible to achieve in the mass state. Democratization, or the more limited notion of parliamentarization, was recommended because it would lead to better leadership and greater controls over bureaucratic power.

A third major issue which Weber addressed vis-à-vis the implications of bureaucracy concerned individual freedom. Weber often posed, but seldom directly answered the question, "Given the basic fact of the irresistible advance of bureaucratization . . . [h]ow can one possibly save *any* remnants of "individualist" freedom in any sense?" (*Ibid.*, p. 1403). The posing of one or another version of this question usually took brief, scattered, and metaphorical form, and its answering, although clear enough, was generally implicit, revolving around the notions of duty, vocation, or ethical conduct.

For Weber, bureaucracy and individual freedom were like bureaucracy and democracy in some respects mutually supportive. Thus, the equality and levelling associated with bureaucracy encouraged freedom and spontaneity, and the material fate and hence the independence of the masses rested on bureaucracy. However, levelling also brought with it new forms of inequality, and the bureaucratization of political, economic, and other organizations also set new limits on freedom. Thus, as with all of his antinomies, Weber saw the relationship between bureaucracy and freedom as paradoxical, as a dilemma.

Bureaucracy, according to Weber, threatened the autonomy of individuals both within and outside of bureaucracy. By definition, it was "formally the most rational known means of exercising authority over human beings" (*Ibid.*, p. 223), and it "means fundamentally domination through knowledge" (*Ibid.*, p. 225). Unfreedom within bureaucracy is more directly stated in the first essay:

> The individual bureaucrat cannot squirm out of the apparatus into which he has been harnessed. In contrast to the "notable" performing administrative tasks as a (*sic*) honorific duty or as a subsidiary occupation (avocation), the professional bureaucrat is chained to his activity in his entire economic and ideological existence. In the great majority of cases he is only a small cog in a ceaselessly moving mechanism which prescribes to him an essentially fixed route of march. The official is entrusted with specialized tasks, and normally the mechanism cannot be put into motion or arrested by him, but only from the very top. (*Ibid.*, pp. 987–988)

This characteristically metaphorical raising of the question of freedom had both gains and losses as will be seen in the other examples below.

Weber foresaw the possibility of a "shell of bondage" (*Ibid.*, p. 1402), a "house of serfdom" (quoted in Mommsen, p. 100) which would surpass even Egyptian bureaucracy in its complete rationality, persistence, and inescapability. At the end of the rationalization process Weber apparently saw a polar night, an iron cage, a machine:

Not summer's bloom lies ahead of us, but rather a polar night of icy darkness and hardness. ("Politics as a Vocation," p. 128).

The Puritan wanted to work in a calling; we are forced to do so. . . . In Baxter's view the care for external goods should only lie on the shoulders of the "Saint like a light cloak, which can be thrown aside at any moment." But fate decreed that the cloak should become an iron cage. . . . No one knows who will live in this cage in the future, or whether at the end of this tremendous development entirely new prophets will arise, or there will be a great rebirth of old ideas and ideals, or, if neither, mechanized petrifaction, embellished with a sort of convulsive self importance. (**The Protestant Ethic and the Spirit of Capitalism,** pp. 181–182)

Together with the dead machine it (this "living machine") is at work to set up the iron cage of that bondage of the future, in which perhaps some day men, helplessly, will be forced to integrate themselves into a purely technical good and this means a rational administrative and maintenance officialdom which is to decide over the direction of their affairs is the ultimate and only value. (Quoted in Löwith, *loc. cit.*, p. 118)

Indeed, there is nothing, no machinery in the world, which works so precisely as does this human machine nor so cheaply! . . . When a purely technical and faultless administration, a precise and objective solution of concrete problems is taken as the highest and only goal, then on this basis one can only say; away with everything but an official hierarchy, which does these things as objectively, precisely, and "soullessly" as any machine. ("Max Weber on Bureaucratization in 1909," pp. 125–126).

In such a mechanistic world, what kind of people would we find but cogs, parcelled-out souls, specialists without spirit, "curdled spirits?" Thus:

Already now, through private enterprise in wholesale manufacture, as well as in all other economic enterprises run on modern lines, *Rechenhaftigkeit*, rational calculation, is manifest at every stage. By it, the performance of each individual worker is mathematically measured, each man becomes a little cog in the machine and, aware of this, his one preoccupation is whether he can become a bigger cog. (*Ibid.*, p. 126)

[T]he great question is therefore not how can we promote and hasten it [bureaucratization], but what can we oppose to this machinery in order to keep a portion of mankind free from this par- celling-out of the souls, from this supreme mas- tery of the bureaucratic way of life. (*Ibid.*, p. 128)

For the last stage of this cultural development, it might well be truly said: "Specialists without spirit, sensualists without heart; this nullity imag- ines that it has attained a level of civilization never before achieved."[51] (**The Protestant Ethic and the Spirit of Capitalism**, p. 182).

The power with which these seemingly bleak metaphors resonate is undeniable. Unfortunately, that very "irresistible style" has led some revisionist students of Weber to miss the precise, tentative, cau- tious, qualified nature of these poetic images of the "iron cage" and "parcelled-out souls." More impor- tantly, many have allowed these scattered metaphors to deflect their attention from Weber's relatively direct discussion elsewhere of the possibilities of freedom in a bureaucratic world. Weber's solution was, as usual, to find a middle ground, this time pro- vided by the mediating category of vocation, between the individual and society, between freedom and necessity, and between the ethical ideal of autonomy and what could realistically be achieved in an increas- ingly bureaucratized world. His mediating category is, again, "vocation."

We have already encountered Weber on the sci- entific, political, and bureaucratic vocations. But Weber also considered vocation in a more general sense, when he discussed freedom as a mode of individual conduct conditioned by the social-struc- tural environment. He argued that there was no easy way out of this dilemma: for Tolstoy's ques- tion, "What shall we do, and how shall we live?" Weber provided Goethe's answer, "[B]ear the fate of the times, like a man." ("Science as a Vocation," pp. 143, 155). This measuring-up to the times involved experiencing the problem of freedom within rationalization with full clarity, with neither utopian delusions nor unnecessary pessimism. By exercising what Romain Rolland later called "pes- simism of the intelligence, optimism of the will," the individual could choose, either for or against predominant trends. Given a disenchanted world, the individual should apply the principles of ratio- nality to his own conduct. This reasoned, individu-

alistic opposition within the iron cage involved the choice between two ethics.

What Weber means by the "ethic of ultimate dis- position" is the unconditional espousal of some (reli- gious or political) value, not considering other possible ends, and not critically examining the appro- priateness, likelihood, or possible unintended conse- quences of the means chosen. Thus, for Weber, the ethic of ultimate disposition implied an all or nothing position for example, consistent militancy or consis- tent pacifism which ran the risk of becoming irre- sponsible fanaticism. On the other hand, the ethic of responsibility, which recognized that people must take into account the foreseeable results of their actions and balance the ethical costs of a given means against the intended ends, risked turning into oppor- tunism. Although this was an ideal-typical distinc- tion, as we have seen in our discussion of the political vocation Weber clearly valued the ethic of responsibility. The balance between the two ethics was especially necessary for politicians, but it was also one that all people needed to find. In effect, Weber placed these ethical demands on all of us. As we argued earlier, one contribution of social science according to Weber was the provision of the clarity needed to make such choices.

Weber consistently applied these principles of reasoned choice and self-clarification to his own political and social-scientific conduct. Weber was led by reasoned choice and self-clarification to support responsible freedom within rationalization, thus securing a place for individual autonomy. Although it is not clear whether the freedom of individual action was Weber's paramount value, it is clear that the con- flict between rationalization and individual responsi- bility was for him the great world-historical theme.

In his concern for individual freedom within rationalization, in his recommendations of parlia- mentary, political-vocational and bureaucratic-voca- tional reform, as well as in his conception of the role of social science, Weber reveals himself as a liberal thinker. He believed in progress through the reconsti- tution of societal institutions, and he was trying to secure a place for individual autonomy while at the same time recognizing the "reality" of an increas- ingly rationalized world.

Quite often, Weber has been characterized as a pessimist. Certainly, very few other social thinkers have used metaphorical imagery any bleaker when discussing the future. However, we suggest that his philosophy of history involved a provisional and con- tingent vision of an indeterminate future which could

---

51 The quotation is from Nietzsche.

be changed. A reading of Weber's image of the future which stresses its optimistic and activist aspects leads us to see the tentative and qualified nature of his so-called "predictions." Like the Hebrew prophets, he spoke of his future conditionally, he was not despairing of it, and he recommended specific changes in human conduct in order to forestall it. His work served to awaken people to certain bleak possibilities which he was then prepared to suggest specific ways of avoiding. This is related to Weber's general insistence on the need to face the world in a "matter of fact," realistic, and intellectually honest way. Only when we are prepared to acknowledge that "the Truth is the Truth," and combine that pessimism of the intelligence with optimism of the will, can we as individuals make the necessary decisions.

Before leaving Weber's sociology of politics, we shall discuss briefly his "class, status, and party" argument, a theme which has generated a great deal of comment, debate, and elaboration, despite his having devoted but a few pages to it himself. As part of his discussion of political communities (in Chapter 9 of Volume II of **Economy and Society**), Weber distinguished three conceptually distinct spheres of power. "Class" is the term that he used for economic power, "status" referred to social power, and "party" meant political power. For Weber, these three dimensions of power are not isomorphic, that is they are not related to one another in a perfect, one-to-one fashion. Thus, although some individuals and groups might be powerful in all three spheres, social reality is often much more complex than that. Sometimes, the economically powerful have neither social honour nor political clout, or they have one but not the other. Similarly, those with social prestige might not be economically or politically powerful, and those with political power do not always enjoy high status or economic privilege.

Weber's brief outline of the complexities of power is often explained as a critique of the Marxist emphasis on and understanding of the importance of economic power, viz., class. In particular, Weber discusses various "class situations," first drawing the obvious distinction between the "propertyless" and the "propertied."[52] However, Weber suggested that possession of property is not the sole determinant of one's life chances in industrial society.[53] The "proper-

tied" include those who profit from rent, investments, and the ownership of productive enterprises, and their life chances are good. Yet the "propertyless" include white collar employees, civil servants, and technicians, who themselves also attain good life chances through the selling of certified skills and credentialized training in the marketplace. Also, according to Weber, in industrial societies the main struggle between people in different class situations entails institutionalized disputes between wage-earners (or their union representatives) and managers, rather than workers and the actual owners of productive enterprises, who tend to remain invisible or unrecognized. In addition, classes are unlikely to become homogeneous because of the persistence of individualistic competition. In Weber's view, these modern circumstances make it unlikely that class situation (essentially, Marx's "class-in-itself") would lead to political action by a "social class"[54] (basically, Marx's "class-for-itself"). To be clear, Marx himself had argued that a class-in-itself would become a class-for-itself only under certain social circumstances. In effect, Weber was suggesting that modern circumstances make the transformation to a "social class" or "class-for-itself" less likely than Marx (or certain Marxists[55]) believed.

Weber did discuss status in the sense of prestige or social esteem, that is the way in which individuals subjectively evaluate their own position or those of others in a social hierarchy, so he did use the concept in the way in which it tends to be employed by present-day sociologists.[56] However, Weber was mainly interested in status *groups*. A status group (*Stände*) is a real group or cohesive community, exhibiting a distinctive lifestyle or subculture, and enjoying either positive or negative social honour. Unlike classes, status groups are communities, even

---

52 Sometimes, Weber referred to them as the "positively privileged" and "negatively privileged," respectively.

53 So, Weber provides us with an early and rudimentary version of what later became developed as "human capital" theory.

---

54 Actually, Weber distinguished three categories of class. The first category was defined in terms of "life chances" relating to "market situation." The second, intermediate category had to do with social action flowing from "class interests." The third category related to historical struggles between classes as political entities, which Weber referred to as social classes.

55 Contrary to what some commentators have claimed, Weber did not mean Karl Marx when he alluded to "a talented author" (**Economy and Society**, p. 930) who had mistakenly argued that classes necessarily become political groups. The reference is to Georg Lukàcs, a Sunday afternoon regular at the Weber home in Heidelberg.

56 Also, the term "socioeconomic status" is sometimes used to refer indirectly to class by sociologists who do survey research or rely on government statistics for their data. Anthropologists tend to use the term "status" to refer to one's position in a social structure, and this is linked to the sociological concept of "role."

in industrial society. Status groups can be occupational, religious, or ethnic ones. They may even be based mainly on lifestyle differences, including perhaps sexual orientation, although to our knowledge Weber never discussed this particular possibility. The action of any status group is not necessarily explicable in strictly economic terms. Also, status groups usually practice some degree of social closure or exclusion: social interaction with outsiders is restricted or controlled. An extreme case of a society characterized by ethnic segregation (legitimated both legally and religiously) is the caste system of classical Indian society. A somewhat less extreme case, this time of occupational segregation, is the estate system found in feudal European societies. For Weber, these two examples of closed societies convincingly demonstrate that sometimes societies are stratified by status group rather than class.

For Weber, a "party" is a purposively rational organization which has as its goal the acquisition of power in some larger structural entity. However, this does not mean simply a political party, such as the New Democrats. "Party" also includes trade unions (e.g., CUPE), professional associations (e.g., the Canadian Medical Association), lobby groups (e.g., the Federation of New Brunswick Faculty Associations), and special interest associations (e.g., Friends of The Christmas Mountains). Like *social* classes and status *groups*, parties are groups, not mere aggregates. Unlike social classes and status groups, parties also have formal organization and an administrative staff, set up according to rules of association established in the political, legal, and regulatory spheres. The existence of parties serves to moderate power struggles among classes (or status groups) in contemporary society by routinizing and institutionalizing the conflict between such communities with their distinct interests.

There are several other important aspects of Weber's sociology of politics. We shall mention only a few. His general definition of the state, and his incomplete analysis of the relationship between bureaucracy, parliament, collegial bodies, and other administrative organizations within the modern rational state, is one area which students might be interested in exploring. Another is his analysis of the rise of the Western city, in all its variations in Ancient and Medieval times. Weber viewed the city as the locus of usurpation and *non-legitimate domination*, and thus revolutionary change. Both of these topics are of course related to ones we *have* discussed in this section, particularly the relationship between bureaucracy and democracy and

the relationships among classes, status groups, and parties. In this connection, it would be interesting to review Weber's arguments concerning the political potential of the three major classes and his views of the three main political parties in the Germany of his day. It would also be instructive to relate Weber's notion of "status group" to his analyses of ethnicity. Finally, a more complete understanding of the development of Weber's sociology of politics would require the reading of some of his more polemical speeches, letters, and articles on nationalism, the war effort, the Kaiser, and so forth.

Conclusion

In this chapter, we have attempted to introduce you to the interpretive sociology of Max Weber. We have necessarily focussed on certain aspects of his thought at the expense of others which some might consider to be equally or more important. We have also ignored some of the complexities of Weber's thought, and we have tried to keep our comments concerning criticisms of Weber to a minimum. These other matters can in our view be left to more advanced courses. Our aim has been to introduce you to Weber's thought, to induce you to read Weber's own writings, and to clarify the major themes in those writings.

It is fairly easy to discern the impact of Max Weber's thinking on key figures within many of the most important perspectives within sociological theory today. For example, it is arguable that the Frankfurt School's Jürgen Habermas has been as much influenced by Weber as by the more readily recognized Marx and Freud. Among the phenomenological sociologists, Peter L. Berger has made his debt to Weber—as mediated by earlier thinkers such as Carl Mayer, Albert Salomon, and Alfred Schütz—very clear. Structural functionalists—those few that remain—have obviously been influenced by Talcott Parsons's understanding of Weber's work, and many of the neo-functionalists surrounding Robert K. Merton started their careers by "correcting" what they took to be certain Weberian errors relating to his having been from another time and place. Ironically, both the proponents of the influential methodological notion of "value-neutrality" and C. Wright Mills, one of the major critics of the opportunism which often flowed from that approach, were indebted to Weber. Indeed, Mills is responsible for introducing some of Weber's most significant work to the English-speaking audience. Among the so-called "conflict" theorists, Randall Collins clearly links his work back to Weber. Some feminist theorists have found the notion of social closure articulated in Weber's work on class, status, and party to be useful for understanding gender and ethnic inequality, particularly with respect to access to highly rewarded and prestigious occupations. Neo-Marxist sociologists of most stripes cannot afford to remain indifferent to Weberian arguments: two who have not are Poulantzas and Wright. Contemporary symbolic interactionists, dramaturgical analysts, and ethnomethodologists should perhaps acknowledge what they owe to Weber more than they have. To this list we can add the many mid- to late-twentieth century interpreters of Weber's general contribution to social theory or particular aspects of his thought, including such significant figures not already mentioned as Martin Albrow, Stanislav Andreski, Carlo Antoni, Raymond Aron, Reinhard Bendix, H.H. Bruun, S.N. Eisenstadt, Ephraim Fischoff, Julien Freund, Anthony Giddens, Stephen Kalberg, Herbert Löthy, Arthur Mitzman, Wolfgang J. Mommsen, Robert A. Nisbet, William Outhwaite, Guenther Roth, Benjamin Nelson, George Ritzer, Wolfgang Schluchter, Otto Stammer, Leo Strauss, Bryan S. Turner, and Dennis Wrong.

Max Weber's Writings

Below are listed the titles of English translations of Weber's major works, as well as some minor ones and a number of collections of readings to which we refer in the text.

The Agrarian Sociology of Ancient Civilizations. Translated by R. I. Frank. London: New Left Books, 1976.

Ancient Judaism. Translated by Hans H. Gerth and Don Martindale. New York: The Free Press, 1952.

Economy and Society. Edited by Guenther Roth and Claus Wittich. Totawa, N.J.: Bedminster Press, 1968.

From Max Weber: Essays in Sociology. Edited by Hans H. Gerth and C. Wright Mills. New York: Oxford, 1946.

General Economic History. Translated by Frank Knight. New York: Allen and Unwin, 1927.

"Max Weber on Bureaucratization in 1909," in J. P. Mayer, Max Weber and German Politics: A Study in Political Sociology, 2nd ed. London: Faber and Faber Ltd., 1956, Appendix I.

Max Weber: The Interpretation of Social Reality. Edited by J.T. Eldridge. Don Mills: Thomas Nelson and Sons (Canada) Ltd., 1971.

On the Methodology of the Social Sciences. Translated by E. A. Shils and H. A. Finch. Glencoe: The Free Press, 1949.

The Protestant Ethic and The Spirit of Capitalism. Translated by T. Parsons. New York: Charles Scribner's Sons, 1958.

The Rational and Social Foundations of Music. Translated and edited by Don Martindale, Johannes Riedel, and Gertrude Neuwirth. Carbondale: The Southern Illinois Press, 1958.

The Religion of China. Translated by Hans H. Gerth. Glencoe: The Free Press, 1951.

The Religion of India. Translated by Hans H. Gerth and Don Martindale. Glencoe: The Free Press, 1958.

"Socialism," in J. E. T. Eldridge, ed., Max Weber: The Interpretation of Social Reality. Don Mills, Ontario: Thomas Nelson and Sons (Canada) Ltd., 1972, pp. 191–219.

The Sociology of Religion. Boston: Beacon Press, 1963.

Weber: Selections in Translation. Edited by W. G. Runciman. London: Cambridge University Press, 1978.

Some Commentaries on Max Weber

The main secondary sources which have influenced our understanding of Max Weber's social theory are listed below.

Bendix, Reinhard. Max Weber: An Intellectual Portrait. Garden City, N.Y.: Anchor Books, 1962.

Bendix, Reinhard and Guenther Roth. Scholarship and Partisanship: Essays on Max Weber. Berkeley: University of California Press, 1971.

Bruun, H. H. Science, Values, and Politics in Max Weber's Methodology. Copenhagen; Munksgaard, 1972.

Freund, Julien. The Sociology of Max Weber. New York: Vintage Books, 1969.

Giddens, Anthony. Politics and Sociology in the Thought of Max Weber. London: Macmillan, 1972.

Mayer, Carl. "The Sociology of Max Weber." Course given at the New School for Social Research, New York, 1969.

Mitzman, Arthur. The Iron Cage: An Historical Interpretation of Max Weber. New York: Alfred A. Knopf, 1970.

Mommsen, Wolfgang. The Age of Bureaucracy: Perspectives on the Political Sociology of Max Weber. Oxford: Basil Blackwell, 1974.

Weber, Marianne. Max Weber: A Biography. Translated and edited by Harry Zohn. Toronto: John Wiley and Sons, 1975.

5

Emile Durkheim

Introductory Note

All references appear in parentheses in abbreviated form in Part Three. The following abbreviations have been used throughout the chapter:

Rules   **The Rules of Sociological Method** (Chicago: University of Chicago Press, 1938).

DL   **The Division of Labor in Society** (New York: Macmillan Co., 1933).

Suicide   **Suicide** (Glencoe, Ill.: Free Press of Glencoe, Illinois, 1951).

Dualism   "Le dualisme de la nature humaine et ses conditions sociales," **Scientia**, XV (1914), 206–21.

Lukes   Steven Lukes, **Emile Durkheim: His Life and Work** (Penguin Books, 1973)

The Subject Matter of Sociology: Social Facts

Like so many of the early sociologists, Durkheim set out to delineate the proper subject matter of sociology and to distinguish sociology from other disciplines, particularly biology, psychology, philosophy, and economics. For Durkheim, the proper subject matter of sociology consists of "social facts."

Social facts are "ways of acting, thinking, and feeling, external to the individual, and endowed with a power of coercion, by reason of which they control him." In Durkheim's view, social facts are qualitatively different from biological and psychological phenomena; they are derived from society as a whole or from one of its partial groups, not from the individual; they constitute the exclusive domain of sociology and are in no way studied by other established disciplines. They are produced by group living; they are rooted in group sentiments, values, attitudes, beliefs, etc.; they are transmitted from generation to generation by word of mouth or by education; and they are manifested in legal codes, religious faiths, moral rules, popular aphorisms and proverbs and the like. One might be tempted to equate them with what has become known in modern sociology as social norms, but it is clear that Durkheim intended social facts to have a wider meaning, to include, for example, such phenomena as "social currents" that may even lead to non-normative behaviour such as suicide and mob atrocities.

Social facts are distinguished from other phenomena by two characteristics: externality or exteriority and coercion or constraint. In saying that social facts are external to the individual, Durkheim meant that social facts are external in origin and, in a manner of speaking, constitute an objective environment that exists independently of the individual. But how is it possible for social facts to be external to the individual, when individuals are the only possible bearers of social facts? Durkheim's reply was that, while inextricably bound up with the life of the individual, social facts have a *"different substratum*; they evolve in a different milieu; and they depend on different conditions."

Durkheim regards social facts as things in their own right (*sui generis*), as realities that cannot be deduced from or reduced to psychological facts. While both social and psychological facts are mental in nature, collective representations (ideas) are, in Durkheim's view, qualitatively different from individual representations. Does this mean that Durkheim posits some sort of "group mind" that exists apart from individuals? Some of his critics have accused him of this sort of illegitimate reification, and perhaps with some justification. Durkheim's reply is that in nature elements frequently combine to form new phenomena with properties that are entirely different from those of the elements. We refer to this process as "emergence." Just as the hardness of bronze or the fluidity of water are not to be found in the ingredients from which they are formed, so the properties of social facts are not to be found in individual consciousness as such. Individuals are the units of society, to be sure, but by living together they form a new reality that is qualitatively different from that of the units. In this sense social facts are external to individuals.

Social facts "emerge" out of group life; they crystallize and in most cases they acquire a tangible form, as in legal codes and moral rules. There is a truly collective, as opposed to common aspect to them. They are not social facts simply because they are universally held by the group or are common to the majority of its members. If they are common to the members of a group, they are common because they are collective, and not collective because they are common.

Durkheim was aware that those who championed such ideals as free will, absolute autonomy of the individual, and self-determination would not respond favourably to his definition of social facts as coercive and constraining, for this would in their minds diminish the dignity of man. Durkheim's reply was that those very ideas that we cherish as our own are not of our own making; they come to us from the outside. "How can they become part of us except by imposing themselves upon us?." The best evidence of this is the socialization of the child. Does this mean that the individual is nothing but a passive receptacle of social forces?

On the contrary, Durkheim writes: "Because beliefs and social practices thus come to us from without, it does not follow that we receive them passively or without modification. In reflecting on collective institutions and assimilating them for ourselves, we individualize them and impart to them more or less personal characteristics. ... It is for this reason that each of us creates, in a measure, his own morality, religion, and mode of life. There is no conformity to social convention that does not comprise an entire range of individual shades." (**Rules**, pp. lxvi-lxvii). To be sure the range of variation is limited, more in some areas e.g., religious and moral codes) than in others (e.g., economic life), and behaviour that exceeds the appropriate limits is met with sanctions.

The presence of sanctions constitutes the very proof of the existence of social facts. Durkheim was well aware that social facts could be defined in a number of ways, as for example, in terms of the individual's commitment to them, but, in choosing to define social facts in terms of constraints and sanctions, he was able to identify the objective, external signs by which they could be recognized and studied. This meant that social facts could be studied scientifically.

Social facts cover a wide range of phenomena and vary in degrees of crystallization and organization. On the one hand, there are the "social currents—trends and tendencies in a population, including the spontaneous outbreaks of mob behaviour. Then there are legal codes, religious beliefs, popular aphorisms, etc.—what we might call institutional norms, which differ from social currents by the fact of being institutionalized, crystallized, and in many instances, codified. Durkheim also regarded as social facts certain morphological and structural features of a population—volume, density, channels of communication, etc. The common feature of these different forms of social facts is that they are collective products of group life.

Social Facts as Things

In the opening lines of Chapter II of the **Rules**, Durkheim enunciates his "first and most fundamental rule" of sociological method: *"Consider social facts as things"* (p. 14). This seemingly simple statement is not an easy one to understand. It rests on a distinction between "concepts" and "things." In Durkheim's view, there is a difference between things as they are in reality and the ideas we have about them. A true science studies "things," but during the incipient stages of a science's development it is frequently the case that the human mind not only perceives the phenomena under study, but also speculates on their nature and fashions crude concepts in order to make sense of them. This is especially likely to occur with social phenomena. We all have ideas about such things as the nature of man, the purpose of the family, the function of religion, the character of crime and punishment, the evolution of society, and the like, and we govern our behaviour accordingly. But these ideas have not been scientifically established; they simply reveal our ideas about reality.

Through a process of deductive reasoning the more disciplined minds begin with such ideas and construct complex theoretical systems, which are nothing more than logical extrapolations of untested ideas. In Durkheim's view, the sociology of his time had not yet acquired the status of a true science; it dealt almost exclusively with concepts rather than things. For example, Comte, while espousing the principles of natural science, began with a preconceived notion that the human species necessarily evolves toward an ever more complete state of perfection, and then he developed an entire sociological system upon that premise. But, as Durkheim argues, such an evolutionary theory could only have been established by an already completed science. Theories, such as those of Comte and Spencer, are largely ideological. Durkheim insisted that sociology must avoid the use of concepts that have not been established scientifically.

How are we to establish the validity of concepts scientifically? Durkheim provides us with three rules to follow:

Rule Number One: *"All preconceptions must be eradicated."* (**Rules**, p. 31)

Sociology must free itself from lay concepts, which are frequently rooted in sentiments. Because we have a vested interest in the ideas we have about the social world, since we govern our behaviour accordingly, we tend to resist efforts to subject them to the cold, dry, objective, analytic eye of the scientist. To develop as a science, sociology must extricate itself from emotionally charged popular opinions, i.e., the preconceptions we have about the social world.

Rule Number Two: *"The subject matter of every sociological study should comprise a group of phenomena defined in advance by certain common external characteristics, and all phenomena so defined should be included in this group."* (**Rules**, p. 35)

Durkheim insists that in order to develop a true science, it is necessary to define at the outset the phenomenon it intends to study. And the definition must be rooted in the inherent properties of the phenomenon. "It must characterize them by elements essential to their nature, not by their conformity to an intellectual idea" (**Rules**, p. 35). This is not easy, since the inherent properties are not always visible, and there is no way to know in advance how significant each of the visible properties is. Nevertheless, in Durkheim's view, it is especially important during the early phases of research, before the facts have been carefully analyzed, to focus on the most objectively verifiable, externally visible characteristics, even though we may find in time that the less obvious characteristics are more significant. The important point is that the defining characteristics must be objective; internal human experiences, such as social

solidarity, suicidal inclinations, feelings of sacredness, etc., must be identified by some objective external measure, just as changes in the temperature become known through changes in the size of a column of mercury in a thermometer. Durkheim used legal codes, statistics on suicide, and religious dogmas as such objective measures in his substantive works. Lastly, systematic knowledge of phenomena can only be gained if all the phenomena that fit the definition are included in the study. For example, if we define "work" as activity that benefits society and then simply focus on gainful employment in our researches, not only will we fail to observe a whole host of societally useful activities, such as housework, but, more importantly, we will have a confused understanding of the phenomenon of work.

Rule Number Three: *"When . . . the sociologist undertakes the investigation of some order of social facts, he must endeavor to consider them from an aspect that is independent of their individual manifestations."* (**Rules**, p. 45)

To acquire an objective understanding of a phenomenon, it is necessary to consider it in its general form, and not in its particular expression. Scientific laws are universal and general. For example, we all have moral obligations toward our family members, but we do not always carry them out fully, nor do we all carry them out in the same way. Yet these moral rules are intended to apply to everyone in the group equally. Thus, to understand such moral conduct, it is better to consider the rules and only secondarily the individual's carrying out of the rules. Since these rules frequently crystallize and acquire a definite form, as in legal codes and religious faiths, they possess a general, universal, and constant character, and consequently serve as reliable subject matter for a science.

In insisting that social facts be regarded as things, Durkheim is not asking us to reduce social phenomena to material phenomena—that would be contrary to his view of social facts—but rather to put ourselves in the same frame of mind as the physicist, chemist, or physiologist when analyzing social occurrences. But in so doing, Durkheim is presenting us with a very particular view of science, one that has been drawn into question by other thinkers (Cf. Simmel and Mead). Durkheim's view of science clearly falls into the positivistic tradition, although Durkheim refused to use this word to describe his own methodological principles.

Despite claims to the contrary, Durkheim was forced to make a number of assumptions about social facts. Social facts are things that exist in nature independently of the viewing mind; they are governed by invariable natural laws which are external to and independent of human volition; they possess determinative qualities and often constrain human behaviour; they cannot be known in advance of their occurrence and cannot be arrived at through introspection; they can be known only through their external, objective, visible characteristics.

Explanation of Social Facts

After establishing the principles by which social facts can be identified, Durkheim proceeds to elaborate a set of rules for explaining social facts. The first principle rests on a distinction between "efficient causes" and social "functions." Accordingly, any social fact can be examined from the standpoint of its utility, function, or value, or from the standpoint of the causes that originate it and make it what it is. But, we should not confuse these two questions. "To show how a fact is useful is not to explain how it originated or why it is what it is. The uses which it serves presuppose the specific properties characterizing it but do not create them. The need we have of things cannot give them existence, nor can it confer their special nature upon them. It is to causes of another sort that they owe their existence"(**Rules**, p. 90). For example, human beings need food to eat and water to drink, but these human needs can in no way be used to explain in a scientific way the properties and origin of food and water.

In Durkheim's view, social thinkers such as Comte and Spencer make the mistake of thinking that they have explained a phenomenon when they have identified the social need that it satisfies. This tendency is found in modern structural-functional theory. But it is clear that Durkheim regarded causes as quite different from functions and insisted that each be taken full account of in the explanation of any social phenomenon.

By cause and function, Durkheim meant social cause and social function. This is clearly set out in his second principle: a social fact must be explained in terms of antecedent social facts, and the function of a social fact must be understood in relation to some social, not individual, end. The argument supporting this principle is a lengthy one. In Durkheim's view, Comte and Spencer reasoned psychologistically, that is, they explained social facts in terms of psychological variables. For Comte and Spencer, "the most complex forms of civilization are only the developments

of the psychological life of the individual" (**Rules**, p. 99). For example, family organization is explained in terms of the sentiments parents have for their children and children for their parents; the institution of marriage is accounted for in terms of the individual advantages it provides for the individuals involved; punishment is explained in terms of the anger which misdeeds arouse, and so forth. But, this type of explanation is completely antithetical to our understanding of social facts. As noted in the previous two sections, social facts are external to the individual and impose themselves from without. It makes no sense to explain them in terms of the individual's inclinations, drives, needs, etc., as these reside within the individual.

This is not to say that human needs, impulses, desires, etc., play no role in the determination of social life. Quite clearly, we act to satisfy these needs, and not infrequently we intervene in the social process and may even play a part in the generation of new social phenomena. But, these needs themselves are effects of antecedent causes. It would be extremely presumptuous of man to think that the phenomena of the world, social and material, simply marshall themselves around the needs of man, not only in the present but in the future that is yet to come. The explanations of Comte and Spencer are not only psychologistic or individualistic, but also teleological, and, on these accounts, are unacceptable to Durkheim. Social phenomena must be explained sociologically.

But what are these antecedent social facts that may be used to explain social phenomena? What, as we say today, are the independent variables in our analysis of social facts? Durkheim's reply is the "internal constitution of the social group." His argument is that if the very fact of human association (group life) determines social phenomena, then the structure of that human association should have some effect on the facts of the social life therein created. Thus, Durkheim sought certain morphological or structural characteristics of the social milieu as his explanatory factors. He identified two sets of factors: the number of people in the group (population volume) and the density of the population. His critics have argued that, in attributing causal significance to the volume and density of a population, Durkheim betrayed his own methodological principle that social facts must be explained by social facts, since population characteristics are in essence physical or material. However, it is clear that Durkheim was not referring to the purely physical aspects of populations; he was referring to the social interactive aspects ("dynamic density")—the degree and intensity of interaction among a people.

The physical characteristics of populations frequently, though not always, serve as objective measures of the "dynamic density." However, it is possible for distant people to communicate frequently, as often occurs with modern means of communication, and for people living in close proximity to have very little social intercourse. Thus, other factors may have to be taken into account when identifying the appropriate independent variables of a social milieu. Such factors as social organization, channels of communication, intergenerational mobility, etc., may serve this purpose. What can be said of whole societies can be said of partial societies, as for example, the family, professional groups, universities, etc. But, in each case, the morphological features of the group serve as the independent variables in our analysis.

Lastly, how do we establish a causal relationship between the social milieu and the social facts we wish to explain? How do we set out to test our hypothesis that there is a "cause" and "effect" relationship between them? Durkheim's reply is through the method of "concomitant variation." Controlled experimentation is impossible in sociology. The historical method of Comte defies the logic of causation. The method of agreement and difference, whereby values of a dependent variable are compared against a plurality of possible antecedent causes in an effort to sort out the causal factors, is frequently ineffective. The method of concomitant variation or correlation overcomes these difficulties. Factors that vary concomitantly, Durkheim reasoned, must be related in some manner or fashion. They may be related as cause and effect; but, then again, two factors may both be effects of some prior cause. It is also possible that between the first and second factor there occurs a third "intervening" variable. How are we to sort out the cause and effect relationships? Durkheim tells us that there is no way of determining cause and effect relations mechanically. It is necessary at some point to introduce theoretical reasoning. The method of concomitant variation is a methodological procedure for ordering data, the explanation of which requires theory.

The Nature of Society: Society as Sui Generis

The conception of society as a reality in its own right (*sui generis*) is as unalterably linked with Durkheim as the statement "The history of all hitherto soci-

ety. . . ." is associated with Marx and Engels. Evidence suggests that Durkheim developed his view of social phenomena while still a student at the Ecole Normale Supérieure, largely through the combined influences of Renouvier, whose works he studied, and Boutroux, one of his teachers. From Renouvier he acquired the view that the whole is greater than the sum of its parts, that a system cannot be explained by its component units. From Boutroux he gained an appreciation of the distinction between sociology and psychology and the relation of sciences to one another. Like Comte, Boutroux had argued that the various sciences constitute a chain or hierarchy; each had its own distinct subject matter and could not be reduced to the science that preceded it. Just as the vital aspects of biology cannot be explained in terms of the physico-chemical properties of matter, so social phenomena cannot be explained in terms of the psychological or biological characteristics of man. Each science constituted a separate order of data and had to be explained in its own terms. Thus, early in his life, Durkheim committed himself to the view that society is a reality *sui generis*, a reality that is qualitatively different from the psychological life of the individual, and one that required social factors to explain it. This view of society, which is frequently described as "social realism," pervades Durkheim's theoretical and substantive work. His commitment to it was enhanced through his reading of Comte and Spencer.

Durkheim did not simply assert this view of society *a priori*; he supported his contention with empirical evidence, with criticisms of opposing theories, and with theoretical arguments of his own. Durkheim noted that suicide and crime rates vary by social group; these differences could not be explained by psychological, organic or material factors, which tend to be considerably more constant than group structures. Durkheim also noted that individuals in crowds and in social situations such as ritual festivals and ceremonies feel and behave differently than when they are alone; thus, he argued that there must be something about the fact of association that accounts for this difference. That individuals would sacrifice themselves for the sake of the group in fits of patriotism and religious zeal persuaded Durkheim that social and cultural beliefs are not only powerful forces but are quite different from individual beliefs and motivations and, therefore, comprise a different order of data. Durkheim found a number of theories to be quite inadequate; his criticism of them helped to strengthen his convictions. Individualistic theories of the State, such as those of Hobbes and Rousseau,

Durkheim felt to be self-contradictory, for why, he reasoned, would the individual willingly create a state that dominates and constrains him? The state cannot be explained in terms of individual motives. Durkheim also rejected theories that explain the development of civilization and the forms of society in terms of man's physico-organic nature (e.g., race and heredity), for the latter, Durkheim argued, are constant, while the former vary greatly. Durkheim challenged Spencer's explanation of the rise and development of civilization in terms of eudemonistic motives (pursuit of happiness) on empirical grounds; there was no evidence that happiness increased with the growth of civilization. The theoretical viewpoints that Durkheim found most compatible were those of "scientific rationalism" and "emergence." By scientific rationalism, Durkheim means that "there is nothing in reality that one is justified in considering as fundamentally beyond the scope of reason," and "there is no reason to set a limit to the progress of science." (cited in Lukes, p. 74) The theory of emergence, as has been mentioned above, stems from the observation that in nature elements often combine to create new phenomena that possess properties that are qualitatively different from those of the elements. The influence of these theories, especially the latter, can be found throughout Durkheim's works.

Compared with conceptions of society found in individualistic theories, the view of society as *sui generis* shifts logical priority from the individual to society. It is not the individual that determines society; quite the contrary, it is society that determines the individual, and it is society that stamps individual man with his distinguishing characteristics. Note the following:

> All social life is made up of ... relations established between a plurality of individuals. ... but we shall see ... that individuals are much more a product of common life than they are determinants of it. If from each of them we take away everything due to social action, the residue that we obtain, besides being picayune, is not capable of presenting much variety. Without the diversity of social conditions upon which they depend the differences which separate them would be inexplicable. It is not, then, in the unequal aptitudes of men that we must seek the cause for the unequal development of societies. DL, p. 338.

But this type of social realism creates theoretical problems for some critics. One question that frequently puzzles students pertains to the origin of society. If society precedes the individual, how do we account for the origin of social phenomena?

First, all societies are born of other societies, and are not created through deliberate decisions of individuals. Thus, the question takes us back to the origin of the very first society. But, the answers to this question are themselves very questionable, and this would not change the method for explaining social facts in history. Individuals participate in the generation of social phenomena through the fact of association, but, "they are not the cause of it, nor do they give it its special form, they only make it possible."

Normal and Abnormal Social Phenomena

In making a distinction between normal and abnormal social phenomena, Durkheim sought to develop a basis for using social science to solve social problems. Unlike Weber, who insisted that science and ethics constituted two unbridgeable realms of human experience, that science could not be used as a basis for making value judgments, Durkheim sought precisely to establish a scientific foundation for ethics. If one could distinguish between social physiology and social pathology, if one could identify an objective criterion of social pathology, then social science could be used to treat social ills.

The distinction between normal and abnormal social phenomena is based on the analogous distinction between the health and sickness of the individual organism. In Durkheim's view, just as a physician distinguishes between a healthy organism and a diseased one, so the sociologist must distinguish between normal and "morbid" or "pathological" social phenomena. To be sure, the task is much more difficult for the sociologist, but the possibility of so doing, for Durkheim, is "beyond doubt." How is this to be done?

Durkheim argues that social phenomena are normal if they are found generally throughout society; all departures from the general and the average are morbid or pathological. However, by average is not always meant the empirical average, for a social fact frequently can be found in a society that does not correspond to the normal conditions of that society. This is the case with social and cultural remnants from the past that no longer serve useful social functions. There are two points of reference for normality: the species in question, since what is normal for one species is not necessarily normal for another species, and, secondly, the stage of development of the species.

Critics have found a number of difficulties with this distinction, not the least of which has to do with what some regard to be an implicit conservative bias. Durkheim takes the existing state of society more or less as "given" and regards departures from this state as pathological. In the view of some, this tends to ignore the possibility of historical alternatives and fails to give an adequate account of social conflict.

Since crime and suicide are found in all societies, Durkheim concluded that they were normal. Just as unpleasant and even painful states of the individual organism, such as occur in parturition, must be seen as biologically normal, so a certain amount of crime and other forms of aberrant conduct must be seen as socially normal. It is clear that Durkheim's distinction between normal and abnormal social phenomena does not parallel the distinction found in modern sociology between normal behaviour and deviance. In Durkheim's view a certain amount of what we would call deviant behaviour is normal, especially in a society that is changing.

The Nature of Man: Homo Duplex

Both proponents and critics of Durkheim have focused on his "social realism," his view of society as *sui generis*. Proponents of Durkheim praise this view of social phenomena as one of Durkheim's most significant contributions to sociology; it did much to establish sociology as a separate social science. Critics of social realism have argued that this view is too one-sided, that it fails to take into account sufficiently the fact of the individual, that it tends to regard the individual as nothing but an abstraction, an insignificant figure totally submerged in society. However, both of these positions are unfortunately one-sided interpretations of Durkheim's work.

Durkheim argued not that the life of the individual is totally a product of social forces; that would be contrary to his own views against analytic reductionism. For Durkheim, social phenomena are qualitatively distinct from individual phenomena; each is real and each constitutes a separate order of data—to be understood in its own terms. In 1914, Durkheim published an article in an Italian journal, **Scientia**, in which he outlines his conception of human nature. He argues that our psychic life consists of two qualitatively different but equally viable aspects: the personal and the impersonal. The first, consisting of sensations and sensory tendencies, is immutably

rooted in the individual organism and has as its object only the individuality of the person. Necessarily egotistical in concern and purely individual in experience, the personal aspect is different from and antithetical to the social. The social aspect, consisting of conceptual thought and moral activity, derives its reality, not from the organism, but from that which is external to individual man and common to a plurality of men. While a person individualizes universal concepts and moral values, the latter nevertheless are derived from a reality which is trans-individual and collective, i.e., society. In Durkheim's words:

> There is in us a being that represents everything in relation to itself and from its own point of view; in everything that it does, this being has no other object but itself. There is another being in us, however, which knows things *sub specie aeternitatis*, as if it were participating in some thought other than its own, and which, in its acts, tends to accomplish ends that surpass its own. **Dualism**, p. 328

Durkheim goes on to say that the two realms of psychic existence are not only different in their source and character but are by nature antithetical and antagonistic. "They mutually contradict and deny each other." But more importantly, the personal or individual and the impersonal or social, whether in the sphere of conceptual thought or moral values, bear a relationship of a necessarily irreconcilable opposition or inner dialectic. Neither the purely individual nor the social aspect of our psychic existence can be reduced to the other without loss in both. "The ego cannot be something completely other than itself, for, if it were, it would vanish. . . . On the other hand . . . the ego cannot be entirely and exclusively itself, for if it were, it would be emptied of all content." It is this "inner contradiction," "this perpetual division against ourselves," that distinguishes us as human beings and it is this irreconcilable opposition between the individual and the social that makes society possible.

We should not regard this article as a concession to his critics which Durkheim felt obliged to write during the latter stages of his career, for the image of man contained therein is clearly visible in his early writings. In **The Division of Labor** the view of man as *homo duplex* underlies the very distinction between mechanical and organic solidarity, and in **Suicide** it serves as the basis for his typology of suicide.

The Study of the Division of Labour

Originally his doctoral dissertation, **The Division of Labor in Society**, published in 1893 while Durkheim was at the University of Bordeaux, has been subjected to varying interpretation of its principle concerns and major contributions. Some have argued that it is a study of social evolution; others that it is a study of the organization of modern society; still others that it is a study of the foundations of social order. Perhaps it is best to let Durkheim speak for himself on this matter. In the "Preface to the First Edition," Durkheim outlines the question that inspired him to write the book:

> This work had its origins in the question of the relations of the individual to social solidarity. Why does the individual, while becoming more autonomous, depend more on society? How can he be at once more individual and more solidary? Certainly, these two movements, contradictory as they appear, develop in parallel fashion. This is the problem we are raising. **DL**, p. 37

Durkheim noticed that the close-knit ties that bind traditional society have broken down. The individual has become more autonomous in modern society; yet society hangs together, and the individual appears to be even more closely bound to society. In the "Preface" Durkheim hints at a possible solution to this seeming contradiction—a "transformation of social solidarity due to the steadily growing development of the division of labor." (**DL**, p. 38) Durkheim sets himself three tasks: to determine "the function of the division of labor, that is to say, what social need it satisfies," to determine "the causes and conditions on which it is dependent," and to "classify the principle abnormal forms it presents, so they will not be confused with the others." (**DL**, p. 45) In defining his problem in this manner, Durkheim is consistent with the rules of sociological method outlined above.

Durkheim agreed with a long line of thinkers, from Adam Smith to Herbert Spencer, that modern society developed out of a more primitive society, bringing with it an increased division of labour, increased specialization and differentiation of occupational roles, increased social heterogeneity, as well as increased individuation. And Durkheim acknowledged that increased population pressure played a part in the development of a more elaborate division of labour. However, he disagreed with most of the explanation given by others regarding this development. In the course of the book, Durkheim disposes of all individualistic, psychological, and teleological explanations, those that attribute cause to such things as the pursuit of happiness, desire for economic gain, anticipation of the results, and man's thirst for civilization.

Durkheim noticed that implicit in the division of labour in modern society there is a moral imperative—"*Make yourself usefully fulfill a determinate function*" (**DL**, p. 43). It is our duty to specialize, to become unlike one another in our social roles. Violations of this rule are not punished by law, but failure to comply frequently leads to personal disadvantage and social disapprobation. For Durkheim, moral imperatives, in this context, are expressions of social solidarity. Durkheim argues that there are two natural bases of solidarity: one based on likeness or resemblances among people, and the other based on complementary differences, as for example in conjugal solidarity. The division of labour corresponds to the latter type of solidarity.

But social solidarity is a subjective phenomenon. In order to study it scientifically, it will be necessary to find an objective measure of it. For Durkheim the visible, objective measure is law. He notes that the frequency and intensity of human interaction varies with the development of legal and moral codes; thus law could serve as a good index of social solidarity. Durkheim was aware that customs, many of which are not codified, also serve to maintain solidarity, and some of them may even be opposite to the law, as for example, the smoking of marijuana in university dormitories, but these constitute a small fraction of the total number of imperative rules of conduct. Thus, law would serve as Durkheim's objective indicator of social solidarity.

The next task was to classify laws. Durkheim, as we should expect, rejects the distinctions used by jurisconsults, since these are lay concepts that cannot be used for scientific purposes. Since unity of causes produces a unity of effects, we should classify law in terms of the sanctions that are brought to bear upon those who violate them. There are two types of laws: penal or repressive laws, those that involve punishment or suffering inflicted on the agent, and restitutive laws, those that require "*the return of things as they were.*" With the method of analysis identified and the concepts defined, Durkheim then attempts to find the type of social solidarity to which each of the two types of law corresponds.

Collective Conscience

Durkheim's analysis of punishment led him to his concept of the "collective conscience." He noted that crime calls forth punishment, but the punishment is frequently disproportionate to the amount of damage done by the crime. For example, murder is regarded as the greatest of crimes, but, compared with such disasters as major economic crises or stock-market crashes, a single homicide does considerably less damage to society. Durkheim rejects explanations of crime in terms of actual or imagined harm to society. He comes to the conclusion that crime evokes punishment because it offends our public sentiments, because it shocks the collective conscience.

The collective conscience is the totality of values, beliefs, and sentiments which we hold in common. The important aspect of the collective conscience is that it is *collective* in nature and origin; it possesses a life of its own apart from the individuals who participate in it. It is a reality *sui generis* that binds individuals and plays a major role in the maintenance of social solidarity, especially in primitive societies.

The *conscience collective* has been translated from the French as "collective conscience" and "collective consciousness," the reason being that the French word, *conscience*, has a meaning equivalent to that of two English words, "conscience" and "consciousness." There is an evaluative and cognitive aspect to the French word; it embraces both moral and religious beliefs and sentiments, on the one hand, and concepts, on the other.

Mechanical and Organic Solidarity

The two types of laws correspond to two types of social solidarity. Penal law with repressive sanctions symbolizes a type of social cohesion that results from a conformity of the particular consciences with the collective conscience. In such a society, the individuals resemble one another, and are attracted to one another by reasons of likeness, but this is not the sole or primary basis of social solidarity. Social solidarity stems from the fact that the psychic life of the individual is fused with the psychic life of society as a whole, i.e., with the collective conscience. This type of solidarity, Durkheim calls "mechanical."

Cooperative law with restitutive sanctions, governing such activities as domestic relations, social contracts, commercial relations, legal procedures, public administration and constitutional matters, corresponds to a type of social solidarity expressed in the division of labour. In a society with a highly developed division of labour, social solidarity is maintained not by likeness and resemblance, but by difference. Personalities are highly differentiated one from the other and are not fused with the collective conscience. Individuals depend upon one another, not only or primarily for economic reasons, but for social reasons. Durkheim argued that differentiated personalities complete and round out one another and become solidary by virtue of comprising differentiated aspects of a common whole. This type of social solidarity, Durkheim called "organic."

The above distinction led to Durkheim's typology of societies. Accordingly, a society maintained by *mechanical solidarity* (primitive society) has a very rudimentary division of labour; solidarity is based on likeness and blind obedience to prescriptive traditions embedded in the collective conscience; the legal system is based on repressive sanctions; moral and legal responsibility is collective; the collective conscience is strong, and individualism is underdeveloped. A society maintained by *organic solidarity* (modern society) has a very elaborate division of labour; solidarity is based on cooperation and interdependence of differentiated personalities; the legal system is based on restitutive sanctions; one's moral responsibility is to fulfill a specialized social function; the collective conscience is considerably weakened, and individualism flourishes. These types of societies must be seen as "ideal types" (Cf. Weber), as models for purposes of analyzing social change.

Development of the Division of Labour

Durkheim concludes that the function of the division of labour is to maintain social solidarity in modern society, just as the function of the collective conscience is to maintain social cohesion in primitive society. But, it must be remembered that we are talking about "ideal types"; no known society is entirely based on one or the other form of social solidarity. Further, and perhaps more importantly, modern, differentiated society with its elaborate division of labour developed out of early forms of society maintained by mechanical solidarity.

Durkheim argues that the division of labour advances as the collective conscience becomes less significant; religion recedes, as science and secular thought develop; and the social organization of society shifts from the segmental type (series of homogeneous segments) to the highly organized differentiated type we find today. However, unlike

Comte and Spencer, who accounted for the development of society in social evolutionary terms, that is, in terms of some inherent principle of human development, Durkheim found it necessary to explain the transformation in terms of external factors. There is nothing inherent in the human species that naturally leads to the development of civilization. The process had to be explained; it could not be assumed.

Durkheim disposes of alternative explanations, in particular the explanation claiming that the division of labour has its origin in the unceasing quest of man to increase his happiness. Against this view, Durkheim argues that happiness results when man is in harmony with the conditions of life, and this is independent of the evolutionary process. Further, there is no evidence that happiness increases with the advancement of civilization. The suicide rate is clearly a measure of unhappiness, and that rises with the advancement of civilization. Durkheim concludes that the explanation for the division of labour cannot be found in the inherent properties of human nature, but rather had to be sought in the "surrounding environment."

What are the primary causes of the division of labour? These are to be found in the "social milieu." Durkheim argues that the increase in population volume and density ("condensation of society") is the primary cause. However, it is not the physical aspects of population that brings about this result—that would involve the use of a material fact to explain a social fact—it is the "moral" or "dynamic" density of the population that counts. Population pressure may stimulate intra-social relations and lead to greater moral and dynamic density, but it does not always have this effect. It can on occasion lead to destructive conflicts, social divisions, and emigration of populations. It is only in an already constituted moral unity, i.e., a solidary society, that population pressure gives rise to greater moral or dynamic density.

Increased population volume and density intensify the struggle for existence. Darwin found that the struggle for existence in the animal world led to increased differentiation among the species. Durkheim reasoned that somewhat of the same process occurs with the human species. He argued that the increased specialization and differentiation of social functions was society's way of surviving in a competitive environment. Rather than struggling directly with one another, members of a society, by differentiating themselves and engaging in cooperative activities, improve the chances of survival of the group. "The division of labor is . . . a result of the

struggle for existence, but it is a mellowed *denouement.* Thanks to it, opponents are not obliged to fight to a finish, but can exist one beside the other. Also, in proportion to its development, it furnishes the means of maintenance and survival to a greater number of individuals who, in more homogeneous societies, would be condemned to extinction." (**DL**, p. 270)

It is important to note that it is society that transforms itself in relation to its environment. Individuals could not possibly have foreseen the advantages of the division of labour until it had already advanced. It is society that divides pre-existing labour; individuation is not a cause but a result of this process; the division of labour does not devolve upon already differentiated individuals, the division of labour makes individuals what they are.

Durkheim also identifies a number of secondary factors that play a part in the development of the division of labour, among them, the progressive indetermination of the collective conscience, the collapse of traditional institutions, and the waning influence of hereditary factors in determining social roles. The collective conscience becomes increasingly universalized and generalized, thus allowing the individual to extricate himself from its influence. When moral imperatives become phrased in universal and general, as opposed to specific terms, individuation becomes possible. It is not that the collective conscience disappears in modern society; quite the contrary, it is still an important source of social solidarity, but it provides only general principles of moral conduct. With migration into the cities and considerable intergenerational mobility, traditional values, beliefs, and world-views perpetuated from generation to generation through the family break down and make room for new modes of conduct. Lastly, Durkheim argues that hereditary factors play a less significant role in determining social functions. As new modes of activity are brought into existence through the development of the division of labour, they become less and less subject to the determinative forces of heredity, since the latter only provide us with general tendencies and not with specific functions.

The Study of Suicide

Published in 1897, **Suicide** is one of the great classics in sociology. It is one of the first major works to use statistics to study social phenomena, and it is rich in theoretical insights. Why should Durkheim study suicide? Some have suggested that he may have been moved to do so after his close friend, Victor Hommay, took his life. But, there are less personal reasons: suicide was a growing social problem in the nineteenth century; there were a number of studies of suicide using non-social factors as explanatory variables that Durkheim may have wanted to challenge; the subject matter could be precisely defined and measured; and perhaps others. In any event, **Suicide** helped to establish the sociological enterprise, for Durkheim was able to take what seemed to be the most individual and private of acts and account or it sociologically.

Durkheim began his study with a definition of suicide. Suicide refers to "all cases of death resulting directly or indirectly from a positive or negative act of the victim himself, which he knows will produce this result." (**Suicide**, p. 44) Note that Durkheim defines suicide without any reference to the intentions of the individual; these could not be observed objectively. But is not suicide an act that is committed by an individual and that affects only him alone? Should it not be studied by psychology rather than sociology? Durkheim's reply is that, while each individual may commit suicide in isolation from other individuals, the combined suicides in a given population constitute a collective phenomenon. The suicide rate in any particular group is remarkably stable, and when changes occur, they occur in a given direction. Further, suicide rates vary quite consistently by groups. Thus, Durkheim was convinced that the suicide rate does not simply summarize the number of the individual suicides, but rather expresses the collective state of the whole. It is "itself a new fact *sui generis*, with its own unity, individuality and consequently its own nature—a nature, furthermore, dominantly social." (**Suicide**, p. 46)

To further persuade his readers, Durkheim considered a number of non-social explanations of suicide. Using the method of concomitant variation, he showed that these factors could not explain the suicide rate of given populations, because the suicide rates did not vary concomitantly with the factor considered. In this manner, he disposed of a number of existing theories of suicide, theories that attribute cause to psychopathic states of the individual (insanity, alcoholism, etc.), "psychological" states (race, heredity), "cosmic" factors (climate, seasons, geography), and the process of imitation. What's left? Social causes, of course. Durkheim presented a series of statistics to show that suicide varies with the nature and social organization of the group. For example, Protestants have a higher suicide rate than Catholics or Jews; single adults have a higher suicide rate than married adults; citizens in aging and decaying societies have a higher rate than those in younger societies.

But what is it about the social organization of groups that gives rise to suicide? Durkheim isolated two factors: the degree of integration of the group and the degree of social regulation. Extremes along either of these dimensions of group life may lead to suicide. Logically, there are four different possible causes and, hence, four different types of suicide. Durkheim provides detailed analysis of only those that are known to occur frequently, viz., egoistic, altruistic, and anomic suicide. The fourth type, fatalistic suicide, is mentioned in a footnote.

The Three Major Types of Suicide

In egoistic suicide, "the individual ego asserts itself to excess in the face of the social ego and at its expense." To the extent that man lives in a "state of nature" is the extent to which he is less in need of society and consequently less subject to its influence. This is the case with older men, children, and women, who in varying degrees feel a "lesser need for self-completion through something not themselves (i.e., society)." Because their needs are more closely related to the needs of the "unsocialized" individual organism, they are subject to the natural constraints of the latter and consequently are more immune to the suicidogenic elements in society. However, once man has drunk of the "social wine," he becomes dependent upon it for his very existence and is therefore subject to its influence. It becomes part of his *raison d'etre*, and from this point on it is impossible for the person to live a purely individual egotistical existence. Society superimposes itself on the individual, man becomes "socially intoxicated," but the pre-social element in his nature is not erased; it remains to assert itself in the face of its newly acquired antagonistic rival. It is at this point that the self-assertion of the individual ego over the social ego acquires suicidogenic potential.

In altruistic suicide the individual ego is completely engulfed in the social ground that sustains it and is unable to give expression to that part of his human nature that is purely individual. "The individual . . . has no way to set up an environment of his own in the shelter of which he may develop his own nature and form a physiognomy that is his exclusively." His problem is not that he sets himself adrift from society through the self-assertion of his individual nature, but rather that "he is *only* an inseparable part of the whole." "While the egoist is unhappy because he sees nothing real in the world but the individual, the intemperate altruist's sadness, on the contrary, springs from the individual's seeming wholly unreal to him. One is detached from life because, seeing no goal to which he may attach himself, he feels himself useless and purposeless; the other because he has a goal but one outside this life, which henceforth seems merely an obstacle to him." (**Suicide**, p. 225) Excessive social integration, thus, produces effects similar to those of excessive individualism. Both in Durkheim's view, are consequences of phenomena transcending natural limits.

Anomic suicide results when "society's influence is lacking in the basically individual passions, thus leaving them without a check-rein." In Durkheim's view a disjunction between means and needs leads to an intolerable condition for all living creatures. In the animal kingdom a spontaneous equilibrium exists between the needs of the organism and the environment. But man, being a social creature, envisions ends beyond his physical nature and consequently has a "natural" desire to transcend his immediate condition. If this were not so, there would be no progress, and man would not be civilized. Thus, man's ever-increasing desire to transcend himself is born with society. The insatiable appetite of the individual ego, while linked with an organic substratum, is not a product of the biology of the individual. It comes into being with the advent of civilization. In Durkheim's view, it is not the "pre-social" organism that needs to be tamed by social restraints; on the contrary, it is society that unleashes "our capacity for feeling," which in itself is "an insatiable and bottomless abyss." Once stimulated, our desires become unlimited: "the more one has, the more one wants, since satisfactions received only stimulate instead of filling needs."

In the absence of restraints, insatiable desires are suicidogenic: "Inextinguishable thirst is constantly renewed torture."

But such restraints cannot be found in the individual *per se*. "Nothing appears in man's organic nor in his psychological constitution which sets a limit to such tendencies." Only a regulatory force that is exterior to individual consciousness and superior to his being can set limits to man's insatiable human passions, and that is the function of society. But social restraints cannot be totally arbitrary; to function properly they must take into account the "legitimate" needs and natural talents of the individual. And they cannot be absolute; they set only relative limits which "make men contented with their lot while stimulating them moderately." Normally a precarious equilibrium exists between the forces that impel the individual to pursue potentially insatiable desires and the restraining forces of society. However, during periods of social change, whether of economic crises or industrial advancement, this delicate balance is upset, thus releasing the forces that lead to anomic life conditions. Suicide is largely a consequence of social causes and conditions, as Durkheim points out, but we should not fail to notice Durkheim's use of his dualistic conception of man when explaining the three types of suicide. Egoistic suicide is characterized by excessive individualism, altruistic suicide by "excessive groupism," and anomic suicide is characterized by an imbalance between the insatiable desires of the individual and social constraints.

Social Pathology of Modern Society

Normally man's insatiable desires are kept in check by the regulative forces of society. Society fixes the limits to which each class may legitimately aspire, and individuals are able to set realistic goals for themselves. However, when society is disturbed, either by some crisis or by rapid change, it becomes incapable of exercising a regulating influence; the normative order breaks down, and man is thrust into an intolerable condition Durkheim called anomie.

This, in Durkheim's view was the general state of Western European society at the turn of the century. It was occasioned in large measure by the rapid industrial growth of the preceding one hundred years. During this period, industrial relations were freed of all regulation. The binding force of religion lost its influence in economic matters. Occupational organizations, such as the guilds, were no longer effective sources of regulation, and government was unable to coordinate the rapid proliferation of occupational roles. The net result was a society that lacked effective regulation, one in which industrial unrest was prevalent.

But this state of affairs is not a normal consequence of the division of labour, as some had maintained. It was clearly an abnormal form, for the normal function of the division of labour is to bring about social solidarity. It was Durkheim's view that during this period of rapid change, society had momentarily lost its ability to regulate economic functions.

However, Durkheim was confident that, in time, new organs of society, in particular, occupational corporations, would emerge spontaneously to reconstitute the equilibrium that was temporarily upset.

Social Institutions and Contracts

The view of society as a set of contractual relations established by naturally free, prior existing, autonomous individuals is a product of modern Natural Law theory. This is the view of society that flourished in the Enlightenment period. In the 19th century, it is adopted by such thinkers as John Stuart Mill and Herbert Spencer, and it is in opposition to this view of society that much of Durkheim's work can be seen. This is particularly the case in **The Division of Labour**. In Chapter Seven, Durkheim addresses the matter of contracts directly.

In Spencer's view, society is maintained through a vast system of particular contracts, which individuals enter freely in order to pursue their self-interests. The division of labour is the result. Social regulation is at a minimum, and social solidarity is simply the outcome of relations of exchange. The typical social relation would be a purely economic one, such as found in the market-place.

Durkheim has several criticisms of this view. First, social solidarity cannot be explained by self-interest. Interests can relate men only for short periods of time. Underlying self-interest is latent conflict, which would break out in the absence of durable social bonds. Contracts based on self-interest could not possibly bind society. Contractual relations are themselves made possible by social institutions which underlie them. Thus, both contract law and non-contract law increase with the division of labour. Rather than diminish with the advancement of the division of labour, social regulation increases. Society and its institutions are prior to contractual relations and are the very foundation of them.

6

Georg Simmel

Unlike most of the sociological thinkers who made important contributions to the development of the discipline, Georg Simmel did not found a school or intellectual tradition which considered itself to be his heir. To be sure there are those who have been profoundly moved by Simmel's works and others who have marvelled at his insights into the relations and interactions of everyday life. But there are few who have declared themselves disciples of Simmel. In part this has to do with the fact that Simmel's best work was his highly concrete and penetrating studies of specific human interactions. Although he tried to provide sociologists with a formalized methodology, what proved to have been of lasting import was the content of his own sociological investigations. Instead of giving sociology a rigorous method, he gave the discipline a series of unique masterpieces which can be marvelled at or copied with varying degrees of proficiency.

Georg Simmel was an outsider. Both of his parents were born into the Jewish faith but his mother was converted to Lutheranism, his father to Catholicism. Cut off from his Jewish roots, a malicious anti-semitism was to plague his academic career until close to the very end of his life. (Simmel was baptized in the Lutheran Church, but he left the Church during World War I). Simmel was born on March 1, 1858 in the heart of Berlin. He was the youngest child in a family of five girls and two boys. Simmel's father died in 1874 and he was taken under the paternal wing of Julius Friedländer who encouraged his interest in music (Simmel studied piano and violin) and who left him a comfortable inheritance which enabled Simmel to pursue an academic career even in the face of some considerable adversity.

Simmel attended the Humboldt University in Berlin where he studied history, ethno-psychology (*Völkerpsychologie*) and philosophy. His doctoral dis-

sertation in philosophy bore the title: "Psycho-ethnographic Studies Concerning the Beginnings of Music." In order to become a professor in Germany at that time a candidate had to prepare a second dissertation or *Habilitationsschrift* which would be presented to the faculty. Simmel had prepared a study of Kant's theory of matter for his *Habilitation*. But Simmel did not receive an official position at the university until 1900; he had been teaching as a *Privatdozent* (a private teacher who receives tuition directly from his students and is given a lecture room by the university) since 1885. Even though Simmel was an extremely popular lecturer (his lecture room was often filled to capacity) he was passed over when it came time to make regular faculty appointments. He wasn't much liked by Dilthey, and Roethes' anti-semitism and jealousy of Simmel's popularity with students (combined with his scholarly mistrust of sociology) were in part responsible for Simmel's slow career progress. In 1900 Simmel was at last appointed extraordinary professor, a regular position which did not allow him, however, to train doctoral students.

In 1908 a position as full professor in the Faculty of Philosophy at the University of Heidelberg became vacant and Simmel applied for the job. Max Weber supported his candidacy. But there were still powerful enemies who tried to put obstacles in his path. For example, one of Simmel's opponents wrote the following in a letter to the Minister responsible for university appointments:

"Whether Prof. Simmel is baptized or not, I neither know nor wished to inquire. But he is an Israelite through and through, in his external appearance, in his mannerisms and his mental set . . . I can in no way believe that one edifies Heidelberg when the world-views and life perspectives represented by Simmel, which sufficiently enough diverge from our German-Christian-Classical training, are guaranteed an even broader area than they already have among the faculty."

Simmel did not get the position. Not until 1914 did Simmel receive the call to become a full professor. He died at the University in Strasbourg 4 years later of liver cancer.

Formal Sociology: Simmel's Kantian Legacy

Like Durkheim and Weber, Simmel attempted to carve out a niche for sociology as an independent science, as a science with its own particular subject matter. The fundamental sociological question which Simmel posed for himself is related to the question which Kant saw to be fundamental for his own epistemology. If Kant had asked the question "how is knowledge possible?" and answered it by demonstrating how the *a priori* creative and organizing categories of the mind act together in the unity of consciousness to produce knowledge, Simmel asked the question "how is society possible?" and answered it by showing that the forms of sociation can be identified as that which form the basis of all human interaction. But unlike Kant who was interested in the *ideal* foundation of epistemology (theory of knowledge), Simmel was interested in the *real* foundation of society. The similarity between Kant and Simmel lies in the fact that both men were looking for the foundation of their respective concerns— knowledge and society.

Sociology for Simmel is not the study of social facts (Durkheim) or the study of social action (Weber), but the study of the forms of sociation. "(I)f society is conceived as interaction among individuals," wrote Simmel, "the description of the forms of this interaction is the task of the science of society in its strictest and most essential sense." (pp. 21–22) By *forms of sociation* Simmel probably meant something akin to the more common concept of *social structure* in contemporary sociology. (But Simmel was clear in his view that the forms were constituted by the interactions among human beings. In this literal sense we can say that Simmel was an interactionist). These forms of sociation are the substantial elements of interactions, the content of the interaction is accidental. The forms are invariant, the content is variable. For example, conflict is a form of sociation which can be studied by sociologists. (Simmel was extremely interested in conflict and wrote about it in a penetrating way). However, if we are interested in conflict as

a form of sociation—or, as we might say today, a basic pattern of social interaction—then it is irrelevant to us whether the conflict is found on the football field, in a family, on the battlefield or in an election campaign. We can study conflict as conflict by ignoring or bracketing the specific content i.e., the purposes, interests, ends, of individuals and groups involved in the conflict situation. Simmel describes the character of "pure" or "formal" sociology in the following terms:

> The study of this second area may be called "pure sociology," which abstracts the mere element of sociation. It isolates it inductively and psychologically from the heterogeneity of its contents and purposes, which, in themselves, are not societal. It thus proceeds like grammar, which isolates the pure forms of language from their contents through which these forms, nevertheless, come to life. In a comparable manner, social groups which are the most diverse imaginable in purpose and general significance, may nevertheless show identical forms of behavior toward one another on the part of their individual members. We find superiority and subordination, competition, division of labor, formation of parties, representation, inner solidarity coupled with exclusiveness toward the outside, and innumerable similar features in the state, in a religious community, in a band of conspirators, in an economic association, in an art school, in the family. However diverse the interests are that give rise to these sociations, the forms in which the interests are realized may yet be identical. And on the other hand, an identical substantive interest may take on a form in very different sociations. (p. 22)

Simmel openly grants that the forms do not have a reality in themselves. (Simmel was no Platonist). We do not speak "grammar," but our spoken and written language has a grammatical structure which we can abstract and study. Grammar is only realized in speech or writing and even bad grammar can be judged only insofar as it is manifested in linguistic communication. The forms of sociation constitute the grammar social life. We interact with one another not in general but in specific, regular and finite patterns. Form and content are never found in isolation from one another, but by a process of mental abstraction we can separate them from one another analytically. We find that one and the same form may be present in a variety of different groups with different purposes and interests (contents). Similarly we may find that the same purpose or interest may give rise to different forms of sociation. (For example, sexual interest is satisfied through a variety of different family forms).

Pure or formal sociology does not study society, it studies the regular patterns of social interaction. This is the peculiar province of sociology which it shares with no other science. But in addition to formal sociology, Simmel proposed two other sociological endeavours: *general* and *philosophical* sociology. General sociology concerns, in his own words "the whole of historical life insofar as it is formed societally." It is not entirely clear exactly what Simmel meant by this general sociology which has as its subject matter social history, but clearly Simmel was concerned with the development of societal forms in the course of history. In any event, he apparently did not consider general sociology to be a science in the same sense as formal sociology.

There is an even greater confusion surrounding the concept of philosophical sociology. In part this concerns the philosophical implications of sociology. But Simmel also views it as the epistemological foundation of the social sciences. At times Simmel appears to go so far as to suggest that philosophical sociology is a fundamental ontology for history and the social sciences. For our purposes, we can ignore the problems arising from the ambiguities surrounding general and philosophical sociology and concentrate solely on pure or formal sociology, which is what Simmel meant by scientific sociology in the strict sense.

Society and Sociology

Simmel rejected two extreme notions in social science. The first was that the individual was the only true reality, that everything properly studied by science should be reduced to the individual units which constitute it. For example, we may talk about "the Roman Army," but this is nothing but an abstraction whose reality can be entirely fathomed by studying the individuals which constitute it. According to the second notion to which Simmel was opposed, everything is part of society. Thus, sociology becomes the super-discipline under which all other disciplines are subsumed.

In relation to the first position, Simmel argued that the individual is no less and no more "real" than society. One can indeed study individuals as individuals, but one can also study society as society. For Simmel it is all a matter of what standpoint one chooses.

One can, for example, study a painting from a distance of 2 feet or a distance of 10 feet. The kinds of things that emerge at these two distances are not the same. One is no better than the other. Each will reveal something different about the masterpiece under observation. Furthermore, the individual human being is also an "abstraction," following this line of reasoning, since the individual is a composite of organs, tissues, experiences, etc. What Simmel is trying to show is that in our social science there is no ultimate starting point or substratum. Different starting points will yield us different kinds of knowledge.

Simmel rejects the second position because it expands sociology into something so encompassing that it becomes in fact meaningless. By trying to transform everything into a sub-species of sociology, we trivialize sociology. Society is not, for Simmel, a super-organism. Simmel thus parts company with many of the evolutionists and social organicists of his day. Society is neither a substance nor an organism but a web of interactions. Thus, according to Simmel, to be strict in our use of terms, we should talk not about society, but about sociation. Even though stable institutions which we tend to see in structural terms (the family, the church and so on) appear to have an objective permanence about them, regardless of what we human beings may do, they "are nothing but immediate interactions that occur among men constantly, every minute, but that have become crystallized as permanent fields, as autonomous phenomena."

Simmel's own view is derived from his understanding of the character of sociology as a specific science. There is no science of the totality of phenomena; every science selects its subject matter according to its interest. By examining the fundamental relations among these abstracted phenomena, science is able to discover the essential elements, patterns or structure of these relations. "Sociology asks what happens to men and by what rules they behave, not insofar as they unfold their understandable individual existences in their totalities, but insofar as they form groups and are determined by their group existence because of interaction. It treats the history of marriage without analyzing particular couples; the principle underlying the organization of offices, without describing a 'typical day' at a particular office; the laws and consequences of the class struggle, without dealing with the development of a particular strike or of particular wage negotiations."(p. 10) Thus, sociology as a science is not concerned with specific contents, but with the forms of sociation. Sociology, according to Simmel, is not interested in what happens in society, but rather what happens *through* society, i.e. *through* social interaction.

Like Durkheim, Simmel felt compelled to defend sociology from encroachments by psychology. But unlike Durkheim, who developed an organismic and substantialist theory of society which he saw as the exclusive province of the science of sociology, Simmel did not see some social substance or organism as the datum of sociology, but viewed social interactions (forms of sociation) themselves as the area of its concern. Now Simmel believed that all sociation depends upon psychological states fear, love, jealousy, anger, etc. However, when two or more people interact with one another, the interaction cannot be explained on the basis of the psychological states of the individuals concerned. Sociology concentrates upon the interaction as an objective datum, leaving out the psychological states without which the interaction would never have occurred. Although Simmel shared Durkheim's goal of providing a foundation and program of study for sociology which would be independent of the science of psychology, Simmel's approach, it has been argued, did not go far enough in providing a distinctively social basis for the new science.

Simmel in Action

Although Simmel's emphasis upon form may give the impression that his sociological analyses are lifeless abstractions purged of any content, the reader will be pleasantly surprised to discover that in fact Simmel's treatments of the most mundane of human actions are stimulating and penetrating. To read Simmel is to have the "aha" experience, viz., he provides us with new and deeper insights into the relations of everyday life.

Let us consider his treatment of sociability which he sees as the play-form (autonomous form) of sociation. Sociability is an interesting form of sociation for it is not only a pure sociological category, an abstraction, but a real interaction which we all enter into in the course of our daily lives. Each of us has the experience of being sociable with others for no other reason than indulging our desire for being sociable. We may call it small talk or chit chat, or we may even try to fool ourselves and others into thinking that we are talking about matters of substance when in fact we are really just talking with others to talk with others and for no other reason. What distinguishes sociability from other forms of sociation is the fact that when we are sociable we have no other purpose or interest or ulterior motive in interacting with others. Sociability is the pure form of interaction; it is stripped of every content (interest, purpose, goal). "It exists for its own sake and for the sake of the fascination which, in its own liberation from these ties, it diffuses."(p. 43)

People are part of groups because they can achieve some purpose thereby. They can satisfy their need of food, shelter, clothing, and so on; they can form a church and worship; they can raise money for medical research, etc. But people are also part of groups because they take pleasure in interacting with others. Whenever this need or want of human interaction is the motive of interaction we have a case of sociability. For this reason Simmel calls sociability "the play form of sociation." Since sociability has no purpose outside of itself, its existence is entirely dependent upon the individuals engaging in this form of interaction. Thus, the character and quality of the interaction will be dependent upon the specific personalities of the individuals engaged in this pursuit. But, paradoxically, the personalities of the individual concerned cannot become overemphasized, for then the playfulness of this form of sociation is destroyed. What regulates the conduct of the individual in sociability is *tact*: "where no external or immediate egoistic interests direct the self-regulation of the individual in his personal relations with others, it is tact that fulfills this regulatory function. Perhaps its most essential task is to draw the limits, which result from the claims of others, of the individual's impulses, ego-stresses, and intellectual and material desires." (p. 45)

By now you should have gotten the impression that sociability is a form of sociation which is in some sense unreal. In other words, it is a process in which the serious, goal-directed, purposeful side of social life is suspended temporarily. For this reason sociability is an unstable form of sociation. We have all experienced a situation in which a sociable interaction is brought to an abrupt end: for example, when small talk at a party becomes too personal, when light conversation turns to business, when someone in the course of a conversation says something tactless. Simmel thus writes about 'sociability thresholds.' The upper threshold is the objective, the lower the subjective: "These thresholds are passed both when individuals interact from motives of objective content and purpose and when their entirely personal and subjective aspects make themselves felt. In both cases, sociability ceases to be the central and formative principle of their sociation and becomes, at best, a formalistic, superficially mediating connection." (p. 47)

According to Simmel, sociability is an artificial world since the objective contents, purposes and materials of 'real' life are by definition excluded. All games are instances of sociability. But there is a problem here, for in the games that we play we often try to simulate real-life situations: we compete for scarce resources, we try to beat others at the game, we try to take from others what they possess, etc. But there is an important difference between these contents of 'real life' and those found in games, for Simmel: "In the game, they lead their own lives; they are propelled exclusively by their own attraction. For even where the game involves a monetary stake, it is not the money (after all, it could be acquired in many ways other than gambling) that is the specific characteristic of the game. To the person who really enjoys it, its attraction rather lies in the dynamics and hazards of the sociologically significant forms of activity themselves. The more profound, double sense of 'social game' is that not only the game is played in a society (as its external medium) but that, with its help, people actually 'play' 'society'."(p. 50)

The Importance of Numbers

One of Simmel's most memorable contributions to sociological theory is his work on the significance of numbers for social life. Simmel believed that, aside from any other factors, the number of people involved in interactions shapes, limits, constrains, promotes and otherwise conditions the form of these interactions both positively and negatively. There are certain qualities which a small group possesses which are lost when the group expands beyond a certain limit. A large group requires certain features to maintain itself which a smaller group does not require. For example, Simmel believed that socialism can only succeed in groups of limited size. Since socialism ("justice in the distribution of production and reward") depends upon an accurate assessment of individual achievement and reward, such a system becomes practically impossible to institute in a large group or society where the differentiation of individuals in the general division of labour makes just such an assessment next to impossible.

What is true of socialism is equally true for certain religious sects. Mennonite and Hutterite groups on account of their religious doctrine and practice cannot become very large. In a way they are destined to remain dependent upon larger societies in which they live. Similarly, the growth of the early Christian communities caused both a change in the sociological and religious character of early Christianity.

Another kind of group which begins to disintegrate as it becomes very large is the aristocracy. In part this is due to the political nature of the aristocracy, i.e. it is a relatively small estate which dominates a much larger mass. In addition to this, however, the aristocracy is limited by personal, kin and marriage ties which "must be ramified and traceable throughout the whole group."

Just as certain kinds of groups disintegrate or begin to change their character when they reach a certain size, so too are there constraints imposed upon the workings of large groups. For example, Simmel believed that large groups can only be moved by simple ideas. (Simmel was probably influenced in his view by the writings of the French social psychologist Gustave Le Bon). The very size of the group reduces the group response to events to the lowest common denominator. When under the influence of an extremist movement the masses can easily fall prey to an emotional radicalism which overwhelms the individual. In fact, the group calls forth an unconditional allegiance on the part of the individual so that he must subordinate his own beliefs and judgments to those of the group.

In addition to subjecting the influence of large and small numbers upon groups and societies, Simmel also focussed his attention on the 'lower limit of the numerical series,' beginning with the isolated individual and then considering the dyadic and triadic relationships.

The two key elements relevant to the singular individual are *isolation* and *freedom*. But isolation for Simmel is not the mere 'absence of society': "On the contrary, the idea involves the somehow imagined, but then rejected, existence of society. Isolation attains it unequivocal, positive significance only as society's effect at a distance—whether as lingering-on of past relations, as anticipation of future contacts, as nostalgia, or as an intentional turning away from society. The isolated man does not suggest a being that has been the only inhabitant of the globe from the beginning. For his condition, too, is determined by sociation, even though negatively."(p. 119)

In one sense freedom is a lack of ties to other individuals. But freedom can also be something positive for sociated individuals. In the first place, the individual in society has demands placed upon him from every tie. He is claimed by his family, his political party, his social club, his professional association, his church, his employer, etc. Each of these claims asserts itself as though it had a monopoly upon the time and attention of the individual. It is incumbent upon the individual to choose among these competing claims and in this choice lies his sociological freedom, according to Simmel. Second, in a social context freedom of the individual implies the extension of his will or power over other individuals. Whenever we talk about freedom of individuals sociated with other individuals we are referring to the struggle to dominate others.

We can see here and in Simmel's further treatment of the dyadic and triadic relationship that something which appears at first sight to be so simple and easily understood as a singular individual, a group of two or group of three is in fact a complex

An Assessment

Although Simmel gave us a formalistic methodology, he is best remembered for his concrete analysis of everyday experiences and relationships. In addition to the matters discussed above, Simmel wrote about the tragedy of modern culture in which human beings find themselves in a world of things which is also a world devoid of meaning. He also analysed the social significance of money and examined the social changes that accompany the increasing use of money as a means of exchange: (i) increase in freedom of social relationships (ii) larger and more impersonal business enterprises (iii) establishment of voluntary associations (iv) the alteration of the style of personal life (depersonalization, specialization, fragmentation of personal relationships).

In his later years Simmel seemed to lose interest in sociological concerns preferring to think of himself as a cultural philosopher. And yet Simmel gave the discipline certain masterpieces of insightful studies which maintain their freshness and relevance to the present.

(NOTE: All citations above from Simmel are taken from **The Sociology of Georg Simmel**, translated, edited and with an introduction by Kurt H. Wolff, The Free Press, New York, 1967.)

7

Vilfredo Pareto

Vilfredo Pareto's contribution to the development of sociology is the subject of dispute within the discipline. Clearly, his influence upon certain American sociological theorists such as Talcott Parsons and George Homans has been profound. Yet, the writings of Pareto have been limited in their impact. The great interest which was shown in his writings during the 1930's (especially at Harvard University) had no parallel at other non-ivy league institutions at that time, and interest began to wane even in pro-Pareto centres shortly thereafter. It is interesting to note that the same conditions which favoured an increasing concern with the theories of Karl Marx should also support the development of partisans of Pareto's thought. (Interestingly, however, the revival of interest in Marx and Marxism which occurred during the late sixties and early seventies was not accompanied by a parallel growth in interest in Pareto. Perhaps this is due to the fact that the Marxism of the sixties was a response to conditions of relative privilege, while the Marxism of the thirties was a response to conditions of relative want.)

Unlike the works of Marx which display a developmental continuity practically from the outset, the writings of Pareto fall neatly into two categories: those written before 1898 reflect the views of an economic liberal and, politically, of an *homme de la gauche*. His later writings mirror the pessimism of a disillusioned reformer, of a self-conscious elitist and general misanthrope. Some have argued that his later views provided a foundation for fascist political and social theory. (Shortly before his death in 1923, Pareto was appointed to the Italian senate by Benito Mussolini who claimed to have been one of his disciples).

Pareto's father was a minor Genovese aristocrat who had fled Italy in the 1830's on account of his radical political views and for supporting the revolutionary Mazzini. He sought refuge in France where he met and married Marie Metenier who bore him three children. Vilfredo Frederico Domaso Pareto was born in Paris during the auspicious year of revolution—1848. At the age of 7, however, Pareto's father returned to his native Italy where his son received his professional training. Following in his father's footsteps, Pareto became a civil engineer, completing a thesis on "The Fundamental Principles of Equilibrium in Solid Bodies" in the year 1870. The notion of equilibrium was to play a major role in his sociological theorizing. Indeed, Pareto's sociological positivism was derived from the principles of the logico-experimental method common to the physical sciences and engineering.

Pareto's academic career did not begin until he was well over forty years of age. After completing his engineering degree he became the director of the Rome Railway Company. Then he managed an iron ore company in Florence. He did not, however, abstain from politics during this period. An economic liberal, Pareto consistently defended free trade doctrine and radical democratic principles in public. When the right-wing government was defeated in 1876 by the moderate left, Pareto turned against the latter which adopted protectionism as government policy. The general corruption of the government added fuel to Pareto's criticism of it. In fact, he ran as a candidate in Florence in 1882 but lost his bid at a political career. His anger and frustration grew after his electoral defeat, although he still maintained an allegiance to liberal and democratic ideals.

Through the intervention of his friend, the economist Maffeo Pantaleoni, Pareto was chosen by the famous mathematical economist Leon Walras as successor to his chair of political economy at the University of Lausanne in 1893. Pareto established his own reputation as an economic thinker of some stature with the publication of his **Cours** d'économie politique in 1896–97. The seething frustration that Pareto felt at his political helplessness in Italy came to a boil in the year 1898. It was then that he made a complete break with the ideals of his youth. He turned his back upon liberalism, humanitarianism and democracy arguing that they were founded upon non-rational sentiments and feelings which impeded a scientific grasp of social and political reality. Interestingly, however, he maintained his commitment to the free trade doctrine and much of his criticism of socialism was based upon his critique of state intervention in the economy. (In this respect he remained faithful to the teachings of Herbert Spencer whose writings he had previously studied.) Although somewhat of an oversimplification, it may be said that Pareto maintained a commitment to the assumptions of liberal economic theory while at the same time turning against liberal-democratic political theory. (The argument of contemporary "liberal" theorists that socialist economic practices will necessarily lead to the erosion political liberty would cut no ice with Pareto).

Of his later writings two of the most important of his books, especially for the development of sociological theory, were **Les Systèmes Socialistes** (1902) and **Trattato di sociologia generale** (1916). In the former work, socialist doctrine was subjected to critical examination and Marxism was especially singled out for attack. According to Pareto, socialism, and particularly the Marxian variant, was a non-scientific doctrine which arose from certain non-logical sentiments but which was paraded about as though it were founded upon scientific principles. For Pareto, Marxism was nothing more than a religion whose adherents were not conscious of its religious character. To be fair, it must be said that Pareto had a great deal of respect for Marx's hard-nosed critique of political economy. It was with the utopian and millennarian aspects of Marxism, with its—in Pareto's view—mythologically founded revolutionism and messianic vision of the future that he quarreled.

The **Trattato di sociologia generale** forms the core of Pareto's contribution to sociological theory. Expanding on some of the themes found in the **Systèmes Socialistes**, Pareto constructed a theory of society based upon the pervasiveness of non-logical actions in human intercourse. Almost all of Pareto's ideas which made an impact upon later sociological thinkers are to be found in his terribly uneven *magnum opus*.

Pareto began to withdraw from society in 1898 after having inherited a small fortune. He moved to a house in Celigny where he acquired an enormous wine cellar which became famous for the quality of its contents. Living an increasingly reclusive existence with his companion Jane Regis and his legions of Angora cats, Pareto became more and more extreme in his vituperative attacks on socialism, humanitarianism, pacifism, and political democracy. He retired from regular teaching at the university in 1907.

Pareto's Concept of Sociology

Pareto was a positivist who believed in the unity of the scientific method. If sociology were to be a science then it should not differ methodologically from the physical sciences. Concepts such as "system" and "equilibrium" used to describe the physico-chemical phenomena in the physical sciences had the same force in sociology. Indeed, Pareto attempted to develop a sociological science which would examine human society as a system in equilibrium or tending to equilibrium. This is regarded by some to be his most important contribution to the development of sociological theory, because it allowed for the retention of the organic analogy without its crude and untenable assumptions. Society is a system of interdependent parts, but the system is in a state of equilibrium which means that (i) there is a tendency to retain a given structure of societal form or (ii) there is a tendency to retain a given rate and direction of social change, which is "built into" the social system. The state of a social system at any time is the result of: (i) extra-social, extra-human factors (physical environment), (ii) external social factors (other concurrently existing societies or earlier states of the same society) and (iii) inner elements of the social system (interests, knowledge, residues, derivations, etc.). When the equilibrium of a society is disturbed, forces come into play which tend to re-establish the previously existing state of the system. Thus, regardless of the nature of social disruption (revolution, reaction to crime, wars, etc.), things are eventually restored to their original form.

Although Pareto rejected the romanticist and organicist view that society was a reality independent of and beyond the sum of its parts, nonetheless, he rejected the opposite view according to which the isolated individual was the only and ultimate reality in society. In opposition to this passive and static understanding of individuals and society, Pareto attempted to develop a dynamic theory. Just as in a physico-chemical system the actions of one element have an effect upon the other elements of the system, so too do the actions of one (or more) individual(s) have a bearing upon the relations of the other individuals in the society. To be sure, Pareto does not go as far as Cooley and especially Mead who study the developmental changes within the individual—the process of internalization—as a result of social interaction, but he does recognize the importance of interaction in the external constraints imposed upon individuals and in the changes in behaviour and ideas which can be observed by the scientist.

Nonlogical Action: The Theory of Residues and Derivations

As an economist Pareto was concerned primarily with actions which can be described as logical. Actions are logical when the actor adopts specific means which have a very high degree of probability of bringing about some desired end. This kind of behaviour can be studied by examining the choices open to the individual in terms of a game theoretical matrix. However, Pareto realized that a very large proportion of human behaviour is not logical. Now Pareto does not mean by this that such behaviour is illogical, although, to be sure, some of it may be. Action is nonlogical for Pareto whenever the actor's subjective perception and explanation of his action differs from the perception and explanation of the same action by some scientific observer who has an objective and exact understanding of the action as a means to attaining some end. (This will be discussed in some detail below). What is of sociological interest for Pareto are the nonlogical actions which he believed were pervasive in human society. In order to develop a generalized system of human interaction Pareto felt that he had to encompass in his theory both the logical actions studied by economics and the nonlogical actions which occur outside of the economic sphere.

Let us consider the character of nonlogical actions more closely. In general, nonlogical actions for Pareto are those which are not based upon the scientific application of discrete means to specific, concrete ends. But there are various kinds of nonlogical actions. Some actions are nonlogical because their ends are unrealizable, illusory or otherwise unreal. (This is obvious from the point of view of the scientific observer who has objective knowledge about the ends of the actions in question). On the other hand, there are those actions which, for whatever reason, cannot realize or attain ends which are objectively realizable by some other means known to the scientific observer. There are yet other types of nonlogical

actions. There are those actions in which both ends and means are nonlogical from the objective, scientific point of view. Finally, there are those actions in which both means and ends are logical, but the actor engages in such action for other reasons, reasons which are nonlogical in character. In other words, the subjective intention of the actor in relation to the action is different from the objective appreciation of the same action by the scientific observer.

Put more simply, Pareto argued that most human beings very often do things for reasons of which they are themselves unaware. We very often do things for very mundane and not infrequently "base" reasons. But at the same time we seem to have a need to tell ourselves and others that our reasons for doing this or that are noble, honourable, or at least rational. Pareto's interest is precisely in these rationalizations of ours that we fabricate in order to convince ourselves that we really know why we do what we do and that the reason why we do what we do is based upon some rational principle or general theory such as justice, equality, God's law, etc. For example, Pareto raises the case of man who, like most men, has a horror of the act of murder and for this reason he refrains from committing murder. Yet he does not say to himself that he refrains from murdering because he has some deep-seated horror of it. Rather he says that murderers are punished by the gods. This gives a cosmic significance to his act of abstaining from committing murder.

There are two elements to this rationalization—in this case that murderers are punished by the gods. The first element is the manifestation of a sentiment or sentiments. The sentiment is one of horror at the thought of murder. Corresponding to this sentiment is the thought "murder is evil," "to kill is bad," or simply "don't kill." The second element is the rationalization itself—the gods punish murderers. Now Pareto believed that the first element which he called a *residue* was fairly constant and substantial in human society. The second element which he called a *derivation* was variable. Indeed, human beings in almost all societies have a horror of murder and yet the theories they make up by means of which they explain their action (refraining from committing murder) vary greatly from one society to another, from time to time and place to place.

It is important to note here that both residues and derivations are concerned not with behaviour directly, but with theories or beliefs about the determinants of behaviour. Furthermore, the residues, or constant elements need not, although they may, be expressed directly in the rationalization. In fact, in the majority of cases the proposition which gives expression to the residue is only implicit in the theory or rationalization. It is to be teased out by the scientific investigator. The constant elements in these theories are called residues because they are what remains after the variable elements are reduced to their essential expressions. On the other hand, derivations have been so labelled by Pareto due to the fact that they are particular rationalizations which are derived from one and the same residue. Pareto illustrates this clearly in the following observation taken from **Mind and Society**, para. 1416, p. 897 (**Mind and Society** is the title of the English translation of the **Trattato di sociologia generale**):

> A Chinese, a Moslem, a Calvinist, a Catholic, a Kantian, a Hegelian, a Materialist, all refrain from stealing; but each gives a different explanation for his conduct. In other words, it is a case of a number of derivations connecting one residue that is operative in all of them with one conclusion which they all accept. And if someone chances to invent a new derivation or refute one of the existing ones, his achievement has no practical consequences and the conclusion remains the same.

After having examined a great variety of rationalizing theories in a great number of societies (Pareto was extremely knowledgeable about the history of classical antiquity) he was able to distill 6 classes of residues which correspond to fundamental human sentiments.

The first class of residue is that of the instinct for combinations. This instinct is manifested in "experimental" or "innovative" behaviour. Things which have hitherto remained apart are brought together to produce something new. Those human societies in which the class I residue is prominent tend to be progressive, dynamic and somewhat unstable societies, according to Pareto. (Incidentally what is true for societies is also true for individuals. Some individuals more than others evince behaviour which is expressive of class I residues).

The second class of residues is called "group persistence" or "persistence of aggregates." This corresponds to the conservative sentiments. We see evidence of this class of residues in the traditional beliefs, customs and practices of society. Furthermore, Pareto believed that the behavioural manifestations of this residue are largely to be found among the masses. Unlike many anarchist and socialist thinkers Pareto believed that the masses were funda-

mentally a *conservative* force in history. Ascending elites could manipulate the masses in their drive for social dominance, but the masses themselves were doomed to serve as the tools of these rising elites. (Pareto also believed that manifestations of this residue are also found among certain kinds of elites—see below. Yet, this residue is always predominant among the masses according to him).

Class III residues represent the "need of expressing sentiments by external acts." Class IV residues are those "connected with sociality." Class V residues are those which express the "integrity of the individual and his appurtenances." Finally, class VI represents "the sex residue."

These six classes of residues are the substantial building blocks of all human society. All of the myriad beliefs, practices, customs, religions, philosophies, in short all the derivations which we can enumerate in human history can be reduced to one or more of these six classes of residues. Pareto, like Marx in this respect, had a theory of base and superstructure, or substance and form. Historical changes are primarily changes of form or of superstructure, but they are not fundamental or substantial. The course of history for Pareto is precisely what it was for Giambatista Vico the 18th century philosopher of history, that is, *corsi e ricorsi*, an eternal return. This view of course is in line with Pareto's concern with systemic equilibrium.

The Circulation of Elites

In his later years, Pareto was openly elitist and antidemocratic in his politics and in his sociological "science." He believed that in every human grouping some would rise to the top, that some would be more proficient at whatever it was they did than others. For example, if we consider all people who play chess as a class or category of persons, then some will be better chess players than others. Theoretically we could devise a hierarchy of all chessplayers according to their chessplaying ability. The same could be done for any activity in which a number of people engage. The moral character of the activity is completely irrelevant here. Some pickpockets are better than others and some humanitarians are better at being humanitarians than others. Those who are the best in the class of chessplayers, pickpockets, humanitarians, etc. are said to be the elite.

Pareto drew a distinction between two kinds of elite: there is the *governing elite* which consists of all those directly or indirectly involved in the use and manipulation of power and the *non-governing elite* which includes all other elite members. Pareto himself was a staunch supporter of meritocracy in an open system of competition and mobility. However, he recognized that some people had an advantage over others in the race for the attainment of elite status. Those born into families with great wealth, social prestige or political connections obviously have a greater opportunity of achieving elite status than those who are born poor and without social standing. Pareto favoured a system in which everyone has a more or less equal chance of attaining elite status because that would ensure that talent, enterprise and effort would become the predominant means of entry into the elite and not family connections and wealth. An elite which inherits its status is lazy and complacent; an elite which wins its elite status is vigorous and hearty. In the former case society is weakened, in the latter case it is strengthened.

Now within the elite groupings Pareto drew a distinction between two categories or types of elite personalities: foxes and lions. The "foxes" (Pareto took both terms from Machiavelli's most famous work **il principe** or **The Prince**) are those whose behaviour predominantly manifests class I residues. These individuals love to put new combinations together, to create alliances, to scheme, to intrigue, to take risks, to innovate. On the other hand, the "lions" are those who demonstrate in their behaviour a preponderance of class II residues. These are the traditionalists, the conservatives, the defenders of the status quo. They use muscle more often than cunning in achieving their ends.

Within the governing elite there is an invariable historical pattern which manifests itself. A governing elite of "foxes" is inexorably replaced by an ascendant elite of "lions." When the lions have consolidated their power, the foxes begin to chip away and eventually their craft and cunning win them power. Foxes and lions replace one another in the governing elite in the same way as day follows night and night follows day. Political change for Pareto can never be anything other than a change of elites. The masses play a role only insofar as they are manipulated and used by one or the other elite group to bolster or achieve their own political dominance. Pareto despised humanitarianism and democracy because they deny the reality of elitism and they spread a false doctrine of equality. Furthermore, Pareto believed that a political elite which embraces humanitarianism and democratic principles is shirking its responsibilities to itself and the country and will inevitably be replaced by an elite made of sterner stuff.

Although Pareto didn't concern himself with the non-governing elite to anywhere near the same extent as he did with the governing elite, nevertheless he did show that a similar kind of elite typology exists within the non-governing variety. In the economy, for example, he identified those elite individuals who demonstrated a preponderance of class I residues in their behaviour and distinguished them from those other elite individuals who evinced a behaviour which is compatible with class II residues. The former he called *speculators* since they were the risk takers, the wheeler-dealers, the pathbreakers and innovators in business, the entrepreneurs. The latter he labelled *rentiers* since, like the aristocrats of old, they were traditionalists and conservative, individuals who invested conservatively in trusted endeavours, industries and stocks. In the economic realm the speculators and rentiers were the respective counterparts of the foxes and lions in the governing elite.

Truth versus Usefulness

The theory of residues and derivations developed by Pareto calls into question the truth value of a large number of statements which we make in the course of our lives. The normative statements we make (i.e., statements about how we should act ethically, politically, religiously, etc.) cannot be verified empirically. Hence, according to Pareto, these statements are neither true nor untrue. They are simply unverifiable. But this objective aspect of such propositions, i.e., their truth value is of no great interest to the sociologist. Rather the sociologist should be concerned with the reasons why certain people come to hold these non-verifiable beliefs. In order to answer this question Pareto suggests that we look for the use-value or utility which such beliefs have for the individuals concerned.

Now the utility of a doctrine has nothing to do with its truth value (i.e., with its experimental or logical validity), according to Pareto. As Pareto says: ". . . a doctrine may be ridiculed on its experimental side and at the same time respected from the standpoint of its social utility. And *vice versa*." (para.73, p. 38).

Accordingly, Pareto enumerates four classes of propositions in which the relationship between truth value and utility differ. The first class of propositions are those which correspond to experience (hence empirically verifiable) but which are held to be true not because of their empirically verifiable character but rather on account of certain sentiments which may be harmful or beneficial to individuals and society. The second class of propositions include those which correspond to experience but which are rejected because they violate certain sentiments. If such propositions were accepted then society would suffer. The third class of propositions consists of those which are not experientially true but which are held nonetheless due to the fact that they accord with certain sentiments. These sentiments are beneficial to individuals and society (and, as Pareto suggests, "often exceedingly so"). The fourth and final class of propositions which Pareto isolates includes all those which are not experientially verified but which are held because of their agreement with certain sentiments. However, in this case, these sentiments benefit some, but are a liability to other individuals. Furthermore, at times they benefit society and at other times they are detrimental to society.

Pareto, not unlike Marx, believed that the ruling ideas of any epoch are the ideas of the ruling class, or elite in Pareto's terminology. (The real difference between Marx and Pareto in this respect concerns the fact that Marx believed that an end to the circulation of elites—or ruling classes—was at hand, in the proletarian revolution, whereas Pareto believed that the circulation of elites would continue as long as organized social life exists on earth). Ascending elites may advance certain propositions in order to secure their own power. By means of these doctrines they can galvanize the masses to act on their behalf. Even though these doctrinal beliefs cannot be realized, nevertheless they may goad individuals into action which takes them to a point closer to the utopian goal. Without these unrealizable ideals set before them these individuals would not have attained these more modest victories.

In connection with his concept of utility Pareto introduced a distinction between an aggregate of individuals and society as a whole. In a pure economic analysis one can, according to Pareto consider the aggregate satisfaction of individuals (Pareto refers to this kind of utility as "ophelimity"). Here we are concerned with the welfare of individuals and not with the welfare of society as a whole. When we consider the wants of individuals and their satisfaction we cannot assume that the wants are the same. Hence, we cannot in this way treat the community as a unity or whole. We have seen for example in the above four propositions that certain beliefs benefit some members of society while acting against the interests of other members of society. Hence, Pareto argued that in addition to the classical economic concern with the welfare of individuals in the aggregate, sociologists should be concerned with the welfare of the system and sub-elements of the social system directly. Indeed, the maximum welfare of aggregated individuals may not be the same as the maximum utility of society as a whole. Both Parsons and Coser, two leading American sociologists, point out that in this respect the thinking of Pareto converges with that of Emile Durkheim who objected to the one-sidedness of the utilitarian emphasis upon the individual as a unit of analysis.

8

Sigmund Freud

Sigmund Freud 1856–1939

Sigmund Freud was a Viennese physician who was the founder of psychoanalysis: a method of treating neurotic disorders based upon a theory of mind and·psycho-sexual development elaborated by Freud and his circle of co-workers and students. Working with a senior colleague, Dr. Joseph Breuer, in treating several female patients suffering from hysteria[1] (from the Greek word στεροv—"uterus," since it was thought that hysteria was a disease confined exclusively to women), Freud discovered the existence of the unconscious, or rather, of unconscious mental processes which reside within every human being.[2] Freud and Breuer discovered that the distressing symptoms would moderate or even disappear when patients were asked to concentrate on them and freely associate to them under hypnosis. Freud hypothesized that the symptoms represented a compromise between the conscious and unconscious parts of the mind. The content of the unconscious must be highly objectionable to the individual's conscious mind and yet be highly charged with some kind of psycho-biological energy. The unconscious, Freud postulated, contains wishes, impulses, thoughts, beliefs, etc. which have their origin in the instinctual, biological constitution of the individual and the species.[3] Freud believed that these wishes, impulses, etc. were the result of two fundamental instincts—love and aggression (death).[4] The free expression of these instinctual demands would make any kind of social life impossible. Society might come to resemble Hobbes' state of nature in which the life of the individual was "solitary, poor, nasty, brutish and short." The human neonate is a "primitive" organism driven by instinct, instinct which must be tamed, controlled, channelled and sublimated over the course of childhood and adolescence. And yet this process of psychological and sociological development can never entirely extinguish the phylogenetic traces of instinct or the ontogenetic scars of individual psycho-sexual growth. In order to understand the unconscious and the force of repression we should first consider Freud's stages of psycho-sexual development.

1 Rycroft defines hysteria as: "Medical diagnostic term for (a) illnesses characterized by the presence of physical symptoms, (b) the absence of physical signs, or any evidence of physical pathology, and (c) behaviour suggesting that the symptoms fulfil some psychological function." Charles Rycroft, **A Critical Dictionary of Psychoanlysis**, Harmondsworth: Penguin, 1972, p. 64. Freud's patients presented one or more of the following symptoms: blurred vision, impairment or loss of speech, paralysis, loss of appetite, anxiety, convulsions, and hallucinations.

2 Although the unconscious is one of the fundamental concepts of psychoanalysis, there is much confusion concerning its meaning. See the discussion in the following: S. Freud, **The Unconscious**, Collected Works, Vol. XIV, pp. 161–215; id. **The Ego and the Id**, Collected Works, Vol. XIX, pp. 3–18.

3 Freud, following established scientific usage, referred to individual development as *ontogeny* and the development of the species as *phylogeny*.

4 The theory of the instincts underwent considerable revision over the years. In his earlier works, Freud posited the self-preservative instinct (e.g., hunger) and the sexual instinct (i.e., love). These two instincts were really connected by the force of Eros or libido, sexual energy, the difference between them being related only to direction: self-preservation demanding the inward direction of love (self as object or narcissistic libido) and the sexual instinct sending its energy toward objects in the environment (object libido). Fundamentally this was a monistic theory of instinct. But in his speculative pamphlet **Beyond the Pleasure Principle** (1919) Freud argued the plausibility of a dualistic instinct theory. Accordingly, all living matter is subject to the influence of two opposing forces: the one bringing organisms together for the perpetuation and extension of life, the other seeking to return living matter to the inorganic state out of which it emerged. For a long while, Freud had resisted the appeal of this dualistic theory partly because the death instinct was so often hidden from view as it was inextricably interwoven with expressions of Eros. Freud, however, offered the examples of the sado-masochistic perversions and of the self-reproaches in melancholia and paranoia where the death instinct manifested itself most clearly.

Freud believed that instinctual erotic energy or libido becomes centred on erotogenic zones, areas or organs of the body which attract sexual energy to them which is then discharged. This discharge of energy produces feelings of pleasure.[5] Prominent erotogenic zones include: the skin, the mouth, the anus, the urethra and the genitals, but in theory any area or organ may become an erotogenic zone. Accordingly, Freud argued that infants and young children were not the asexual creatures of the Victorian understanding but rather "primitive" beings pulsating with sexual energy, receiving sexual pleasure from stimulation of the erotogenic zones. To say the least, Freud's views on childhood sexuality appeared scandalous in late nineteenth century European society and they met with great resistance both from within and without the medical establishment. When Freud's notions gradually gained respectability, they paved the way for a new and more realistic understanding of the psychic life of children.

The first stage of psycho-sexual development—the oral stage—takes its name from the organ which becomes the first source of sexual pleasure—viz., the mouth. The mouth is the organ of connection to the breast, the source of nourishment and comfort. For Freud, in addition to being the conduit of nourishment for the infant the mouth is also the organ whose stimulation is the source of sexual pleasure. In the normal course of development the child gradually renounces the pleasure associated with the sucking action at the breast, although the prevalence of thumb sucking in older children shows how unwilling many are to make the sacrifice. Furthermore, the mouth also is an instrument of aggressive impulses. It seeks to bite the breast, to incorporate it, to make it part of its own body. The biting of the nipple by older infants is a behavioural manifestation of this aggression. A small amount of interest may be retained in the mouth as an organ of sexual interest in normal development as evidenced by the pleasure which adults take in kissing and in other employments of the labia during foreplay.

When a reluctance to renounce the pleasure associated with labial stimulation dominates the course of development, a fixation on the mouth and on oral pleasure may be the result. Because this oral

attachment meets with stern rebuke from society, this fixation is repressed, i.e., forcibly kept from the conscious mind.[6] With the onset of puberty a fresh infusion of instinctual energy may provide a new urgency to the unconscious fixation which makes new and insistent demands on the individual. A struggle would then ensue between the instinctual desire and the forces of repression resulting in a neurotic symptom such as anxiety or leading to sexual perversion.

The second stage of psycho-sexual development is called the anal stage. Here the mucous membrane of the anus and excretory tract become sources of sexual excitation and pleasure. This stage corresponds chronologically with the period of toilet training which involves issues of mastery and control. A struggle often develops between the child and the parents over when and where the child will perform the excretory function. In this struggle of wills, the child may give vent to considerable amounts of aggression. When the child does perform the function as the parents desire, he proudly presents the successful result to the parents as a precious gift, i.e., as a part of the child's own body which has become detached from it. The child may also identify the column of faeces in the rectum with the penis and come to understand that, like the faeces, the penis too may become detached from the body. In the following citation we can appreciate the complicated connections which result as part of the dynamics of the anal stage:

> Children who are making use of the susceptibility to erotogenic stimulation of the anal zone betray themselves by holding back their stool till its accumulation brings about violent muscular contractions and, as it passes through the anus, is able to produce powerful stimulation of the mucous membrane. In so doing it must no doubt cause not only painful but also highly pleasurable sensations. One of the clearest signs of subsequent eccentricity or nervousness is to be seen when a baby obstinately refuses to empty his bowels when he is put on the pot—that is, when his nurse wants him to—and holds back that function till he himself chooses to exercise it. He is naturally not concerned with dirtying the bed, he is only anxious not to miss the subsidiary pleasure attached to defecating. Educators are once more in the right when they describe children who keep the process back as 'naughty'.

---

5 Freud recognised that pleasure was not entirely the result of a discharge of instinctual energy, for the build up to sexual climax is experienced as pleasurable and it involves an increase of undischarged energy. See the discussion in: S. Freud, **Three Essays on the Theory of Sexuality, Collected Works**, Vol. VII, pp. 208–212.

---

6 Repression is not the result of social disapprobation alone. There is a biological component in instinctual repression as well, according to Freud.

The contents of the bowels, which act as a stimulating mass upon a sexually sensitive portion of mucous membrane, behave like forerunners of another organ, which is destined to come into action after the phase of childhood. But they have other important meanings for the infant. They are clearly treated as a part of the infant's own body and represent his first 'gift': by producing them he can express his active compliance with his environment and, by withholding them, his disobedience. From being a 'gift' they later come to acquire the meaning of 'baby'—for babies, according to one of the sexual theories of children are acquired by eating and are born through the bowels.

The retention of the faecal mass, which is thus carried out intentionally by the child to begin with, in order to serve, as it were, as a masturbatory stimulus upon the anal zone or to be employed in his relation to the people looking after him, is also one of the roots of the constipation which is so common among neuropaths. Further, the whole significance of the anal zone is reflected in the fact that few neurotics are to be found without their special scatological practices, ceremonies, and so on, which they carefully keep secret.[7]

When the child has achieved mastery over the excretory function (which in some cases is not achieved until late in childhood) and has renounced the pleasure associated with it (or it has become an unconscious fixation) a new erotogenic zone becomes the focus of libidinal cathexis[8] or occupation. To this point the anatomical differences between the sexes play no significant role in individual psycho-sexual development. This holds for the next stage as well. Both male and female children discover that touching or rubbing the genitals is pleasurable. But no notice is taken of the difference between the phallus and the clitoris as male and female appear to be endowed with a phallic appendage. However, the discovery of the anatomical distinctions between the sexes has a different psychological impact upon male and female children. When the male child recognizes that females do not have a penis, he develops anxiety over

the possible loss of his own appendage. After all, the faeces are detachable from the body and now he is faced with an entire class of people whom, he believes, once had a penis (in the phallic stage) but from whom it has been severed. Little girls on the other hand when they discover that "theirs" doesn't measure up to what males possess suffer a blow to their narcissism and develop an envy for the male appendage.[9] The overcoming of the phallic stage leads directly to the final struggle so crucial to the development of mature adult sexuality: the Oedipus Complex. Freud took the name from the play **Oedipus Rex** by Sophocles. The play concerns the life of a tragic figure whose fate, foretold by the oracle, was to kill his father and bed his mother. Horrified by this prophesy his father exiled his son to a far-off country where the boy grew up without knowledge of his true parentage. But as fate would have it Oedipus returns and unknowingly slays his father and beds his mother. His punishment is the loss of his eyes. For Freud, Sophocles was telling the story of the great human drama, the most significant struggle in the lives of all children.

But the Oedipus Complex is different for males and females. The little boy begins to covet his mother as his exclusive love object and accordingly develops an aggressive rivalry with his father. The little boy is caught between desire for the mother and fear of his father which exacerbates the castration anxiety already of concern to him during the preceding phallic stage. At the same time, the male child also loves his father as his protector and as an ego ideal with whom he can identify. The son's relation to his father is thus emotionally ambivalent.

The female Oedipus complex, sometimes referred to as the Electra Complex, must take a different route if the little girl is to develop a normal adult heterosexual orientation. What draws the little boy closer to the heterosexual choice of object, i.e., his love for his mother, must force the little girl to renounce the mother as an object choice. (Freud freely admitted that his attempts to explain the development of female sexuality were tentative and he remained somewhat unsatisfied with his theories of female sexuality.) Like the little boy, the little girl takes her mother as the first sex object. The little girl, however, in discovering that her mother is not complete, i.e., lacks a penis,

---

7 **Three Essays on the Theory of Sexuality**, London, Hogarth Press, 1953, pp. 186–87.

8 The term "cathexis" is an English translation of the German term *Besetzung* from the word *besetzt* which means "occupied," "taken," or "loaded." In this case, and in the cases of many other of Freud's technical terms, the German uses ordinary language whereas the English translation resorts to foreign-based neologisms.

---

9 In fact there are a number of possible responses to the recognition of this anatomical difference between the sexes. A large number of neurotics unconsciously believe that females possess a penis. There may be a trace of this in popular culture more generally.

turns to her father and in so doing identifies with the mother who has given birth to the father's child. The little girl thus expresses her envy for the father's penis in the wish to have a child, especially a male child, by the father. (Freud remarked that there is no love on earth as deep as the love of a mother for her child, especially her male child.)

For Freud the great problem for the development of character and sexuality for little girls is envy, for little boys anxiety. Each sex has its own cross to bear but in Freud's view the crosses are different.

Following upon the Oedipal drama, a latency period ensues in which the sexual development of the first five or six years of childhood is forced into the unconscious to be reactivated again by a fresh burst of sexual energy at the onset of puberty. All the pregenital stages of development must now become subservient to the primacy of genital sexuality in the service of heterosexual genital coupling. Should one or more elements of pre-genital sexuality (such as anal sex, oral sex, sado-masochism etc.) replace the heterosexual genital coupling then we have what Freud referred to as perversion. The perversion consists not in the pleasure which is obtained from one or more of these pre-genital erotogenic zones—indeed they may be part of a normal sexual repertoire which leads to heterosexual genital climax. Rather, the perversion consists in the replacement of genital intercourse as the final aim of sexual satisfaction with one of the pre-genital configurations.[10]

We are now in a position to understand the unconscious and why instinctual repression is a *conditio sine qua non* both of mature psycho-sexual development and of civilization. The repression of unconscious wishes connected with pre-genital sexual pleasure and the Oedipus complex is necessary for the establishment of the primacy of the genitals. Furthermore, the development of civilization can only occur on the basis of the repression of instinct. The price to be paid for civilization is discussed at length in Freud's **Civilization and Its Discontents**. (see below).

Yet something important is missing in the foregoing, namely, the relationship between the elements of the personality and the instincts, the unconscious and the force of repression. According to Freud, the most primitive element of personality is the psychical representative of the instincts. It is the part of the individual psyche where the psychological meets the biological. Freud called it the 'id'—*das Es* in German, literally the 'it'—a term which he borrowed from the philosopher Friedrich Nietzsche via the physician George Groddeck. The id is largely unconscious and is ruled by the pleasure principle. In other words the id is driven by the demands of instinct which it seeks at all costs to satisfy. The id does not take 'no' for an answer but relentlessly pushes for satisfaction of instinct. The id relates to the world in a thoroughly narcissistic manner as though it were omnipotent. This blind subservience to the pleasure principle puts the individual at odds with reality and thus poses a great danger to his continued existence. In order to preserve itself the organism must develop a faculty which can listen to the demands of a reality whose power is greater than its own. Freud draws an analogy here between the membrane of a cell and its contents whereby the former is extruded to protect the latter from the threats to it from the environment. The counterpart of this membrane in the personality Freud calls the ego (in German *das Ich* or the 'I'). The ego comes under the sway of the reality principle as it seeks to guide the individual to act in conformity with the demands of the environment. The ego thus represents the faculty of reason within the individual. In terms of the relationship between ego and id Freud uses the metaphor of a spirited horse and its rider:

> The ego's relation to the id might be compared with that of a rider to his horse. The horse supplies the locomotive energy, while the rider has the privilege of deciding on the goal and of guiding the powerful animal's movement. But only too often there arises between the ego and the id the not precisely ideal situation of the rider being obliged to guide the horse along the path by which itself wants to go.[11]

But there is yet a third element of the personality which is often considered as the highest of the three and is seen to distinguish human beings from other animals. This agency is the source of human conscience, of morality, attention to duty and of the ideals which we come to hold both in relation to ourselves and to society as a whole. Freud saw this psychical agency standing over the ego, watching it, judging it, berating it for its shortcomings. This agency he called the 'super-ego' (*das Über-Ich*—literally the 'over-I').

---

10 Perversion is the opposite of neurosis for Freud. In neurosis the symptom represents a compromise between an unconscious impulse and the force of repression whereas in perversion the instinctual impulse is acted out compulsively.

11 **The New Introductory Lectures**, Collected Works, Vol. XXII, page 77.

Young children are creatures of instinct and do not know the pangs of conscience. They do not know what is dirty or shameful and they are reprimanded by their parents or other agents of civilization when they, for example, play with faeces or expose themselves in public. But with the successful renunciation of the pleasure associated with the stimulation of the erotogenic zones repression makes the activities associated with these zones into something shameful, disgusting or dirty. The function of the parents in condemning the young child for doing these things is now taken over by the individual himself. The super-ego may rightly be seen as the agent of society within the individual. It provides the ego with an ideal against which it can measure itself and at the same time punishes the ego for falling short of this ideal.

But the matter is not clear cut and the super-ego can create great problems for the individual and society as a whole. The super-ego receives its energy from the id and is connected to the id in an intimate fashion. Because of this the super-ego holds the ego responsible not only for the ego's action, but for the (unconscious) wishes in the id. The ego becomes the scapegoat for the id in face of the super-ego's inability to distinguish between the actions of the ego and the unconscious, repressed wishes in the id. The fate of the ego is a hard one as Freud points out:

> We are warned by a proverb against serving two masters at the same time. The poor ego has things even worse: it serves three severe masters and does what it can to bring their claims and demands into harmony with one another. These claims are often divergent and often seem incompatible. No wonder that the ego so often fails in its task. Its three tyrannical masters are the external world, the super-ego and the id. When we follow the ego's efforts to satisfy them simultaneously—or rather, to obey them simultaneously—we cannot feel any great regret at having personified this ego and having set it up as a separate organism. It feels hemmed in on three sides, threatened by three kinds of danger, to which, if it is hard pressed, it reacts by generating anxiety.[12]

Strong evidence for the working of the super-ego was presented to Freud in paranoid delusions where the ego feels that it is constantly being watched, and in melancholia (depressions) where the ego feels worthless and empty as a result of the (undue) harshness of the super-ego. We shall soon see that accord-

ing to Freud one of the greatest problems facing modern civilization concerns the growing power of the super-ego as a result of the growth in repression.

Having reviewed the bases of Freud's instinct and personality theories, we can now begin to look at his more sociological writings.

Totem and Taboo

Freud believed that in the course of growth the individual recapitulates the developmental history of the species; ontogeny recapitulates phylogeny. In 1912 Freud published a major work in which he applied the insights of psychoanalysis to explain the origins of two widespread phenomena of anthropological interest. Totemism is a system of religion and kinship found in many societies studied by anthropologists. The two key features of totemism are a prohibition against the killing and eating of the totem animal by clan members and one against the marrying or the having of sexual relations with a member of the same clan. Taboo is a Polynesian word meaning both 'sacred' and 'dangerous' or 'unclean'. It refers to the power of persons or things which is the source of ritual restrictions in relation to them. Taboo serves to protect important persons (such as chiefs and priests) from harm and the weak from the might of the powerful; it is a defence against dangers associated with coming into contact with the dead; it prevents interruptions of life processes such as birth, death, marriage; it seeks to safeguard human beings from the wrath of the gods and to protect young children from harm. Totemism and taboo are intimately linked by Freud since "(t)he most ancient and important taboo prohibitions are the two basic laws of totemism: not to kill the totem animal and to avoid sexual intercourse with members of the totem clan of the opposite sex."[13]

The key to understanding totemism and taboo in early human cultures lies in the *psychological ambivalence* anchored deeply within the primitive psyche. But Freud goes further than this and finds this same psychological ambivalence in obsessional neurotics, in children during the Oedipal stage of development and in everyone when they dream. The basis of the ambivalence lies in the existence of two opposed currents of feeling, one of tenderness and love, the other of hostility and aggression. The former, tender current is conscious, the latter, aggressive impulse unconscious. The identical mechanism in taboo and obsessional neurosis is illustrated by Freud in the following:

---

12 Ibid.

13 **Totem and Taboo**, Collected Works, Vol. XIII, pp. 31–32.

'A Maori chief would not blow a fire with his mouth; for his sacred breath would communicate its sanctity to the fire, which would pass it on to the pot on the fire, which would pass it on to the meat in the pot, which would pass it on to the man who ate the meat, which was in the pot, which stood in the fire, which was breathed on by the chief; so that the eater, infected by the chief's breath conveyed through these intermediaries, would surely die.'[14]

This woman's neurosis was aimed at her husband and culminated in her defence against an unconscious wish that he should die. Her manifest, systematic phobia, however, related to the mention of death in general, while her husband was entirely excluded from it and was never an object of her conscious solicitude. One day she heard her husband giving instructions that his razors, which had lost their edge, were to be taken to a particular shop to be re-set. Driven by a strange uneasiness, she herself set off for the shop. After reconnoitring the ground, she came back and insisted that her husband should get rid of the razors for good and all, since she had discovered that next door to the shop he had named there was an undertaker's establishment: owing to the plan he had made, she said, the razors had become inextricably involved with thoughts of death. This, then, was the *systematic* reason for her prohibition. . . . The *real* cause of her prohibition upon the razors was, of course, as it was easy to discover, her repugnance to attaching any pleasurable feeling to the idea that her husband might cut his throat with the newly ground razors.[15]

Freud gives several examples of animal phobias in young boys to illustrate this same psychological ambivalence. In a case reported to him by the Hungarian psychoanalyst Sandor Ferenzci, a young French lad developed a strange relationship to the chickens on the farm after one of them had pecked at his penis. The boy gave up human speech in favour of cackling and crowing for a while and later spoke and sang only of poultry. "His favourite game was playing slaughtering fowls. 'The slaughtering of poultry was a regular festival for him. He would dance round the animals' bodies for hours at a time in a state of intense excitement.' But afterwards he would kiss

and stroke the slaughtered animal or would clean and caress the toy fowls he had himself ill-treated."

Here we have a clear expression of the ambivalence of the Oedipus complex, for the fowl which pecked at his penis, the poultry that he slaughtered and later caressed, and the birds with whom he identified were substitutes for his father and all the emotional ambivalence which he directed at his father was transferred to the fowl in the barnyard. "From time to time he translated his wishes from the totemic language into that of everyday life. 'My father's the cock', he said on one occasion, and another time: 'Now I'm small, now I'm a chicken. When I get bigger I'll be a fowl. When I'm bigger still I'll be a cock.'" According to Ferenzci, the child had gratified his sexual curiosity about human family life by his observations of the sexual activity among the poultry in the yard. "He showed that he had formed his choice of sexual objects on the model of life in the hen-run, for he said one day to the neighbour's wife: 'I'll marry you and your sister and my three cousins and the cook; no, not the cook, I'll marry my mother instead.'"[16]

But Freud sought to demonstrate that the Oedipus conflict which played such a decisive role in the life of the individual has a phylogenetic basis which was decisive in constituting the psychological foundations of society. In order to do this Freud had to return to the question of the origins of totemism.

Following Darwin, Freud believed that the earliest humans roamed about in a *primal horde* which was under the absolute authority of a powerful male—the primal father, who had killed off all his rivals, jealously guarded his sexual monopoly over the women, and maintained the weaker males in a state of submissiveness. The weaker males hated the primal father who kept them from the females in the horde and they collectively rose up against him and killed him to get his 'power'. (In order to incorporate his power they ate his body and drank his blood). After committing the murder, however, they felt remorse at what they had done, for they had loved the old man as well. (He kept them warm in the winter and provided them with food.) In order to atone for their sin, they erected a shrine at the place of his murder and every year celebrated a festival where they symbolically re-enacted the murder and cannibalism. Furthermore, in order to ensure that these deeds would never happen again, they agreed to renounce their claims to the women in the horde and to seek their

---

14 Citation from **The Golden Bough** by James Frazer. Op cit. p. 28.
15 Op. cit. p. 96.

16 Op. cit. pp. 130–31.

'brides' from other groups. This *incest taboo* became the cornerstone of a stable society. At the same time, the *primal parricide* led to the development of religion, conscience, ethics and morality as well as our sense of guilt. The Oedipal wishes which each individual harbours have their origin in these early experiences of the human race. Freud based this view in part on the evolutionism of Lamarck according to whom acquired characteristics could be transmitted from one generation to the next. Thus the practice of totemism expressed the two great renunciations of instinct which made civilization possible.

Group Psychology and the Analysis of the Ego

In this work published in 1921 Freud turned his attention to the psychology of the human group. This represented in part a return to the sociological and anthropological material which he presented in **Totem and Taboo**. In this later work, however, Freud took up the views then current in social psychology, especially those expressed by Gustave LeBon, William McDougall and William Trotter, on the characteristics and foundations of groups.

Freud lists the following characteristics of groups in relation to the individuals who make them up:

1. Individuals in groups yield to instinctual forces on account of some invincible power due to numbers of the group
2. Individual acts and sentiments are contagious within groups
3. Individuals in a group are highly suggestible, there being something hypnotic about group interaction
4. Individuals in groups act in ways that are distinctly more primitive and more childish than they would in isolation and individuals in groups experience a lowering of their intellectual ability
5. Groups are largely driven by instinctual impulses and passion; they have a sense of omnipotence; they entirely lack in critical thinking and are open to influence; they may change instantly in mood from one extreme to the other; group feelings are simple and exaggerated; they want to be ruled aggressively by strong leaders; they are conservative and respect tradition; groups may also exhibit under suggestion higher moral positions than those exhibited by isolated individuals; groups maintain contradictory ideas without experiencing any conflict between them; groups can easily be swayed by words; they never thirst after the truth.[17]

McDougall agrees with LeBon's characterization of groups but he draws a distinction between organized and unorganized groups. The primitive character of groups outlined by LeBon can be mitigated by means of organization, continuity, structure, differentiation and complexity. For Freud, McDougall is simply urging upon the group the same conditions which pertained to the individual before he was subjected to group forces. Following Trotter, Freud argued that group formation is 'biologically a continuation of the multicellular character of all the higher organisms.'[18]

The common denominator found in all sociological descriptions of group dynamics is the concept of suggestion, or rather suggestibility. Freud proposed to consider the source of this high degree of suggestibility so characteristic of individuals in groups as a direct result of the group bond—Eros or love. The ties which link individuals to one another and to the group are libidinal ones[19] and lovers are highly susceptible to the suggestions of one another. There are in fact two sets of libidinal ties—one between the members of the group, the other between the members and their leader. Freud takes as his two examples of highly structured groups the Church and the army. In both we find erotic ties among the members and between the members and their leader. A good illustration of the centrality of these erotic bonds can be seen when panic sets in among the troops during a military campaign. Freud argues that the panic is often unrelated to an actual increase in danger—in fact the word panic itself connotes the idea that the fear is not real. Rather the "panic fear presupposes a relaxation in the libidinal structure of the group and reacts to that relaxation in a justifiable manner." With the loss or loosening of libidinal ties, the indi-

---

Works, Vol. XVIII, pp. 72–81.

18 Op. cit. p. 87.

19 Libido is an expression taken from the theory of the emotions. We call by that name the energy, regarded as a quantitative magnitude (though not at present actually measurable), of those instincts which have to do with all that may be comprised under the word 'love'. The nucleus of what we mean by love naturally consists (and this is what is commonly called love, and what the poets sing of) in sexual love with sexual union as its aim. But we do not separate from this—what in any case has a share in the name 'love'—on the one hand, self-love, and on the other, love for parents and children, friendship and love for humanity in general, and also devotion to concrete objects and to abstract ideas. Our justification lies in the fact that psychoanalytic research has taught us that all these tendencies are an expression of the same instinctual impulses; in relations between the sexes these impulses force their way towards sexual union, but in other circumstances they are diverted from this aim or are prevented from reaching it, though always preserving enough of their original nature to keep their identity recognizable (as in such features as the longing for proximity, and for self-sacrifice)." Op. cit. pp. 90–91.

---

17 **Group Psychology and the Analysis of the Ego**, Collected

vidual is left alone to face the danger.[20] Freud sees a clear parallel between this generation of fear within the group and the generation of neurotic anxiety within the individual:

> Fear in an individual is provoked either by the greatness of a danger or by the cessation of emotional ties (libidinal cathexes); the latter is the case of neurotic fear or anxiety. In just the same way panic arises either owing to the disappearance of the emotional ties which hold the group together; and the latter case is analogous to that of neurotic anxiety.[21]

Freud, like Durkheim and Comte, believed that group living presupposes altruism on the part of individuals. Yet we must explain how this altruism is able to overcome a primary egoism or what Freud calls narcissism or self-love. Furthermore, there is overwhelming evidence to show that this narcissism coupled with instinctual aggression leads to hostile feelings not only between strangers but also between those people who are bound by affectionate and/or sensual ties. Freud rejects the notion that group bonds can be based upon self-interest alone. As Durkheim had done before him, Freud pointed out that self-interest was too ephemeral, too labile and too limited to maintain the complex structure of the group over long periods of time. The only force which we know that has the power to overcome our narcissism and aggression is Eros. When we are in love our own needs are subordinated to the needs of the object of our love. The same thing happens in the formation and dynamics of groups:

> The same thing occurs in men's social relations as has become familiar to psychoanalytic research in the course of development of the individual libido. The libido attaches itself to the satisfaction of the great vital needs, and chooses as its first objects the people who have a share in that process. And in the development of mankind as a whole, just as in individuals, love alone acts as the civilizing factor in the sense that it brings a change from egoism to altruism. And this is true both of sexual

love for women, with all the obligations which it involves of not harming the things that are dear to women, and also of desexualized, sublimated homosexual love for other men, which springs from work in common.[22]

But there is a problem with this parallel between individual and group psychology, for the kind of object love with direct sexual aims existing between two individuals cannot exist among the members of the group. There is another expression of love, neither narcissistic nor object related, at work in binding the members of a group to one another, and Freud calls this identification.

Identification is one of the oldest forms of emotional bond existing between one person and another. It is present at the beginning of the Oedipus complex when the little boy develops an admiration for his father, accepts him as a model, wants to be like him and take his place. It is an ambivalent process which may assume an affectionate or a hostile colouring. The wish to do away with and replace the father is an expression of the hostile character of identification in the Oedipus complex. But an identification may also become a substitute for a tie to a libidinal object. This occurs in melancholia (depression) which results from the loss of a love object. The lost object is not relinquished but is introjected into the ego and is set up as one element of the ego which is now fractured in two. The one part of the ego reproaches the other for abandoning the individual and the self-reproaches of the ego (suffering) are its way of taking revenge on the lost object. The part of the ego which punishes the other part is the ego ideal or super-ego. As we shall momentarily see, the ego ideal plays an important part in the libidinal organization of groups for Freud.

Finally, identification can arise on the basis of some shared quality among people. In term of group psychology this shared quality is the common tie to the leader of the group. There is a phylogenetic basis to this tie to the leader since the common substance which united the first clan members in the totemic system was the flesh and blood of the murdered father consumed by the band of brothers. This united them in remorse and laid the foundation for civilization.

Since Freud believed that the basis of group psychology rested on the libidinal ties among the members of the group and between the members and their leader, it is not too far fetched to look to the psychol-

---

20 "The typical occasion of the outbreak of panic is very much as it is represented in Nestroy's parody of Hebbel's play about Judith and Holofernes. A soldier cries out: 'The general has lost his head!' and thereupon all the Assyrians take to flight. The loss of the leader in some sense or other, the birth of misgivings about him, brings on the outbreak of panic, though the danger remains the same; the mutual ties between the members of the group disappear, as a rule, at the same time as the tie with their leader." Op. cit. p. 97.

21 Ibid.

22 Op. cit. P. 103.

ogy of love for help in understanding the (erotic) social bond. One of the characteristics of being in love is the tendency to over-evaluate or idealize the love object. A similar case of overvaluation is found in the relation between the hypnotist and his subject. The former has come to occupy the place of the latter's ego ideal. The difference between being in love and hypnosis stems from the fact that the latter excludes the possibility of sexual satisfaction. Freud does not suggest that hypnosis is a good object of comparison with group formation because "it is truer to say that it is identical with it."[23] The only difference, in Freud's view between group formation and hypnosis is quantitative, i.e., the latter is a relation between but *two* people only.

Freud is now in a position to outline the mechanism of structured group formations:

> But after the preceding discussions we are quite in a position to give the formula for the libidinal constitution of groups, or at least of such groups as we have hitherto considered—namely, those that have a leader and have not been able by means of too much 'organization' to acquire secondarily the characteristics of an individual. *A primary group of this kind is a number of individuals who have put one and the same object in place of their ego ideal and have consequently identified themselves with one another in their ego.*[24]

Freud also deals with the matter of social or communal feeling, the sense of social justice and equality, the notion of the common good and the like. For Freud they arise as reaction-formations to feelings of jealousy and envy. This is most clearly manifested in the vicissitudes of sibling rivalry, the model for subsequent rivalries:

> The elder child would certainly like to put his successor jealously aside, to keep it away from the parents, and to rob it of all of its privileges; but in the face of the fact that this younger child (like all that come later) is loved by the parents as he himself is, and in consequence of the impossibility of his maintaining his hostile attitude without damaging himself, he is forced into identifying himself with the other children. So there grows up in the troop of children a communal or group feeling, which is then further developed at school. The first demand made by this reaction-formation is for justice, for equal treatment for all. We all know

how loudly and implacably this claim is put forward at school. If one cannot be the favourite oneself, at all events nobody else shall be the favourite. This transformation—the replacing of jealousy by a group feeling in the nursery and classroom—might be considered improbable, if the same process could not later on be observed again in other circumstances. We have only to think of the troop of women and girls, all of them in love in an enthusiastically sentimental way, who crowd around a singer or pianist after his performance. It would certainly be easy for each of them to be jealous of the rest; but in the face of their numbers and the consequent impossibility of their reaching the aim of their love, they renounce it, and, instead of pulling out one another's hair, they act as a united group, do homage to the hero of the occasion with their common actions, and would probably be glad to have a share of his flowing locks. Originally rivals, they have succeeded in identifying themselves with one another by means of a similar love for the same object. . . .

> What appears later on in society in the shape of *Gemeingeist*, *esprit de corps*, 'group spirit', etc., does not belie its derivation from what was originally envy. No one must want to put himself forward, every one must have the same. Social justice means that we deny ourselves many things so that others may have to do without them as well, or, what is the same thing, may not be able to ask for them. This demand for equality is the root of social conscience and the sense of duty.[25]

Yet, this sense of equality does not extend to the leader: "All the members must be equal to one another, but they all want to be ruled by one person. Many equals, who can identify themselves with one another, and a single person superior to them all—that is the situation that we find realized in groups which are capable of subsisting."[26]

The importance of the leader for the solidarity of the group should not be underestimated, according to Freud. The illusion that the leader loves each of the members to exactly the same degree is a contrivance of the group which, according to Freud "is simply an idealistic remodelling of the state of affairs in the primal horde, where all the sons knew that they were equally *persecuted* by the primal father, and *feared* him equally."[27]

---

23 Op. cit. p. 115.
24 Op. cit. p. 116

25 Op. cit. pp. 120–121
26 Ibid.
27 Op. cit. p. 125

The Future of an Illusion

Freud returned to broader sociological concerns in the last few years of the 1920's, publishing **The Future of an Illusion** in 1927 and **Civilization and Its Discontents** late in 1929. The former work was a short but systematic consideration of religion which built upon certain of Freud's idea's already developed in **Totem and Taboo** and **Group Psychology**. Some of the themes treated in **The Future of an Illusion** were dealt with at greater length in **Civilization and Its Discontents**.

Freud begins his treatment of religion by presenting a brief outline of the human condition. This piece of philosophical anthropology bears a distinct resemblance to the views of Marx in that it gives emphasis to the relations between the humankind and nature and to the problem of the relations among human beings in society. Freud's concern diverges from that of Marx, however, in that he assesses these two fundamental human relations in terms of their impact upon instinctual life. Freud suggests that there is a necessary conflict between the growth of civilization and the satisfaction of instinctual needs. In fact, Freud proposes an elite theory of culture and civilization, for he argues that the majority who renounce the satisfaction of instinct necessary for civilization must be dragged into the civilizing process by the enlightened few.

> It is just as impossible to do without control of the mass by a minority as it is to dispense with coercion in the work of civilization. For masses are lazy and unintelligent; they have no love for instinctual renunciation, and they are not to be convinced by the argument of its inevitability; and the individuals composing them support one another in giving free rein to their indiscipline. It is only through the influence of individuals who can set an example and whom masses recognize as their leaders that they can be induced to perform the work and undergo the renunciations on which the existence of civilization depends. ... To put it briefly, there are two widespread human characteristics which are responsible for the fact that the regulations of civilization can only be maintained by a certain degree of coercion—namely, that men are not spontaneously fond of work and that arguments are of no avail against their passions.[28]

Thus, these two fundamental relations of the human kind are sources of conflict and indeed of pain and suffering for individuals. Nature threatens to drown us, to make us ill, to burn us, to subject us to earthquakes, and eventually to kill us and all our loved ones. Civilization forces us to renounce instinctual pleasure and to suffer abuse, indignity, exploitation, etc. at the hands of our fellows. As a consequence "(m)an's self-regard, seriously menaced, calls for consolation; life and the universe must be robbed of their terrors; moreover his curiosity, moved, it is true, by the strongest practical interest, demands an answer."[29]

But this helplessness and terror are nothing new for adults for they have encountered this same condition in childhood. Then their parents provided a sense of security and well-being.

> For once before one has found oneself in a similar state of helplessness: as a small child in relation to one's parents. One had reason to fear them, and especially one's father; and yet one was sure of his protection against the dangers one knew. Thus it was natural to assimilate the two situations. Here, too, wishing played its part, as it does in dream-life ... (A) man makes the forces of nature not simply into persons with whom he can associate as his equals—that would not do justice to the overpowering impression which those forces make on him—but he gives them the character of a father. He turns them into gods, following in this, as I have tried to show, not only an infantile prototype but a phylogenetic one.[30]

Religion then is powered by a wish based on an infantile and phylogenetic model. Accordingly, religion is an illusion, i.e., a belief which arises on the basis of a wish whose probability of being true is small. Freud deals with each of the major arguments advanced on behalf of religion. The first argument rests on the belief in the wisdom of our ancestors. But our ancestors were wrong about many things and what guarantee do we have that they were right about religion? The second argument concerns the proofs which religion has offered from ancient times.

---

28 **The Future of an Illusion**, Collected Works, Vol. XXI, pp. 7–8. Freud considers the possibility that the hostility of the masses to civilization is itself the result of cultural rather than instinc-tual determinants. In other words, it might be possible to restructure society viz. to reorganize the relations among human beings in such a way as to produce masses sympathetic to the aims and demands of civilization. Freud strongly doubts whether this is possible at all and he certainly rejects the possibility of this happening under the current stage of technological development.

29 Op. cit. P. 16

30 Op. cit. P. 17

But these so-called proofs are no more reliable than our ancestors in this matter. Taken together they represent a mass of self-contradictory arguments which in the end fall back on belief in divine revelation. Finally, it is argued by proponents of religion that it is forbidden to raise the question of religion's authenticity at all. For Freud this argument only exposes the weakness of the religious position.

Having dealt with these three main arguments he considers two fall back positions adopted by the defenders of religion. The first is an argument raised by the early Church Fathers: *credo quia absurdum*, I believe because it is absurd. But Freud asks the obvious question—are we obliged to believe every absurdity and if we are to be selective what criteria do we use to distinguish among the absurd positions we are to consider adopting? The second argument was refined by a contemporary of Freud, Franz Vaihinger, a neo-Kantian thinker who wrote an influential book entitled **Die Philosophie des Als-Ob (The Philosophy of As-If)**. Even though we know there is no God we persist in our religious beliefs and practices *as if* there were a God on account of the benefits to the individual and society which accrue as a result. To this Freud counters that the 'as-if' argument is really a variant of the *credo quia absurdum* view. Second, he argues that it is a viewpoint which could only be held by intellectuals and has little relevance to the religious sensitivities of the common man for whom religious truths are self-evident verities and not finely developed philosophical principles.

Having dealt with the 'rational' arguments advanced by the forces of religion, Freud then considers the social utility of religious belief. Here he deals with the claim that without religion people would not act as morally as they do, that they would be less happy than they are, that the masses would revolt against the rule of law. Freud has grave reservations about these claims on behalf of religion. He grants that religion in the form of the super-ego has played a part in the taming of the instincts. But it has not done enough to justify itself:

> It has ruled human society for many thousands of years and has had time to show what it can achieve. If it had succeeded in making the majority of mankind happy, in comforting them, in reconciling them to life and in making them into vehicles of civilization, no one would dream of attempting to alter the existing conditions. But what do we see instead? We see that an appallingly large number of people are dissatisfied with civilization and unhappy in it, and feel it as a

yoke which must be shaken off; and that these people either do everything in their power to change that civilization, or else go so far in their hostility to it that they will have nothing to do with civilization or with a restriction of instinct ... It is doubtful whether men were in general happier when religious doctrines held unrestricted sway; more moral they were not.[31]

As for fear that the masses would run riot and tear society apart on learning of God's non-existence, Freud advances the thought that the masses will eventually discover this secret for themselves in any event. Thus, it would be preferable to introduce the masses in general to scientific ways of thinking to help them to a secular morality which respects the achievements of civilization and its laws.

Religion can be looked upon as bearing a certain historical truth and even as a necessary stage in human development. When, for example, God issued the commandment "Thou shalt not kill" a great historical truth was revealed. For it was the murder of the primal father, the reaction of the band of brothers to their deed that led them to respect of the will of God, God who was cast in the image of their slain father. But this stage of disguised historical truth will surely be superseded, according to Freud, just as the individual overcomes infantile neurosis in the course of his maturation.

Religion would thus be the universal obsessional neurosis of humanity; like the obsessional neurosis of children, it arose out of the Oedipus complex, out of the relation to the father. If this view is right, it is supposed that a turning-away from religion is bound to occur with the fatal inevitability of a process of growth, and that we find ourselves at this very juncture in the middle of that phase of development.[32]

Historically, religion protected individuals from suffering neurotic disorders. From this point of view Freud considered religion to be the "universal neurosis" of the humankind. Yet Freud believed that we were about to reach a stage in our development where we could relinquish our universal neurosis by means of scientific enlightenment even as psychoanalysis could clear up our personal infantile attachments. The God of Science, Λογο, is not as powerful as the God of religion. But science is founded on observation and measurement and thoroughly grounded in reality. Science is prepared to abandon any theory or truth which does not meet the test of

---

31 Op. cit. P. 37
32 Op. cit. P. 43

reality. In Freuds words: No, our science is no illusion. But an illusion it would be to suppose that what science cannot give us we can get elsewhere.[33]

Civilization and Its Discontents

In this work Freud further develops some of the ideas which he advanced in **Totem and Taboo, Beyond the Pleasure Principle, Group Psychology and the Analysis of the Ego,** and **The Future of an Illusion.** The dominant theme of the work concerns the unhappiness which civilization causes humanity as it forces a renunciation of instinctual gratifications. Both erotic and aggressive trends are renounced or repressed. Freud questions the meaning of life and he concludes that it can only be found in a life of maximum pleasure and minimum pain, i.e., in happiness.

But the possibility of achieving happiness is limited significantly by the suffering which threatens us from the external world, from our fellows and from our own bodies. For Freud there is no royal road to happiness and each individual must choose his own path given these severe limitations.

But why is civilization a source of unhappiness? Surely it has come into being to order our relations to nature and to one another in such a way as to make our lives easier, more comfortable and more secure. The answer, simply put, is that the human kind pays for the advantages of civilization with the renunciation of instinctual gratification and we do this very unwillingly. Our control over the environment which we celebrate in the achievements of science and technology provide many examples of this. For example, the taming of fire could only be accomplished by man renouncing an instinctual urge:

> Psychoanalytic material, incomplete as it is and not susceptible to clear interpretation, nevertheless admits of a conjecture—a fantastic-sounding one—about the origin of this human feat. It is as though primal man had the habit, when he came in contact with fire, of satisfying an infantile desire connected with it, by putting it out with a stream of his urine. The legends that we possess leave no doubt about the originally phallic view taken of the tongues of flame as they shoot upwards. Putting out fire by micturating—a theme to which modern giants, Gulliver in Lilliput and Rabelais' Gargantua, still hark back—was there-

fore a kind of sexual act with a male, an enjoyment of sexual potency in a homosexual competition. The first person to renounce this desire and spare the fire was able to carry it off with him and subdue it to his own use. By damping down the fire of his own sexual excitation, he had tamed the natural force of fire. This great cultural conquest was thus the reward for his renunciation of instinct. Further, it is as though woman had been appointed guardian of the hearth, because her anatomy made it impossible for her to yield to the temptation of this desire.[34]

But the war between the instincts and the requirements of civilization is fought out not only in the technological and scientific realm but in the area of aesthetics, morality and even hygiene. Freud suggests that civilized humanity values beauty in spite of its non-utilitarian character: "We soon observe," he wrote, "that this useless thing which we expect civilization to value is beauty. We require civilized man to reverence beauty wherever he sees it in nature and to create it in the objects of his handiwork so far as he is able." But even more elementary than beauty are cleanliness and order which have indeed become the yardstick of civilization:

> We do not think highly of the cultural level of an English country town in Shakespeare's time when we read that there was a big dung heap in front of his father's house in Stratford; we are indignant and call it 'barbarous' (which is the opposite of civilized) when we find the paths in the Wiener Wald littered with paper. Dirtiness of all kinds seems to us incompatible with civilization. We extend our demand for cleanliness to the human body too. We are astonished to learn of the objectionable smell which emanated from the *Roi Soleil*; and we shake our heads on the Isola Bella when we are shown the tiny wash-basin in which Napoleon made his morning toilette. Indeed, we are not surprised by the idea of setting up the use of soap as an actual yardstick of civilization. The same is true of order.[35]

In addition we measure civilization according to its ideals, ideals which involve universal demands leading to the perfection of all humanity. We value these ideals as great cultural achievements in themselves even if the gap between them and reality leaves much to be desired. And finally we measure civilization

---

33 Op. cit. P. 56

34 **Civilization and Its Discontents,** Collected Works XXI, p. 90
35 Op. cit. p. 93

according to the way in which society regulates the relations among its members.

Freud paints a picture of our uncivilized ancestors which differs little from that of Hobbes and Rousseau. In the course of civilization, and as a necessary prerequisite for it, we find the development of law and justice which are no respecters of persons. This civil development necessarily diminishes the original freedom of the individual in the state of nature, but it has given us a universal security the lack of which created the conditions of the *bellum omnium contra omnes* [war of all against all] in the 'state of nature.' The liberty which the individual was forced to relinquish has been raised anew from time to time as a demand upon civilization for greater individual liberty. Sometimes these demands have been syntonic with the general course of civilized development and have served the forces of progress whereas at other times they have caused their proponents to adopt an attitude hostile to civilization itself. But there can be no doubt that the development of civilization has forced a change in the members of society at the communal level akin to the forced development of instinctual dispositions by organic repression upon the individual.

Freud calls attention to three modes of fostering changes in individual development which have a parallel in the changes in instinctual disposition brought about by the forces of civilization. These are character formation, sublimation and repression or forced renunciation of instinct. The individual learns not only to be clean and orderly but to feel disgust and shame in the face of dirt and disorder. This is first accomplished as a reaction to the instinct satisfied by the free evacuation of the bowels combined with the high valuation placed on the faeces. A similar process must occur on the social level. Sublimation is a process of deflection of instinctual aims into inhibited paths which are socially advantageous. For example, the desire to cut can be sublimated in the activities of a butcher or the precise movements of a surgeon. And finally the forced repression or renunciation of instinct leads to frustration at both the individual and social levels. In the former it may lead to neurosis and in the latter to the development of a hostile attitude to civilization.

It is important to show that the repression of instinct operates at the biological level and is intimately bound up with the unique evolution of the human kind. There can be no doubt but that Freud's views are deeply dependent on the theory of evolution. For example, the development of an erect posture had significant consequences for sexuality which until that momentous evolutionary event was primarily driven by olfactory stimuli making smell the dominant sexual force. With the development of an upright gait, the sense of smell suffered organic repression and the sexual sense became that of sight given the new visibility of the genitals. At the same time the exposure of the genitals required their protection which the development of shame helped to satisfy.

The social benefits of hygiene were also a derivative of the diminution of the olfactory stimuli in the sexual arousal of the male combined with the organic repression of anal erotism. Freud describes this in the following:

> A social factor is also unmistakably present in the cultural trend towards cleanliness, which has received *ex post facto* justification in hygienic considerations but which have manifested itself before their discovery. The incitement to cleanliness originates in an urge to get rid of the excreta, which have become disagreeable to the sense perceptions. We know that in the nursery things are different. The excreta arouse no disgust in children. They seem valuable to them as being part of their own body which has come away from it. Here upbringing insists with special energy on hastening the course of development which lies ahead, and which should make the excreta worthless, disgusting, abhorrent and abominable. Such a reversal of values would scarcely be possible if the substances that are expelled from the body were not doomed by their strong smells to share the fate which overtook olfactory stimuli after man adopted the upright posture. Anal erotism, therefore, succumbs in the first instance to the 'organic repression' which paved the way to civilization. The existence of the social factor which is responsible for the further transformation of anal erotism is attested by the circumstances that, in spite of all man's developmental advances, he scarcely finds the smell of *his own* excreta repulsive, but only that of other people's. Thus a person who is not clean—who does not hide his excreta—is offending other people; he is showing no consideration for them. And this is confirmed by our strongest and commonest terms of abuse. It would be incomprehensible, too, that a man should use the name of his most faithful friend in the animal world—the dog—as a term of abuse if that creature had not incurred his contempt through two characteristics: that is an animal whose dominant

sense is that of smell and one which has no horror of excrement, and that is not ashamed of its sexual functions.[36]

The two-fold force which impelled communal existence forward on the path of civilization consisted of love, in both its sensual and affectionate (i.e., aim-inhibited) modalities, and work, imposed as external necessity and a condition of continued existence. When sexuality became a permanent and continuous need of man and lost the periodicity of his animal cousins, it was necessary to maintain the love object in close proximity. At the same time it was in the interest of the woman and her offspring to be near the stronger male.

It would seem then that the course of civilization should run smooth. Here we find a community of families in which the pairs are bound to one another in an uninhibited libidinous way and the members of society linked by identification and a common interest in productivity, security, etc. But it is at this point that Freud introduces a profound idea, namely, that love itself becomes an obstacle to the process of civilization. There is a tension between the demands of the family and the demands of the community. Since Freud assumed that libido was not only a quality but also a quantity and that there was a fixed amount available to the individual, it seemed reasonable to assume that whatever was expended in the service of the family would be denied the community and vice-versa. Woman, whose initial interest in establishing the permanence of the family soon came into conflict with the demands of the community. Furthermore, the community began to make demands and place restrictions on the sexual lives of its members. Thus, Freud could write: "On the one hand love comes into opposition to the interests of civilization; on the other, civilization threatens love with substantial restrictions." These restrictions include the proscription of incestuous object choices, the imposition of taboos and other customary inhibitions, prohibitions on the manifestations of sexuality in children, the limitation of object choice for the adult to members of the opposite sex and the forbidding of extra-genital sexual satisfactions as perversions.

And so we are faced with a paradoxical development. Eros, which combines individuals and groups into larger wholes creates the conditions during the course of civilization which force erotic expressions into very narrow channels which does significant damage to the libidinal lives of people. The weak may submit to the demands of civilization and suffer distortions in their sexual lives whereas the strong will either ignore the imposition or trade their freedom for a guarantee of security. Empirical evidence shows how leaky the containment of instinctual impulses has traditionally been in the civilized condition.

A further complication arises on the basis of what Freud believed to be an original bisexual disposition in the human being. If this is so, then it is clear that the male and female sexual wishes will not be satisfied by the same object. Furthermore, the very ambivalence of the relationship to the love object signifies that, in addition to the erotic impulse, an aggressive trend will also manifest itself from time to time. And there is no guarantee that the love object will accommodate the expressions of this aggression.

And finally, Freud presented the possibility that organic repression will not only force an end to the dominance of the olfactory stimuli in sexual arousal or of anal erotism, but it may in fact subject the whole of sexuality to the force of repression:

> ... with the assumption of an erect posture by man and with the depreciation of his sense of smell, it was not only his anal erotism which threatened to fall victim to organic repression, but the whole of his sexuality; so that since this, the sexual function has been accompanied by a repugnance which cannot further be accounted for, and which prevents its complete satisfaction and forces it away from the sexual aim into sublimations and libidinal displacements. ... All neurotics, and many others besides, take exception to the fact that 'inter urinas et faeces nascimur [we are born between urine and faeces],' The genitals, too, give rise to strong sensations of smell which many people cannot tolerate and which spoil sexual intercourse for them. Thus we should find that the deepest root of the sexual repression which advances along with civilization is the organic defence of the new form of life achieved with man's erect gait against his earlier animal existence.[27]

Having zeroed in on the sources which potentially prevent the realization of happiness for individuals in civilization, Freud then raises a significant question: why does Eros in bringing together two people to make one unit insist on going further and demand libidinal links among members of the com-

---

36 Op. cit. p. 100

37 Op. cit. p. 106

munity as well, links which necessarily deplete the store of libido available to the family? Why is it not possible for members of the community to be linked to one another through ties of common interest and common labour, leaving the full store of libido to pairs of lovers/mates? Freud answers:

> But this desirable state of things does not, and never did, exist. Reality shows us that civilization is not content with the ties we have so far allowed it. It aims at binding the members of the community together in a libidinal way as well and employs every means to that end. It favours every path by which strong identifications can be established between the members of the community, and it summons up aim-inhibited libido on the largest scale so as to strengthen the communal bond by relations of friendship. In order for these aims to be fulfilled, a restriction upon sexual life is unavoidable. But we are unable to understand what the necessity is which forces civilization along this path and which causes its antagonism to sexuality. There must be some disturbing factor which we have not yet discovered.[28]

The clue to the discovery of this disturbing factor is the great ideal of Western, i.e., Christian civilization: "Thou shalt love thy neighbour as thyself." Freud proposes that we adopt a naive attitude to this injunction, to react to it as we would had we encountered it for the first time. In this phenomenological approach, we discover that it doesn't make any sense. If love is something for which we have a limited capacity, then it is something valuable which should be reserved for family and friends. Should we be too liberal with it we risk doing an injustice to them by putting a concern for strangers on the same level as our intimate relations. If love is spread too thinly, if we had to share it with everyone, then only a tiny fraction would fall to any one individual which would leave it without practical effect. Furthermore, the stranger may not be deserving of love; he may not love me, indeed, he may wish to do me harm. Freud has no objection to following the maxim: 'Love thy neighbour as thy neighbour loves thee,' but the premium placed on unconditional love is impossible and absurd. If it is further argued that it is precisely because your neighbour is undeserving of your love that you should love him, then Freud believes this to be a variant of the position: *credo quia absurdum* [I believe because it is absurd]. These unrealistic

demands made upon us in Christian civilization represent a massive attempt both to hide and to combat an unpleasant truth, a truth which provides a constant threat to civilization itself. This truth is the truth of human nature, the truth of the innate character of aggression and destructive impulses which we harbour not only in relation to our enemies and strangers, but to those whom we love as well.

> The element of truth behind all this, which people are so ready to disavow, is that men are not gentle creatures who want to be loved, and who at the most can defend themselves if they are attacked; they are, on the contrary, creatures among whose instinctual endowments is to be reckoned a powerful share of aggressiveness. As a result, their neighbour is for them not only a potential helper or sexual object, but also someone who tempts them to satisfy their aggressiveness on him, to exploit his capacity for work without compensation, to use him sexually without his consent, to seize his possessions, to humiliate him, to cause him pain, to torture and to kill him. *Homo homini lupus* [Man is a wolf to man]. Who, in the face of all his experience in life and of history, will have the courage to dispute this assertion? As a rule this cruel aggressiveness waits for some provocation or puts itself at the service of some other purpose, whose goal might also have been reached by milder measures. In circumstances that are favourable to it, when the mental counter-forces which ordinarily inhibit it are out of action, it also manifests itself spontaneously and reveals man as a savage beast to whom consideration towards his own kind is something alien. Anyone who calls to mind the atrocities committed during the racial migrations or the invasions of the Huns, or by the people known as Mongols under Jenghiz Khan and Tamerlane, or at the capture of Jerusalem by the pious Crusaders, or even, indeed, the horrors of the recent World War—anyone who calls these things to mind will have to bow humbly before the truth of this view.[39]

But if this innate aggressiveness is so powerful, so ingrained, so insistent upon release, then how is it that civilization is possible at all? Obviously, one part of the answer is provided by instinct theory itself, namely, that opposing the force of death and destruction are the powers of Eros, the powers of love to bind people together into larger unities. But this is

---

38 Op. cit. pp. 108–09

39 Op. cit. pp. 111–12

only a partial answer, for in order to prevent aggressiveness from undoing the work of Eros at every turn within the community, the native aggressiveness must be deflected away from an internal focus and be directed outside the group. It is this necessary reflex which lies at the heart of racism, racial jokes, ethnocentrism, genocide, ethnic cleansing, etc., etc.

> It is always possible to bind together a considerable number of people in love, so long as there are other people left over to receive the manifestations of their aggressiveness. I once discussed the phenomenon that it is precisely communities with adjoining territories, and related to each other in other ways as well, who are engaged in constant feuds and in ridiculing each other—like the Spaniards and the Portuguese, for instance, the North Germans and South Germans, the English and the Scotch, and so on. I gave this phenomenon the name of 'the narcissism of minor differences', a name which does not do much to explain it. We can now see that it is a convenient and relatively harmless satisfaction of the inclination to aggression, by means of which cohesion between the members of the community is made easier. In this respect the Jewish people, scattered everywhere, have rendered the most useful services to the civilizations of the countries that have been their hosts; but unfortunately all the massacres of the Jews in the Middle Ages did not suffice to make that period more peaceful and more secure for their Christian fellows. When once the Apostle Paul posited universal love between men as the foundation of his Christian community, extreme intolerance on the part of Christendom towards those who remained outside it became the inevitable consequence. To the Romans who had not founded their communal life as a State upon love, religious intolerance was something foreign, although with them religion was a concern of the State and the State was permeated by religion. Neither was it an unaccountable chance that the dream of a Germanic world-dominion called for anti-semitism as its complement; and it is intelligible that the attempt to establish a new, communist civilization in Russia should find its psychological support in the persecution of the bourgeois. One only wonders, with concern, what the Soviets will do after they have wiped out their bourgeois.[40]

Freud follows this discussion with a short recapitulation of the development of his theory of instincts. He explains that the reasons he resisted accepting the existence of a destructive or death instinct had to do with the fact that it almost always manifests itself behind the scenes, usually inextricably bound up with erotic elements. But behind the difficulty of the purity of its form, lies the unwillingness of human beings to accept this dark side of their nature. There is a hint that Freud believed that it was more difficult for humanity to recognize the instinct of aggression than it had been for it to accept the sexual instincts. Freud wrote: "I remember my own defensive attitude when the idea of an instinct of destruction first emerged in psychoanalytic literature, and how long it took before I became receptive to it. That others should have shown, and still show, the same attitude of rejection surprises me less. For 'little children do not like it' when there is talk of the inborn human inclination to 'badness', to aggressiveness and destructiveness, and so to cruelty as well."[41]

Freud does suggest, however, that the death instinct can, like its erotic counterpart, become inhibited in its aim and directed to socially beneficial and ego-syntonic expressions. For the raw instinct to destroy and annihilate can be blunted and achieve satisfaction in the mastery over objects and the control of nature. This suggests the possibility that the violent clashes between Eros and death can be mitigated at least to some degree.

Freud then presents us with a concise summary of his thoughts on civilization in relation to the instinctual demands of the human kind:

> I may now add that civilization is a process in the service of Eros, whose purpose is to combine single human individuals, and after that families, then races, peoples and nations, into one great unity, the unity of mankind . . . These collections of men are to be libidinally bound to one another. Necessity alone, the advantages of work in common, will not hold them together. But man's natural aggressive instinct, the hostility of each against all and of all against each, opposes this programme of civilization. This aggressive instinct is the derivative and the main representative of the death instinct which we have found alongside of Eros and which shared world-dominion with it. And now, I think, the meaning of the evolution of civilization is no longer obscure to us. It must

---

40 Op. cit. pp. 114–15.

41 Op. cit. p. 120

present the struggle between the instinct of life and the instinct of destruction, as it works itself out in the human species. This struggle is what all life essentially consists of, and the evolution of civilization may therefore be simply described as the struggle for life of the human species.[42]

But there is yet one further manifestation of the destructive instinct which is more insidious still than the form of hostility and aggression existing between individuals and groups. And amazingly it arises as a result of civilization's attempt to defuse the instinct for aggression, to make it harmless to the work of Eros. We have already encountered this mechanism in our earlier discussion of personality theory, for we are referring here to the formation of the super-ego. The individual conscience has become an internal check on the externalization of the instinct of destruction. As Freud writes:

"conscience," is ready to put into action against the ego the same harsh aggressiveness that the ego would have liked to satisfy upon other extraneous individuals. The tension between the harsh super-ego and the ego that is subjected to it, is called by us the sense of guilt; it expresses itself as a need for punishment. Civilization, therefore, obtains mastery over the individual's desire for aggression by weakening and disarming it and by setting up an agency within him to watch over it, like a garrison in a conquered city.[43]

We first encounter a sense of guilt in relation to actions forbidden by our parents. This is powered by a fear that we will lose their love, i.e., their protection. The second encounter with guilt is from within, from the critical eye of the super-ego. We can hide our actions from our parents who seek to force us to renounce our instinctual satisfactions. But we cannot hide our *wishes* from the super-ego. Even if we renounce instinctual satisfactions they continue to maintain an active subterranean existence in the unconscious. The development of the super-ego, the Trojan horse of civilization in the individual psyche, has become a major source of modern man's unhappiness. "Instinctual renunciation now no longer has a completely liberating effect; virtuous continence is no longer rewarded with the assurance of love. A threatened external unhappiness—loss of love and punishment on the part of the external authority—has been exchanged for a permanent internal unhap-

piness, for the tension of the sense of guilt."

If we recall that the super-ego receives its power to reproach the ego from the id, and the instinctual energy in the id is a function of the force of repression, then it follows that the force which the super-ego has at its disposal to attack the ego will vary directly with the force of repression. But it is the pressure of civilization which forces the repression and renunciation of instinctual satisfactions. Hence, the demands of civilization upon the instinctual life of individuals engender a strong sense of guilt not for actions done, but for an increase in the power of unconscious desires and wishes. The saint experiences himself as a wretched sinner to a greater degree than people who have outlets for their libidinal and aggressive impulses.

And, in conclusion, Freud uses the very fact which prevented his grasp of the significance of the instinct of aggression to make a systematic claim concerning the vicissitudes of both sets of instincts. He surmises that the sexual and destructive instincts are almost always intertwined in some fashion and the repression of both leads to parallel consequences:

I am tempted to extract a first advantage from this more restricted view of the case by applying it to the process of repression. As we have learned, neurotic symptoms are, in their essence, substitutive satisfactions for unfulfilled sexual wishes. In the course of our analytic work we have discovered to our surprise that perhaps every neurosis conceals a quota of unconscious sense of guilt, which in turn fortifies the symptoms by making use of them as a punishment. It now seems plausible to formulate the following proposition. When an instinctual trend undergoes repression, its libidinal elements are turned into symptoms, and its aggressive components into a sense of guilt.[44]

At the conclusion of the book, Freud refuses to allow himself to be cast in the role of prophet concerning the future course of civilization. He refuses to offer the one thing that radicals and traditionalists alike demand—consolation. And yet he does pose *the* significant question for the future of civilization:

The fateful question for the human species seems to me to be whether and to what extent their cultural development will succeed in mastering the disturbance of their communal life by the human instinct of aggression and self-destruction. It may

---

42 Op. cit. p. 122
43 Op. cit. pp. 123–24

44 Op. cit. p. 139

be that in this respect precisely the present time deserves a special interest. Men have gained control over the forces of nature to such an extent that with their help they would have no difficulty in exterminating one another to the last man. They know this, and hence comes a large part of their current unrest, their unhappiness and their mood of anxiety. And now it is to be expected that the other of the 'Heavenly Powers', eternal Eros, will make an effort to assert himself in the struggle with his equally immortal adversary. But who can foresee with what success and with what result?[45]

Freud added the last sentence in 1931 after the Nazi Party had scored significant electoral gains in Germany's federal election.

---

45 Op. cit. p. 145.

9

Charles Horton Cooley

A Brief Biographical Sketch[1]

Charles Horton Cooley was born on August 17, 1864 to Thomas McIntyre and Mary Elizabeth Cooley. He was their fourth child. Thomas Cooley was a professor of law at the University of Michigan Law School and a newly appointed Justice to the Supreme Court of Michigan. Charles was a sickly and lonely child, but he was endowed with willpower, imagination and intellectual ability. He did not remain passive and accept his frail constitution, but opted for rugged experiences in his youth. In 1882, for example, he headed out west and worked with a surveying crew, working strenuously in some very rough country. Shortly thereafter he left for Germany where he enrolled as a student at the Ludwig-Maximilian University in Munich. He stayed less than a year in that city, and, after a brief tour of mountain climbing in the Swiss Alps, he returned to Ann Arbor where he completed his training in mechanical engineering in 1887.

Shortly after graduation, Charles made his first acquaintance with the writings of Herbert Spencer and he was fascinated by the magnificent evolutionary schema they presented. In 1889 Charles left Ann Arbor for Washington, D.C. where he went to work for the Interstate Commerce Commission and later the Census Bureau. He read his first paper "The Social Significance of Street Railways" to the American Economic Association in 1890. In 1892 he was offered a half-time instructorship in Political Economy at the University of Michigan. While teaching part-time at the University, Cooley successfully completed his doctorate on "The Theory of Transportation." He did a minor in sociology, the questions for the examination having been sent by Franklin Henry Giddings at Columbia University.

While still working in Washington Charles married Miss Elsie Jones, a high school teacher of Greek and Latin. After settling in Ann Arbor in 1892, they raised a family of three children. His offspring became the subjects in his domestic "laboratory," and by carefully observing their psychic development, Cooley was able to fashion an important part of the foundation of his social psychology.

Cooley was influenced by the important American psychologists, philosophers and sociologists of his day. His work in social psychology is unthinkable without the pioneering efforts of Giddings, Ward, James, Dewey, Royce and Baldwin. Yet the deeper and more pervasive influences upon Cooley came not from modern men of science, but from writers like Ralph Waldo Emerson and Henry David Thoreau. Cooley also learned much from the great German genius Johann Wolfgang Goethe. [Cooley's works are peppered with observations taken from the writings of Emerson and Goethe].

Cooley published three major works in is lifetime: **Human Nature and the Social Order** (1902), **Social Organization** (1909), and **Social Process** (1918). In the first book Cooley worked out the basis of his social psychology including the theory of the looking glass self. In the second book he expanded on the nature and importance of the primary group and the primary ideals.

After a successful career in research and teaching and pioneering efforts in social psychology, Charles Horton Cooley succumbed to cancer on May 8, 1929.

---

1 Biographical information on Cooley is based primarily upon the account given in Jandy (1942).

Early American Sociology[2]

The individual which had the greatest impact upon the fledgling science of Sociology in the United States in the late 19th century was Herbert Spencer. It was Spencer's commitment to the social Darwinist view of the survival of the fittest and the rugged individualism suggested by this doctrine that found a willing listener in William Graham Sumner, one of the founding fathers of American sociology. When it came to preaching against the evils of government interference in economy and society Sumner was even more extreme in his opposition than Spencer. An evolutionist, like Spencer, Sumner believed that only through unfettered competition and struggle would progress for the human kind be achieved.

Not all fathers of American sociology shared the fatalistic bias of Spencer and Sumner. Lester Frank Ward, another follower of Spencer and the first American to write a sociological treatise, rejected the notion that human intelligence should not be brought to bear upon social problems. The human mind, so argued Ward, through the process of its evolutionary development, has a capacity to become actively engaged in the transformation of the natural and social environment. With the appearance of the teleological, human mind, the evolutionary process had achieved a higher stage of development. Unlike the rest of the animal kingdom, the human kind is able to shape both natural and social forces to its own ends. It is the uniquely human psychic factor generated in the evolutionary process which enables us to do this.

But in spite of Ward's departure from the laissez-faire extremism of Spencer and Sumner (Ward was rather sympathetic to socialistic reformers), he was not able to solve the problem generated by Spencerian organicism. If society is an organism or super-organism, what is the nature of the relationship between the individual and society? What is the nature of human individuality? Furthermore, Ward was never able to reconcile the evolutionist view that the law of evolution governs all phenomena in nature, with the freedom presupposed by the teleological view of the human mind as an active participant in the shaping of the human social and natural environment.

Taking his cue from Ward, Franklin Henry Giddings developed the notion of the psychic factor fur-

ther. Giddings too began within the Spencerian framework, but he argued that human society cannot be explained in terms of the laws of aggregation or the self-limitation of conflict. In order to move from the pre-social to the social condition of the human kind, a psychological factor must be present. This psychological factor is "true self-consciousness" and Gidding's explanation of it immediately calls to mind Cooley's description of the looking glass self. Giddings refers to it in the following terms:

> the distinctive peculiarity is that each individual makes his neighbor's consciousness, feeling or judgment an object of his own thought at the same instant that he makes his own feeling or thought such an object, judges the two to be identical, and then acts with a full consciousness that his fellows have come to like conclusions and will act in like ways.(1894, 57)

Now although Ward and especially Giddings elaborated upon the psychological factor in the genesis and functioning of society, neither of these men developed a systematic social-psychological theory. Nor were they able to solve the problem of the relationship between the individual and society raised by Spencerian sociology.

The issue of the psychological factor in the constitution of society and the problem of the relation of the individual and the aggregate were brought together by two pragmatist thinkers, William James and John Dewey.

In his two volume work, **The Principles of Psychology**, James suggested that the human self did not stand out against society, but was at its very core something social. The opposition between the individual and his society was not one of kind but rather of degree. The individual and society are different sides of the same coin. "Properly speaking", wrote James (1890, 294) "a man has as many social selves as there are individuals who recognize him and carry an image of him in their mind."

John Dewey developed a theory of the social self as part of an attempt to reconcile his Hegelian idealism with new developments in experimental psychology. According to Dewey, the individual consciousness is filled with a universal content. What is universal is obviously that which is shared among individual selves, and that is something social. For Dewey, (1887, 327) "the self has no meaning except as contrasted with other persons. Egoistic feelings are impossible except through a connection with altruistic feelings. 'Mine' requires a contrasted 'thine.' "

---

2 For a fuller discussion of these matters see Cohen (1982) upon which the following section is largely based. Citations from the works of the early Americans in this section are taken from Cohen who has excerpted them from the original sources.

Josiah Royce was one of the foremost American Hegelian philosophers of his time. Like Dewey, Royce believed that human individuals share a universal world which rests upon their social experience. Consciousness of self, for Royce, is the prerequisite for all knowing and this self-consciousness is social in its origin.

> As a fact, a man becomes self-conscious only in the most intimate connection with the growth of his social consciousness. These two forms of consciousness are not separable and opposed regions of a man's life; they are thoroughly interdependent. I am dependent on my fellows, not only physically, but to the very core of my conscious self-hood, not only for what, physically speaking, I am, but for what I take myself to be. Take away the Alter from consciousness, and the conscious Ego, so far as in this world we know it, languishes, and languishing dies. (1898, 201)

It was Royce (1901, 170) who, in another work, wrote: "we first learn about ourselves from and through our fellows..." As Cohen (1982:116–7) has recently suggested, in the writings of Royce "(s)ociety is implicated in every thought of self. Self and society are coordinate concepts, necessarily linked in consciousness, and, therefore, in social theory. Royce clearly understood that no individualistic psychology could comprehend the social basis of all psychic phenomena." For Royce the genesis of the social self can be explained in relationships. Imitation was first investigated by the French psychologist Gabriel Tarde (one of Durkheim's arch foes) in his influential work **Les Lois de l'Imitation**. The American psychologist James Mark Baldwin investigated the process of human self development in children by applying the theory of imitation to explain the empirical data. Baldwin postulated three phases of self development in the child: the projective, subjective and ejective. The first phase of self development corresponds to the child's distinguishing between persons and other non-person objects. These persons are experienced in a different way than non-person objects. By imitating persons the child now seeks to become like the projective objects, to experience himself in a way which he attributes to others. Finally, the child comes to the realization that others have the same experiences in themselves that he has in himself:

> The projective becomes *ejective*; that is, other people's bodies, says the child to himself, have experiences *in them* such as mine has. They are also me's:

let them be assimilated to my me copy. This is the third stage; the ejective, or 'social' self is born. (Baldwin, 1897, 338)

The individual is a microcosm of society. In the very depths of our personal beings, in our selves, we are part of everyone else, thoroughly social creatures. Man is not "a single soul shut up in a single body to act, or to abstain from acting, upon other similarly shut in similar bodies; but as a soul partly in his own body, partly in the bodies of others, to all intents and purposes, so intimate is this social bond..." (153)

G.W.F. Hegel and Adam Smith

The Hegelian influence on the early Americans through the writings of Royce, Dewey and James is apparent. The identity of subject and object with which Hegelian philosophy begins its critique of subjective idealism is precisely the same starting point for the theory of the social self. In a way, the problem bequeathed by Spencer to sociology is the same problem in sociological guise as that left by Kant and Fichte to German idealist philosophy. Instead of the problematic relationship between subject and object, sociology was confronted by the problematic relationship between individual and society. Through his writings and those of his American followers, Hegel pointed a new way to understanding the social nature of the self.

Yet, Hegel, in turn, had been influenced by earlier thinkers whose views helped to shape his own on a variety of issues. One of these thinkers was the Scottish moral philosopher and political economist, Adam Smith, who in his classic work in moral philosophy, **The Theory of Moral Sentiments**, set out a theory of self-development that gave emphasis to the role of sympathy and the imagination in social relations and interactions. To be sure, Smith gives emphasis to the attempt by individuals to fathom what others are experiencing and they do so by comparing their own experiences and feelings in similar situations in which others find themselves. But he also writes about the impact of the imagination of how others imagine the individual to be. Smith relies on the capacities of sympathy and identification which are carried out by the faculty of the imagination to explain what amounts to the social generation of the self. It is Smith who suggested that the self needed a "mirror" or a "looking-glass" to know itself. It is difficult to believe that Smith's ideas did not have a direct impact upon Cooley in this matter beyond the mediating influence of the Hegelians. Here are some selected passages from

Smith which anticipate the main points of Cooley's "looking-glass self."

> The violator of the more sacred laws of justice can never reflect on the sentiments which mankind must entertain with regard to him, without feeling all the agonies of shame, and horror, and consternation. . . . By sympathizing with the hatred and abhorrence which other men must entertain for him, he becomes in some measure the object of his own hatred and abhorrence. . . . Every thing seems hostile, and he would be glad to fly to some inhospitable desert, where he might never more behold the face of a human creature, nor read in the countenance of mankind the condemnation of his crimes. . . . The opposite behaviour naturally inspires the opposite sentiment. The man who . . . has performed a generous action . . . feels himself to be the natural object of their love and gratitude, and, by sympathy with them, of the esteem and approbation of all mankind. (pp. 163–65)

> Were it possible that a human creature could grow up to manhood in some solitary place, without any communication with his own species, he could no more think of his own character, of the propriety or demerit of his own sentiments and conduct, of the beauty or deformity of his own mind, than of the beauty or deformity of his own face. All these are objects which he cannot easily see, which naturally he does not look at, and with regard to which he is provided with no mirror which can present them to his view. Bring him into society and he is immediately provided with the mirror which he wanted before. It is placed in the countenance and behaviour of those he lives with, which always mark when they enter into, and when they disapprove of his sentiments; and it is here that he first views the propriety and impropriety of is own passions, the beauty and deformity of his own mind. (p. 204)

> Our first ideas of personal beauty and deformity are drawn from the shape and appearance of others, not from our own. We soon become sensible, however, that others exercise the same criticism upon us. We are pleased when they approve of our figure, and are disobliged when they seem to be disgusted. We become anxious to know how far our appearance deserves either their blame or approbation. We examine our persons limb by limb, and by placing ourselves before a looking-glass, or by some such expedient, endeavour, as much as possible, to view ourselves at the distance and with the eyes of other people. (pp. 205)

> We suppose ourselves the spectators of our own behaviour, and endeavour to imagine what effect it would, in this light, produce upon us. This is the only looking-glass by which we can, in some measure with the eyes of other people, scrutinize the propriety of our own conduct. . . . When I endeavour to examine my own conduct, when I endeavour to pass sentence upon it, and either to approve or condemn it, it is evident that, in all such cases, I divide myself, as it were, into two persons; and that I, the examiner and the judge, represent a different character from that other I, the person whose conduct is examined into and judged of. The first is the spectator, whose sentiments with regard to my own conduct I endeavour to enter into, by placing myself in his situation, and by considering how it would appear to me, when seen from that particular point of view. The second is the agent, the person whom I properly call myself, and of whose conduct, the character of a spectator, I was endeavouring to form some opinion. The first is the judge; the second the person judged of. But that the judge should, in every respect, be the same with the person judged of, is as impossible as that the cause should, in every respect, be the same with the effect. (pp. 206–07)

The Individual and Society

While the work of Charles Horton Cooley represents a major assault on the individualistic viewpoint in American social theory at the turn of this century, it is by no means a complete departure from early American sociological thinking. Regarded as an "anomaly in sociological literature" George E. Vincent in 1903, Cooley's **Human Nature and the Social Order**, together with his subsequent publications, served to shift sociological thinking in a holistic direction. Cooley's success, however, stemmed not from a wholesale critique of individualism but rather from his formulation of a viewpoint which seemingly acknowledged the freedom and autonomy of the individual, a nineteenth-century liberal presupposition which the Americans were loathe to give up. Cooley wrote at a time when individualism as a fundamental starting point for speculation on man and society was becoming increasingly untenable; not only was it beginning to clash with the presuppositions of a pure sociology, but it was getting bogged down in various forms of instinct theory, which were slowly being discredited. Individualism as a viewpoint on man and society was in crisis; it was no longer a tenable position in sociological thinking, yet it was a basic tenet of American liberalism. Cooley rescued the romantic individual of American liberalism while formulating a theoretical system capable of handling collective phenomena in their own terms. His success, it is claimed, stems from his ability to effect a synthesis of the individualistic viewpoint in American social thought with a rapidly enlarging conceptual apparatus based on the fundamental reality of society—to construct a theoretical system which retained a measure of freedom and autonomy for the individual, or an illusion of it, but which also viewed the individual as a social creature who derived his essential features from life in society.

Cooley's liberal world-view is clearly evident in his interpretation of social institutions. An institution "is simply a definite and established phase of the public mind" which represents "the working out of the permanent needs of human nature." (**S.O.** 313–314) Institutions and individuals are linked in a reciprocal relationship of cause and effect, the individual receiving from the institutions the traditions and values of his social heritage and impressing upon them his distinctive character together with the cumulative changes occasioned by changing conditions of life. At times institutions acquire a rigidity which resists subsequent incorporation of new elements; they become mechanical, inflexible, and no longer embody the genuine, permanent and emerging needs of human nature. In fact, all social structures possess this tendency, variously referred to as "institutionalism, formalism, traditionalism, conventionalism, ritualism, bureaucracy and the like." (**S.O.**, 342) At these times man will seek to alter institutions, to bring them more into accord with his needs. But basically, institutions are not the permanent enemies of individual man, rather they are the basis of human freedom and are becoming increasingly so with the passage of time. In Cooley's view the scope of alternatives for individual and social action increases with the advancement of knowledge and the enlargement of social "sympathy"; with increased understanding the mechanical, constraining elements of social institutions are elevated to a "higher plane."

Cooley grants to the individual a sense of personal integrity and a measure of autonomy. In Cooley's view institutions do not envelope the individual entirely; they embody only selected aspects of his whole personality. An institution, Cooley writes, "is made up of persons, but not of whole persons; each one enters into it with a trained and specialized part of himself." (**S.O.**, 319) And a constellation of insti-

tutions does not exhaust the individual's complement of personal characteristics. There is something about man that sets him apart from institutions: "In antithesis to the institution . . . the person represents the wholeness and humanness of life." (**S.O.**, 319) Further; "A man is no man at all if he is merely a piece of an institution; he must stand also for human nature, for the instinctive, the plastic and the ideal." (ibid.)

There is a seeming dialectic in Cooley's interpretation of institutions. Institutions serve as a point of departure for all innovations, providing "a basis for the very individual who rebels against it." (**S.O.**, 321) Progress, Cooley insists, "always begins in a revolt against institutions." (320) A process of interaction of personality and social institutions is at the very heart of all progress. But in Cooley's formulation, the antithesis between the individual and the institution is not irreconcilable; any disjunction between them is simply temporal. Both institutions and individuals are made of the same stuff; they are *not* fundamentally different types of "beings"; thus they cannot by nature be at odds. Cooley attributes to man the traditional liberal qualities of freedom, rationality, liberty, and individuality, and envisions the social structure as their very embodiment and furtherance. Basically, individual and social institutions are different aspects of the same logically prior reality. Cooley writes:

> A separate individual is an abstraction unknown to experience, and so likewise is society when regarded as something apart from individuals. The real thing is Human Life, which may be considered either in an individual aspect or in a social, that is to say a general, aspect; but is always, as a matter of fact, both individual and general. In other words, "society" and "individual" do not denote separable phenomena, but are simply collective and distributive aspects of the same thing, the relation between them being like that between other expressions one of which denotes a group as a whole and the other the members of the group, such as the army and the soldiers, the class and the students, and so on. (**H.N.**, 37)

The Looking-Glass Self

Early in his career, Cooley rejected the individual-society antithesis and the philosophical premise that attributes ontological primacy to the pre-social individual on the grounds that both the individual and society are but different aspects of a logically prior psychical stratum of human existence, (H.N., 41–47) thus levelling any fundamental distinction between them. Society is not a thing in its own right. "Society is rather a phase of life than a thing by itself; it is life regarded from the point of view of personal intercourse." (H.N., 135) Essentially a mental construct, society "emerges" in the dual process of communication and interaction between social beings, neither of which is logically or historically prior to the other. "Society, then in its immediate aspect, *is a relation among personal ideas*" (H.N., 119; emphasis in original) Thus, Cooley concludes: "the imaginations which people have of one another are the *solid facts* of society, and to observe and interpret these must be a chief aim of sociology." (H.N., 121, emphasis in original)

The same mental stratum underlies the self; in Cooley's view the person is a psychical rather than a material fact. (H.N., 120) Paying lip service to the "independent reality of persons," Cooley insists that "the personal idea . . . is the immediate social reality." In fact, "a corporeally existent person is not socially real unless he is imagined." (H.N., 123) On the other hand, persons with no corporeal reality, the dead, often acquire social reality through the imaginations of the living. As far as social relations are concerned, "the personal idea is the real person." (H.N., 118) Essentially it is the imagination that makes the individual real, not material contact; "the self that is most importunate is a reflection, largely, from the minds of others." (H.N., 246) There is "nothing fantastic, unreal, or impractical" about conceiving persons as "facts of the imagination." "On the contrary," writes Cooley, "the fantastic, unreal, and practically pernicious way is the ordinary and traditional one of speculating upon them as shadowy bodies." (H.N., 132–133) Rooted in an undifferentiated instinctual base, the social self is built up through imagination and personal intercourse, and derives its distinguishing features from the ongoing social process. "The social self is simply any idea, or system of ideas, drawn from the communicative life, that the mind cherishes as its own. (H.N., 179) But the choice of ideas constituting the self is not an arbitrary or individual matter; there is a double contingency involving self and other in the process of self-formation. The self is created, sustained and transformed largely through the imaginations of oneself which one attributes to others. Such is the basis of Cooley's "looking-glass self." H.N., 184)

The importance of the imagination, the realm of the psychical, in Cooley's sociology is so evident that it hardly requires further comment. For Cooley "mind" is the very foundation of all human existence—self, society, social organization, morality, freedom, and the like. It is both motive force and essential substance. Thus, distinctions among the "entities" of human experience are necessarily secondary to their fundamental similarity. The point that is being made is that Cooley "translates" the conceptual entities, individual and society, into a common dimension, that of mind, consequently levelling their essential differences. "Self and society go together as phases of a common whole." (S.O., 8–9) We recall that "Mind", for Cooley, "is an organic whole made up of cooperating individualities, in somewhat the same way that the music of an orchestra is made up of divergent but related sounds." (S.O., 31)

Primary Groups and Primary Ideals

The distinguishing features of individual persons and of social institutions are developed in the social process and are not prior to it; thus, they are social both in genesis and in character. However, Cooley postulates a human nature which, while emerging in the context of intimate face-to-face relations, or "primary groups," is universal and permanent and hence logically prior to the social process. Human nature is a cluster of universal "sentiments and impulses" that distinguishes man from the rest of the animal kingdom; it is not present at birth, but comes into being with personal experience in primary groups. It is a "*group-nature or primary-phase of society*" (S.O., 29; emphasis in original) which is everywhere the same, and which everywhere is the foundation of the social order. Interestingly enough, Cooley, who avoided the issue of pre-social determinants, postulates certain "givens" in human nature, but he locates these neither in the constitution of individual man, nor in the more elaborate structure of social institutions, but in the primary group. "What else can human nature be than a trait of primary groups." (S.O., 30)

Primary ideals are those which become the measure of social institutions and "the motive and test of social progress." (S.O., 32) Such social ideals as love, freedom, justice, moral unity, fellowship, sympathy, individuality, loyalty, truth or good faith, service, kindness, rules and laws, and the like, are in Cooley's view the primary needs of mankind. It is in the universal primary group that they are both nurtured and satisfied. To the degree that they are extended into the broader structures of society is the degree to which the latter embody the permanent and genuine needs of the human kind. While there is never a perfect "fit" between primary ideals and social institutions, the "purpose" of the latter is the fulfilment of the former; there is no basic disjunction between them.

A Note on Cooley and Mead

It is immediately apparent to even the most casual reader of their works that Mead was greatly influenced by Cooley, especially in the development of the theory of the self. There are many points of comparison and contrast which could be made between the theories of the two men. A few of the major points of contrast deserve to be singled out here.

First, Cooley assumed the existence of a rudimentary self (or rather self-feeling) at birth. This means that for Cooley the self is not entirely social, but has its roots in biology or physiology. If this is the case, then Cooley has no way to account for the genesis of the social self which he clearly wants to maintain as non-biological. For Mead, the self is something wholly social, the genesis of which can be demonstrated solely with reference to the social process. Cooley's treatment of the self is based upon affect—*self-feeling*. For Mead, the self is primarily a cognitive phenomenon. One can account for the genesis of the latter, whereas the former can only be accepted as a given.

Second, Mead is clearly the more sociological thinker of the two. There is a danger in following Cooley too closely of falling into the idealist trap of viewing the social process as a process that takes place only inside the head of the individual instead of seeing it as an objective social process among interacting individuals. By emphasizing the act, Mead begins with objective social behaviour, and this allows him to introduce social (universal) symbols into the endopsychic process. To follow too closely is to run the risk of not being able to get beyond the individual consciousness. (See, Jandy, 125–126.)

Bibliography

Baldwin, James Mark, **Mental Development in the Child and the Race**. New York: 1897.

Cohen, Marshall J., **Charles Horton Cooley and the Social Self in American Thought**. Garland: New York & London, 1982.

Cooley, Charles Horton, **Human Nature and the Social Order**. Schocken Books: New York: 1964 [1902].

_____ **Social Organization**. Schocken Books: New York: 1963 [1909].

_____ **Social Process**. Southern Illinois University Press: Carbondale and Edwardsville, 1966 [1918].

Dewey, John, **Psychology**. New York: 1887.

Giddings, Franklin Henry, **The Theory of Sociology**. Philadelphia: 1894.

James, William, **The Principles of Psychology**. New York: 1890.

Jandy, Edward C., **Charles Horton Cooley: His Life and Social Theory**. The Dryden Press: New York: 1942.

Royce, Josiah, **Studies in Good and Evil**. New York: 1898.

_____ **The World and the Individual**. New York: 1901.

Smith, Adam, **The Theory of Moral Sentiments**. Indianapolis: Liberty Classics, 1976.

10

George Herbert Mead

Introductory Note

Works of Mead are referred to by the following abbreviations:

MSS **Mind Self and Society**. Chicago: The University of Chicago Press, 1934.

MT **Movements of Thought in the Nineteenth Century**. Chicago: The University of Chicago Press, 1936.

PA **The Philosophy of the Act**. Chicago: The University of Chicago Press, 1938.

OSP **On Social Psychology**, Rev. Edition. Chicago: The University of Chicago Press, 1964.

All references to Mead's work, including the journal articles which Mead published during his lifetime, are cited in full in footnotes at the bottom of the page.

Biographical Sketch

George Herbert Mead entered the world on February 27, 1863, at South Hadley, Massachusetts, as the son of Hiram Mead and Elizabeth Storrs Billings. His father, a minister in the Congregational Church, came from a long line of New England Puritan farmers and clergymen, and, when George was seven years old, he moved the family to Oberlin, Ohio to accept a position as a Professor of Homiletics (the art of preaching) at the newly established Theological Seminary at Oberlin College. His mother, who came from a long line of prominent American families, was an accomplished woman in her own right, having served as president of Mount Holyoke College for a number of years. After the death of Hiram Mead in 1881, she taught at Oberlin College to help provide for the family, which consisted of George and his older sister Alice.

Mead grew up in Oberlin and entered the College at the age of sixteen. Though he was mild-mannered and kindhearted in temperament, he rebelled against the pious atmosphere of the College and sought to liberate himself from the supernaturalism that pervaded his early educational experiences. He is recorded as having said that he spent the second twenty years of his life unlearning what he was taught in the first twenty years. In any event, the influence of his religious puritanical heritage was never fully lost, although it was considerably attenuated by the progressive ideas that found their way into Oberlin College at that time.

Mead's intellectual growth was influenced in a very important way by Henry Northrup Castle, whom Mead met as a student in 1881 at Oberlin College. They became life-long friends, and Mead eventually married Henry's sister Helen. It was Henry Castle who provided the support and encouragement Mead needed to pursue his naturalistic explorations of the mind and the self. The two young men gave vent to their iconoclastic tendencies by attempting to refute church dogma and by immersing themselves in secular literature. Henry Castle encouraged Mead to develop his thought, and, in 1887, four years after they graduated from Oberlin, persuaded Mead to join him at Harvard University to continue his studies. The two became roommates until Mead began tutoring the children of William James and living in the home of his teacher.

Before enrolling in Harvard in the fall of 1887, Mead taught primary school for a short while and worked for three years with a surveying crew of a railroad company that was building a line from Minneapolis to Moose Jaw, Saskatchewan, to connect with the Canadian Pacific Railroad.

At Harvard, Mead studied primarily with Royce and James. The following year he went to Leipzig where he studied the works of Wilhelm Wundt, and later he went to Berlin for further studies in psychology and philosophy. On October 1, 1891, he married Helen Castle, and the two of them proceeded to Ann Arbor, Michigan where Mead was to become an instructor in the Department of Philosophy and Psychology at the University of Michigan.

At the University of Michigan Mead met Charles Horton Cooley, John Dewey, James Tufts, and Alfred Lloyd, who were all teaching there at the time. During his three years at the University of Michigan, Mead began to develop the broad outline of his theory of the mind and the self. The influence of his colleagues, especially Dewey and Cooley, is quite apparent in his later writings. In 1894, Mead followed Dewey to the newly established University of Chicago, where he taught in the Department of Philosophy, Psychology and Pedagogy until his death in 1931. It was here that Mead developed his theory into its present form.

The Works of George Herbert Mead

It was at the University of Chicago that Mead worked out the basic notions of his theoretical system. He was a brilliant lecturer and a beloved teacher, but he had considerable difficulty putting his ideas into print. Accounts of his life note the agony he experienced as he struggled to give written expression to his rapidly evolving mind. It was in the classroom where he lectured, always without notes, that his germinal ideas developed into the forms in which we know them today.

Mead was constantly dissatisfied with his work and was continually outgrowing the expression of his own thought. During the later years of his life, when it became evident that Mead would never publish a systematic treatise on his social psychological and philosophical reflections, a group of student and concerned colleagues arranged to have stenographic notes taken of his lectures. It is these notes, together with student notes and fragments of unpublished writings, that were edited and published after his death in three separate volumes. From class and stenographic notes taken in his course on social psychology came the volume **Mind, Self and Society** (1934); from stenographic notes prepared for Alvin Carus and the class notes of George A. Pappas, taken in Mead's course, "Movements of Thought in the Nineteenth Century," came the book under the same title in 1936; and finally, from a collection of unpublished papers by Mead himself, which were in varying

stages of completeness, and from a large body of student notes on Mead's interpretation of the history of ideas, came the volume, **The Philosophy of the Act**, published in 1938. Mead's Carus lectures, which he read in Berkeley in December, 1930, just before his death, were published in 1932 under the title **The Philosophy of the Present**.

In reading the works of Mead, the student should remember that they were initially presented as lectures to undergraduate classes. The cyclical, repetitious style of presenting material was no doubt an intentional pedagogical technique, but the subject matter itself seems to require constant repetition, since the concepts and ideas used by Mead often presuppose one another and frequently cannot be defined in terms which lie outside of the theoretical framework of the system. Thus, there is no clear, logical starting point. Mead did publish a number of articles in scholarly journals (see Bibliography), but these, too, reveal the same laboured tendency in self expression.

While Mead's ideas were never presented in a systematic manner by the master himself, they nevertheless form a remarkably coherent theoretical system, a system which has made an enormous impact on the discipline of sociology in America. The student who takes the time and trouble to study the works carefully will find his/her efforts well rewarded.

In 1961, thirty years after Mead's death, Arnold M. Rose, one of the foremost spokesmen of the symbolic interactionist tradition, expressed the view that **Mind, Self and Society** was the "most comprehensive formulation" of symbolic interaction theory.[1] While Mead never used the term "symbolic interactionism" to describe his work, there is no doubt that the very foundations of this tradition can be located in the lectures and articles of Mead. Because Mead published very little during his lifetime, his early work never received the widespread attention which had been given to his friends and colleagues, Charles Horton Cooley and John Dewey. However, the record will show that Mead had a profound impact on his students and colleagues at the University of Chicago.

Though Mead taught in the Department of Psychology, Philosophy, and Pedagogy, he attracted a large number of sociology students, among them Ellsworth Faris and Herbert Blumer. When Mead took ill in 1931, the Department of Sociology was

---

1 Arnold Rose, ed., **Human Behavior and Social Processes** (Boston: Houghton Mifflin, 1962) p. 3.

approached to provide someone to teach Mead's course on Comparative Psychology. According to Ellsworth Faris, Herbert Blumer taught the course apparently to everyone's satisfaction.[2] Anselm Strauss also notes that the influence of Mead found its expression primarily in the writing of sociologists (OSP, xi-xiii). Today Mead's influence can be found in almost every branch of sociology, but it is particularly evident in such areas as socialization, studies of identity, role theory, reference groups, labelling theory, occupational studies, deviance, and even the sociology of knowledge.

Mead's Theory of Mind, Self, and Society

American sociology arose in the post-Civil War period in large measure as a response to the unsettling effects of industrialization and urbanization. Reared in a predominantly rural, Protestant, religious tradition, the men who launched the sociological enterprise in the new world were imbued with an ethos of individualism and liberalism, and their approach to the rapidly emerging social problem bore the mark of a frontier tradition.

Unlike their European counterparts, who developed a viable sociology out of a conservative response to the excessive individualism of the Enlightenment, the early American sociologists fashioned their theoretical system on the premises of a liberal-individualistic world-view. As Hinkle and Hinkle write of the early American theorists, "they conceived of social behavior and society as constituted of *individual behavior* and particularly emphasized the motivations of individuals in associations."[3] While such a viewpoint was sufficient to help establish the new science of human behaviour in America, it was inevitable that the individualistic, liberal world-view would eventually come into direct conflict with an evolving sociological perspective based on the concept of the group rather than the individual. In the early decades of the present century, American sociology was faced with a dilemma: how was it to continue to develop a distinctive conceptual apparatus capable of handling the phenomena of collective life upon a foundation of a vigourously individualistic

world-view? There was a conceptual gap between the individual and society, and the social thinkers of the period were trying to close it, but they were not prepared to abandon the liberal ethos. In 1905, Albion Small wrote: "Today's sociology is still struggling with the preposterous initial fact of the individual. . . . Whether we are near to resolution of the paradox or not, there is hardly more visible consensus about the relation of the individual to the whole than at any earlier period. Indeed, the minds of more people than ever before are puzzled by the seeming antinomy between the individual and the whole."[4] It is largely in the works of Cooley and Mead, especially the latter, that a conceptual synthesis between the two discrepant elements—the individual and the social—can be found. It may be for this reason that the sociologists of the period were attracted to Mead.

The Formation of Median Social Psychology

With the encouragement of his friend Henry Northrup Castle, Mead successfully extricated himself from his puritanical, religious background and sought an explanation of mind and self in naturalistic terms. Like so many of his generation of American thinkers who set out to free themselves from their religious heritage, Mead developed a pragmatic outlook that was influenced in a significant way by the evolutionary theories of Charles Darwin.

Mead was not simply taken by the notion of the "survival of the fittest," with which Darwin's name is most frequently associated, but was also favourably impressed by the logic of the system of thought itself; it is the latter that pervades Meadian social psychology.

Darwin, in Mead's interpretation, took up the question of the origin of "forms" ("*species*" being the Latin word for form). This question could not be answered by physical science, since forms constitute the starting point for the physical sciences and are necessarily presupposed. Darwin assumed that forms came into being as a result of a life-process that was everywhere the same. What then accounted for the variations in forms and the survival of some and not of others? For Darwin the answer was to be found in the conditions of the environment. Those forms which were best able to adjust to the conditions of life survived, and new forms came into being in response to changing conditions. For Mead, Darwin-

2 Ellsworth Faris, "The Social Psychology of George Mead," **American Journal of Sociology**, XLIII (1937), 391–403.

3 Roscoe C., Jr. and Gisela J. Hinkle, **The Development of Modern Sociology: Its Nature and Growth in the United States** (New York: Random House, 1954), pp. 1–9.

4 Albion Woodbury Small, **General Sociology** (Chicago: University of Chicago Press, 1905), p. 443.

ism was a theory of the genesis of forms, a theory that explained the origin of forms and their survival largely in terms of the conditions of the environment. While accepting the basic evolutionary ideas of Darwin, Mead reasoned further that the human form in the course of evolution not only gained control of its environment but also acquired the capacity to determine what the environment would be. Thus, the evolutionary process does not simply play itself out mechanically on man; to a significant extent it is shaped by the activities of man himself. Mead also reasoned that such control could only have arisen through society, not through man as an individual, and that society itself was an "emergent" in the evolutionary process (**MT**, 157–61, 166, 196–97, 252–53, 262).

Out of the general intellectual rebellion against the supernaturalism of the puritan tradition emerged a new school of philosophy known as "pragmatism," and Mead was one of its chief proponents, although he credits John Dewey and William James for having developed the field. In Mead's view, the basic postulate of the pragmatic viewpoint was the assumption that the truth of an idea, or an hypothesis, was to be found not in some abstract, metaphysical system but in the utility of the idea or hypothesis in the empirical world. If an idea or hypothesis "works" then it is to be accepted as a provisional truth. The value of an idea is to be found in its practical consequences. In Mead's view the pragmatic doctrine is simply an expression of the scientific methodology (**MT**, 326–59).

Another formative influence on Mead was that of behaviourism, particularly that of his friend and colleague at the University of Chicago, John B. Watson. Mead adopted a behaviouristic approach to social psychology, but he clearly rejected Watson's conclusions about the character of human thought. In contrast to Watson's mechanical, stimulus-response theories, Mead developed a type of behavioural theory which others have labelled "social behaviourism." While Mead, like Watson, took as his starting point the objective, observable conduct of living forms, he differed from Watson in two key respects: he viewed human conduct as an aspect of the social process, and not as a character of the isolated individual; and he regarded mind as an integral component of the human act.

Mead acknowledged his indebtedness to both Dewey and James, not only for their articulation of pragmatism, but also, and perhaps more importantly, for their work on the mind. Dewey had challenged

the notion of the "reflex arc" concept that was prevalent in mechanistic psychology. According to this principle, the behaviour of the individual organism is nothing but a motor response to a sensory stimulus in the environment. Dewey argued that this type of stimulus-response explanation is grossly inadequate to account for human behaviour, because it fails to consider the process of initiating the act on the part of the individual, and it ignores the constant coordination and readjustment of the motor and sensory processes that take place during the act. Dewey's contribution was to draw out the self-initiated and processual characteristics of human behaviour. From James, Mead acquired a view of mind as a selective, attentive, and relational process. James regarded the mind as a "stream" of mental activities with a past and a future, and not as a static state of consciousness, as has been presupposed in traditional psychology. While Mead accepted in large part these views of mind and clearly incorporated them into his theory of the mind and self, he was not able to accept them fully, for, in his view, the theories of Dewey and James failed to identify the mechanism by which the mind and the self arise.

Mead criticized Charles Horton Cooley for presupposing mind and for failing to isolate the mechanisms by which the self arises, but he was favourably disposed to Cooley's approach to the broader questions of social psychology. Cooley proposed a method of analysis whereby the inner experience of the individual could be grasped by placing oneself in the position of the other in one's imagination, a method known as "sympathetic understanding." Cooley also formulated a view of the self as a mental construct consisting of the imaginations which we and others have of ourselves, a "looking-glass" self that reflects the attitudes of others. While there are only three references to Cooley in **Mind Self and Society**, none of which is complimentary, it is generally felt that Mead was profoundly influenced by Cooley during their association at the University of Michigan.

Lastly, we should mention the influence of Wilhelm Wundt, whose work Mead read carefully during his one semester at Leipzig. This, by no means, suggests that Wundt's influence was any less significant in the formation of Meadian social psychology, for Mead derived his concept of the gesture as a preliminary stage of the act directly from Wundt. However, there is little record of Mead's association with Wundt at Leipzig, and it is not clear whether Mead had any direct contact with his European teacher. Mead's main criticism is that Wundt presupposed a mind that was prior to the process of communication, rather than viewing communication as fundamental to the nature of mind.

This is by no means an exhaustive list of formative influences on the thought of George Herbert Mead. There are others whom we could mention, such as Josiah Royce, Alfred Lloyd, James H. Tufts, and Albion W. Small, who were associated with Mead in different ways. Also, there are the writings of such great thinkers as Kant, Fichte, Schelling, Hegel, and Bergson, to name a few, that formed a backdrop for the evolution of Mead's mind. But the influences of Darwin, James, Dewey, Cooley, Watson, and Wundt particularly stand out in the social psychological writings, as the student will discover in his/her reading of Mead.

There is one notion, however, that arises with the development of evolutionary thought. The notion—the concept of "emergence"—is mentioned at this time since it is basic to Meadian theory. As Mead uses this concept, it refers to the bringing into being of novel forms through a reorganization of previously existing elements. Mead gives the example of water which arises from the combination of hydrogen and oxygen. Water is not present in the elements; it is something that arises from them, but, in the process of creation, it acquires a nature that distinguishes it from the elements, a nature that is not reducible to the parts. An "emergent" is a creation that arises in the evolutionary process through the combination of previously existing elements. It is in this sense that Mead talks about the emergence of mind, self, consciousness, rationality, etc., from the social process (**MSS**, 329–334).

To Summarize: The formative influences in Meadian social psychology can be found in the works of Darwin, Dewey, James, Watson, Cooley, and Wundt. The concept of emergence is basic to the understanding of the theory.

The Nature of Mind

Mead's conception of mind developed through a critique of traditional and contemporary theories. Theories of such men as Royce, Tarde, Baldwin, Giddings, Wundt, and even Cooley, which presupposed a mind whose existence was thought to be prior to the social process, were not acceptable because they could not explain that which they took as logically prior—the origin of mind itself. Not infrequently such a mind was regarded as a kind of "spiritual stuff" or transcendental phenomenon, which meant that it could not be investigated with the methods of science.

Behaviouristic psychology was unacceptable because it either ignored mind altogether or reduced it to physiological processes. Mental phenomena, for such behaviourists as Watson, were explained in terms of conditioned reflexes; thought and consciousness were regarded as inaudible utterances of words resulting from the activity of the muscles of the throat. In Mead's view these theories led to conclusions about language that were clearly absurd (**MSS**, 10–11). Equally unacceptable were the traditional psychologies, dating back to Hume, that conceived of the mind as a static entity residing within the organism and merely receiving impressions from the outside world. The work of James and Dewey, which led to a conception of mind as a continuous "flow" of memory images, perceptions, and anticipations of the future, helped Mead to reject the static conceptions of mind. Mead responded more favourably to the dynamic conception of mind which was implicit in parallelistic psychology, but he was not prepared to accept the separation of thought and action which such a psychology tended to assume. Lastly, he rejected outright individualistic psychology which assumed that the mind was an inalienable property of the pre-social individual and that the individual was the repository of human reason. Such theories were unacceptable because they regarded social phenomena as mere accretions of individual minds.

Mead set out to explain the mind in behaviouristic terms, but he did not intend to reduce mental phenomena to physiological processes. "Mental behavior," Mead writes, "is not reducible to non-mental behavior. But mental behavior or phenomena can be explained in terms of non-mental behavior or phenomena, as arising out of, and as resulting from complications in the latter" (**MSS**, 11). In Mead's view, mind is a peculiarly human attribute which arises in the evolutionary process when the impulsive conduct of the biological organism is thwarted or blocked in its effort to adjust to the environment. Mind, then, emerges out of the non-mental behaviour of pre-human biological forms.

The lower animals respond to the environment in an intelligent way, but they do not "understand" the factors that affect their behaviour and cannot conceive of alternatives. The human animal, on the other hand, is able to isolate and to indicate to himself and to others the values and meanings of those features of the environment to which he is responding, and in so doing, he gains control of them, thus enlarging his field of experience. "Mentality," Mead writes, "simply comes in when the organism is able to point out meanings to others and to itself." Such reflective intelligence is characteristic of the mind, and the mechanism that makes this possible is that of language communication. Mind is the mechanism of control over meaning. In this sense, mind is a functional process serving the interests of the organism in its "adjustment" to the environment. As such, it is an integral part of the act.

The mind is not a substance or an entity, nor is the brain the locus of the mind. The mind "lies in the field of conduct between a specific individual and the environment."[5] As a process, it is selective, purposive, volitional, intentional, and teleological in character, and it serves the interests of the individual.

However, while the mind is an experience of the individual, its origin and character are entirely and wholly social. "The processes of experience which the human brain makes possible are made possible only for a group of interacting individuals: only for individual organisms which are members of a society; not for the individual organism in isolation from other individual organisms" Mind, then, is a social product; it arises out of the social process and is made possible by symbols and meanings which are social in nature. To exercise the mind in relation to physical objects is only possible after the individual has acquired a social self and has gained a facility with what Mead called "significant symbols." Thus, social consciousness is historically prior to physical consciousness.[6]

To Summarize: The foci of Mead's critique of existing theories of mind include: presupposition of a mind that is logically prior to the social process, the reduction of mind to physiological mechanisms, the static view of mind, the separation of thought and action, and the individualistic conception of mind. Mead conceptualized the mind as a functional, volitional, purposive, and sensory process, which sustains the life-process by serving the interests of the organism in its adjustment to the environment. Mind emerges out of the social process and is wholly and entirely social in origin and nature. It is made possible by language.

The Nature of the Self

Early in his career, Mead directed his attention to the question of the origin and development of the self. Simply to pose the question in this manner was to depart from tradition, for, in individualistic psychology and in the social psychology of some of Mead's contemporaries, such as Charles Horton Cooley, there was a pronounced tendency to presuppose a self that was logically prior to the social process. In other words, the self was taken as a "given," as a thing that possessed qualities and characteristics—motives, needs, desires, instincts, ideals, etc.—that played a specific determinative role in shaping human conduct. From this point of view the social process was seen as a product of prior minds and selves.

Mead found two problems with these theories. First, such theories could not explain that which they take as logically prior; they could not explain the existence of the self. Second, such individualistic theories of the self could not account for the social process, since the social process can operate, as it apparently does in the societies of the lower biological forms, without the existence of conscious selves. By conceptualizing the social process as logically prior to and as a condition of the emergence of minds and selves, Mead felt that the origin and character of the self could be explained rather than taken for granted.

However, in asserting a social theory of the self, Mead did not simply presuppose the human social process from which minds and selves arose; he accounted for it in terms of a "biosocial" process, which operates in nature. In Mead's view, biological organisms are drawn together by physiological impulses which complete themselves through the involvement of organisms in a common social act, as for example, in the case of reproduction, mutual protection, and the securing of food. It is out of this natural biosocial process that minds, selves and human societies emerge.

The self is not initially there at birth; it emerges in the social process and undergoes continuous development within that process throughout the life of the individual. However, the self is not completely submerged in society. Once it has arisen it can provide social experience for itself; it can play back upon the social process and affect subsequent development of both itself and the process. While Mead referred to the self as a social structure, it is quite clear that he regarded the self as a process, as a "phase" of a larger ongoing social process.

Although the self is dependent on the biological and physiological nature of man, it is qualitatively different from the physiological organism and cannot be reduced to physiological impulses. The specific "content" of the self is derived not from the biological organism but from the social process. While we tend

---

5 George H. Mead, "A Behavioristic Account of the Significant Symbol," **Journal of Philosophy,** XIX (1922), 163.

6 George H. Mead, "What Social Objects Must Psychology Presuppose?" **Journal of Philosophy,** VII (1910), 178.

to organize our bodily experiences about the self, as for example, when we say "my toe," "my face," "my back," the body can act in an intelligent way without involving a self, and the self can experience itself without involving the body. Thus, the self can be distinguished in a very definite way from the biological organism and should not be confused with it.

The distinguishing characteristic of the self is its capacity to be an object to itself. Just as we say "my face," "my book," "my friend," as we refer to certain objects about us, so we say "my self." But what is the nature of the creature whose self it is that I possess? It is a creature which appears to be simultaneously both a subject and an object. But how can one be both subject and object at the same time? One can be both subject and object by taking the attitudes of others towards one's self. One gets outside of one's self, so to speak, and "observes" the self from the standpoint of others. One can experience himself as a self or individual "only insofar as he first becomes an object to himself just as other individuals are objects to him or in his experience; and he becomes an object to himself only by taking the attitudes of the other individuals towards himself within a social environment." Thus, consciousness of self and, indeed, consciousness itself, including consciousness of one's private subjective experiences, is possible only when the individual takes the organized attitudes of the community towards himself.

Such reflexivity is made possible, in Mead's view, by a form of communication involving "significant symbols," which are gestures, usually vocal gestures, that arouse in oneself the same attitudes that they arouse in others. Simply put, reflexivity is made possible by language. Thus, one comes to have a self and become conscious of one's self by applying to one's self the words and meanings which he derives from the community in which he lives. How else can I know myself except by taking the words that you use to describe me to describe myself? "I am what I think you think I am." In this sense, the self is a mental or linguistic construct.

To Summarize: The self emerges in the social process and is not prior to it. It undergoes continuous development within that process and plays a part in shaping it. The self has a character that is qualitatively different from the biological organism and cannot be explained in terms of physiological impulses. It has the capacity to experience itself as an object by taking the attitudes of the community towards itself. It is a social product that is made possible by language.

The Nature of Society

Of the three basic notions in Meadian social psychology, "society" is the least developed. It may be for this reason that "mind" and "self" have received considerably more attention from sociologists and philosophers alike. Part of the neglect may well stem from the ambiguity of the term itself. Is society a process or a structure? Is it reducible to the interaction of biological forms, or is it a phenomenon *sui generis*, a thing in its own right, that is qualitatively different from the biological organisms that participate in it?

Whatever else society is in Mead's theoretical system, it is first and foremost a process, a process from which minds and selves arise and through which they develop, and without which there would be no minds and selves. However, there is a double sense in Mead's use of the term "social process." On the one hand, social process refers to the interaction of logically pre-human biological forms. "The behavior of all living organisms has a basically social aspect: the fundamental biological or physiological impulses and needs which lie at the basis of all such behavior—especially those of hunger and sex, those connected with nutrition and reproduction—are impulses and needs which, in the broadest sense, are social in character or have social implications, since they involve or require social situations and relations for their satisfaction by any given individual organism; and they thus constitute the foundation of all types or forms of social behavior, however simple or complex, crude or highly organized, rudimentary or well developed." It is out of this rudimentary form of social interaction involving biological organisms that human symbolic interaction emerges, and it is the latter which gives rise to and is co-extensive with minds and selves. Thus, there are two types of social processes—biosocial and symbolic—in which man participates, and he participates in these simultaneously.

The basic unit of the social process is the "act," which can be regarded as a "segment" of behaviour, which takes place over time, and which unfolds in a comprehensible and related sequence of activity. For Mead, the act involves an "impulse" (an attitude of readiness to act), a "stimulus" (identification of an object in the environment that will serve as an occasion for the release of the impulse), and the response" (the coordinated action that follows). For example, a student may want to write a sociology essay (impulse), he may go to the library to search for appropriate material (stimulus), and then he may sit down to make notes of the relevant passages (response). A social act takes place in a social environment and involves social objects. In a very important sense, society is a coordinated series of social acts.

However, human societies involve symbolic communication, which in turn presupposes the existence of a common fund of universal symbols and meanings shared by the community. In addition, there are what Mead termed "generalized social attitudes" that call out common social responses, as, for example, in the assertion of a property right that is recognized by the community. For Mead, a cluster of such common responses constitutes an institution, and society is made up of such institutions. Thus, society can quite rightly be regarded as a configuration of generalized social attitudes. In this sense, the notion of society is not unlike what anthropologists refer to as "culture."

While Mead regarded society as a process that evolved naturally through time, it would be quite misleading to say that Mead had no conception of social structure. While he did not assert, as did Durkheim, that society was a phenomenon *sui generis*, as a reality that possessed qualities different from the individuals that made it up, he did set out to explain the conduct of the individual in relation to the social whole. "For social psychology, the whole (society) is prior to the part (the individual), not the part to the whole; and the part is explained in terms of the whole, not the whole in terms of the part or parts." Further, and perhaps more importantly for our present purposes, Mead did envision society, especially modern, industrial society, as an evolving, functionally differentiated constellation of social roles. Note the following: "Ultimately and fundamentally societies developed in complexity of organization only by means of the progressive achievement of greater and greater degrees of functional, behavioristic differentiation among the individuals who constitute them"

To Summarize: Mead regarded society largely as a process of interaction. Man participates in two qualitatively different social processes—biosocial and symbolic—with the latter emerging from but not reducible to the former. In each process, the basic unit is the act, and society can be regarded as a coordinated series of acts. Human societies are organized in terms of "generalized social attitudes" or institutions. They are also organized along functionally differentiated lines.

Biosocial and Symbolic Interaction

We have already drawn attention to the distinction between biosocial and symbolic processes. In this section we will discuss this distinction in the context of interaction and attempt to clarify the relation of the one process to the other.

For Mead, all living organisms are involved in social behaviour by virtue of the fact that the fundamental physiological impulses require a social nexus for their gratification. In his essay, "The Biologic Individual," Mead outlines what he refers to as a "roughly fashioned catalog of primitive impulses." These are the impulses or instincts that initially impel the organism to act. When the behaviour of one individual form serves as a stimulus for another living form to respond, the two forms can be said to be engaged in a common social act. Such cooperative activity, in Mead's view, constitutes social interaction. However, such interaction is the interaction of biological organisms—whether animal or human—and does not involve an interpretation of the act on the part of the participants. It is "unconscious" activity which takes place directly and is not mediated by symbols. Human beings sometimes engage in such interaction, as for example, when one is startled by a shout or loud noise made by another individual.

However, if one is conscious of the meaning of the shout, if one interprets the shout to mean "help" or "look out" the interaction that follows will be structured in term of the meanings and symbols that are shared by the participants in the act. In this sense interaction is symbolic, and it is this kind of interaction in which Mead was primarily interested.

The capacity to engage in symbolic interaction is a peculiarly human attribute which arises in the evolutionary process of man. It emerges out of the biosocial process when impulsive conduct breaks down. "Where the act fails to realize its function, when the impulsive effort to get food does not bring food—and, more especially, where conflicting impulses thwart and inhibit each other—here reasoning may come in with a new procedure that is not at the disposal of the biologic individual." Such reasoning increases the scope of options for the human individual and considerably enlarges his universe of experience.

However, while human reasoning and symbolic communication operate according to principles which are different from those governing the biological organisms, and therefore are not reducible to the latter, rational conduct and impulsive behaviour are not entirely separate spheres of activity; they are related in a very definite way. Mead felt that the primitive impulses of man were subject to infinite modification in the social process; thus, they did not determine human conduct in the same way that instincts determine the conduct of lower forms. The behaviour of man is largely a consequence of the process of symbolic interaction, not the biosocial process. Yet, the behaviour is put into motion by the primitive biosocial endowment of man. We might say that the impulses of the biological organism provide the "undifferentiated motivational energy" which the human individual converts into specific forms of self-conscious behaviour through the medium of symbols. For all intents and purposes, then, we may disregard the contributions of the biological organisms to the behaviour of man, although we must remember that the symbolic interactive process has its origin in the biosocial process.

To Summarize: Biosocial interaction, which does not involve consciousness, stems from primitive impulses which are part of the endowment of the biological organism. Symbolic interaction springs from the biosocial process, but is not reducible to it. In human symbolic interaction the primitive impulses are reshaped in the social process into "attitudes" and "motives" which are specifically symbolic in character.

The Act

At the very outset, Mead identifies a starting point for his social psychology—"an observable activity—the dynamic, on-going social process, and the social acts which are its component elements." He explicitly states that the act is the "fundamental datum" in behaviouristic psychology. Yet as important as the act is in Mead's theoretical system, there is no explicit, systematic treatment of the concept of **Mind, Self and Society**. In **The Philosophy of the Act**, Mead discusses the act from the standpoint of the subject, outlining the four stages of impulse, perception, manipulation, and consummation in considerable detail, but this provides little help to the student who may be struggling to grasp the meaning of the concept from the objective standpoint in the social psychological writings. In this section, we will attempt to put together from various statements in Mead's work a sketch of the main features of the act and the social act from the objective standpoint.

Mead defines an act as "an on-going event that consists of stimulation and response and the results of the response" (**PA,** 364). But the stimulus is not "the given" in the environment which determines

conduct, since temporally and logically prior to the stimulus and the response are the "attitudes and impulses of the individual" which seek out the appropriate stimuli that will set free the response. In Mead's view, the phases of the act constitute "a dynamic whole . . . no part of which can be considered or understood by itself." The act is a process with coterminous and contingent phases.

An important feature of the act is its self-initiated character. As Mead notes, "the organism is not simply a something that is receiving impressions and then answering to them. It is not a sensitive protoplasm that is simply receiving these stimuli from without and then responding to them. The organism is doing something," In Mead's view, the impulses and attitudes sensitize the individual to the environment and determine what the stimulus will be. In Mead's words, "in the process of acting we are continually selecting just what elements in the field of stimulation will set the response successfully free."

By viewing ongoing-social activity, involving an inner and an outer aspect, as fundamental, and by stressing the self-initiated behaviour of the individual, Mead escapes the criticism that had been levelled at the stimulus-response theory. In Watson's behaviouristic psychology, the organism is merely a passive entity responding to external stimuli that are given in the environment. By contrast, Mead views the organism, especially the human organism, as an active and dynamic creature who not only selects from the environment, but also, and more importantly, determines what that environment will be.

While the act is self-initiated, the act is a dynamic whole, which means that it cannot be explained entirely in terms of impulses and attitudes of the individual organism. The earlier and later phases mutually determine one another. As Mead notes: "The later stages of the act are present in the early stages—not simply in the sense that they are all ready to go off, but in the sense that they serve to control the process itself. They determine how we are going to approach the object, and the steps in our early manipulation of it" (**MSS** 11). As one approaches an object, say a hammer, one has some idea of what he is going to do with it when he reaches the object. Thus, the "end in view" plays a significant part in determining the process. We may describe this character of the act as teleological.

While there appear to be four stages of the act—impulse, stimulus, response, and result of the response—these can be reduced to three for our present purposes—impulse, stimulus, and response.

Mead defines an "impulse" as "a congenital tendency to react in a specific manner to a certain sort of stimulus, under certain organic conditions" (**MSS**, 337), but it is clear that he has in mind here the primitive impulses of the biological organism. But as we have already noted, the primitive impulses of man are subject to extensive modification in the life-process. Further, conscious reasoning occurs in man when impulsive conduct is inhibited or blocked. While reasoning is never detached from the impulsive substratum of human life, its "content" is derived not from the biological organism, but from the social process. The impulse phase of the act for humans is expressed in "attitudes" which have a symbolic character to them.

An attitude Mead defines as "the adjustment of the organism involved in an impulse ready for expression" (**MSS**, 362). For all intents and purposes, we can regard human "attitudes" as symbolic and social, rather than organic. A "stimulus" is the "occasion for the expression of the impulse." The stimulus is not the primary cause of behaviour, as the mechanistic behavioural psychologies would have us believe; it is an "object of interest" in the environment which the intelligent organism selects as the occasion for the release of the impulse. "Stimuli are means, tendency is the real thing. Intelligence is the selection of stimuli that will set free and maintain life and aid in rebuilding it." The "response" is the reply of the individual to the stimulus that completes the act initiated by the impulse. The stimulus, then, is the "vehicle" through which the impulse expresses itself in the act.

A "social" act is one "in which the occasion or stimulus which sets free an impulse is found in the character or conduct of a living form that belongs to the proper environment of the living form whose impulse it is." A social act involves some sort of cooperative activity between and among individuals. Its added complexity stems from the fact that the response of one individual may serve as a stimulus for another individual involved in the same act. As we will see later, it is this form of act that serves as the basis for the genesis of the self.

To Summarize: The act is the basic unit of the social process. It is a dynamic whole with three discernible phases—impulse, stimulus, and response. It is a self-initiated, selective, teleological process which relates the organism to the environment. In a social act the environment includes other living forms.

Organism, Objects and the Environment

We tend to regard the environment as pre-existing, as something that is "just there," into which organisms enter and within which organisms live out their lives. This view fails to take into account the determination of the environment by the organism, and by this Mead does not mean simply the erection of buildings and bridges. It is a determination that is given in nature.

It is determination that stems from the sensitivity of the organism to its environment. Objects come to be what they are by virtue of their relations to the living organisms whose environment they form. In themselves, they are meaningless. Mead gives the example of an animal, such as an ox, that can digest grass, entering the world. At this point grass becomes food; it did not exist as food prior to the entry of the ox into the world. In this sense, the ox determines its environment by its sensitivity to it. In the same manner, the eye and the sensory processes of man endow objects with their characteristics and meaning.

Thus, the environment does not simply consist of objects that exist "out there"; rather, it emerges for the organism as a result of its "impulses seeing expression, a process that is selective." "Apart from such an experience involving both the form and its environment," Mead writes, "such objects do not exist."[7] This is not to suggest that objects are figments of one's imagination; rather, it is to state that objects acquire their distinctive characteristics and meaning only in relation to living forms. As Mead writes, "external objects are there independent of the experiencing individual, nevertheless they possess certain characteristics by virtue of their relation to his experiencing or to his mind, which they would not possess otherwise or apart from those relations."

It is important to note at this time that such characteristics, which come into being by virtue of the sensitivity of the organism to its environment, constitute the "meaning" of the objects. Thus, the meaning of things and, reality itself, reside neither in the external world nor in the living form, but, rather, within the interrelations between the two.

Intelligence is the capacity of the organism to sustain the life-process through successful adjustments to the environment. Animals possess such intelligence but they do not possess the capacity to engage in conscious reasoning. Thus, they cannot be aware of the meanings of the objects which consti-

---

7 George H. Mead, "A Behavioristic Account of the Significant Symbol," **Journal of Philosophy**, XIX (1922), 158.

tute their environment, and, therefore, they are unconsciously governed by them. The human individual, on the other hand, possesses reflective intelligence, which makes it possible for him to gain consciousness of the meanings of the objects in his environment. This capacity frees him from the determination of his biological endowment and enables him to greatly expand his universe of experience. For the human individual, both the form and the environment are subject to extensive modification and development. Man's environment is considerably larger and more diverse than that of the environment of lower animals, and this environment is continually being enlarged by the human mind.

One more point needs to be mentioned in this section. It will be recalled that reflective intelligence is the capacity of a human mind that is wholly and entirely social in origin, nature, and content. Thus, the environment of man, including the universe of physical objects, is socially constructed.

To Summarize: The organism creates its own environment through its sensitivity to "objects." Objects exist as relations to the organisms whose environment they form. The meaning of an object is to be found in its relation to the organism. The reflective intelligence of man enables him to comprehend meaning and to enlarge his universe of experience. The environment of man is socially constructed.

Attitudes, Gestures, and Significant Symbols

We have already noted that an "attitude" was part of the impulse stage of the act. It refers to the readiness of an organism that is about to behave in a particular way. When an attitude of one living form serves as a stimulus for another form, implicated in the same social act, to respond and thus to carry out its part of the whole act, we have what Mead called a "gesture." A gesture, then, is part of the social act and is the basic mechanism through which the social process takes place. It initiates the act and calls out a response from another living form. In this sense, the later stages of the act are signalled in the gesture.

However, the response of the second form to the gesture of the first does not normally follow in a mechanical fashion, and does not normally terminate the act. In the social process, the response of the second organism becomes a stimulus to the first and, therefore, becomes a gesture for the first to respond. This type of mutual stimulation and mutual adjustment of living forms Mead referred to as the "conversation of gestures." To illustrate this process Mead used his favourite example of the dog-fight. The bark of one dog stimulates the second to attack or retreat; the response of the second in turn causes the first dog to change its position and its attitude, and so on. Thus, the act is continually being modified in the course of its unfolding. The impulse-stimulus-response process is a continuous, staggered, two-way stream of coordinated activity.

There are two characteristics of the gesture that need to be drawn out. First, the gesture is an integral part of the organization of the social act and is not primarily an expression of the emotional life of the individual. Second, gestures which are not significant symbols, do not involve a consciousness of meaning; they merely call out the impulsive responses of the organism.

The "conversation of gestures" is basically an unconscious process. The interacting forms do not have an awareness of the meaning of their gestures; their responses take place directly and are not mediated by conscious thought or reflection. The dog does not think about the effect his bark will have on the other dog; nor does he adjust his behaviour in terms of his anticipation of the other dog's response. To do that he would have to be able to indicate to himself the attitudes which his gestures evoke in the other dog. He would have to understand the meaning of his gesture, and the gesture would now become a "significant symbol."

To use Mead's words, "gestures become significant symbols when they implicitly arouse in an individual making them the same response which they explicitly arouse, or are supposed to arouse in other individuals, the individuals to whom they are addressed." Gestures that particularly lend themselves to this type of double stimulation are vocal gestures. Thus, it is largely through language that the human individual signifies meanings to himself and to others. For example, if a boy says to a girl, "May I have this dance?" his gestures (words) arouse in himself the same attitudes that they are intended to arouse in the girl. If she says, "Yes," as he hopes she will, her response will arouse in each of them the same attitudes, and they will proceed to dance. In this form of interaction, meaning is constantly being introduced in each successive stage, and the process continues until it reaches a conclusion which may or may not be mutually desired. Even if the conclusion is not desired by one of the participants in the act, the meanings of the gestures are quite clear to each of them throughout the process. This form of interaction is quite different from the dog-fight.

When an individual becomes conscious of the

meaning of his gestures, his gestures become significant symbols. Such consciousness becomes possible when the individual is able to take the attitudes of others toward his gestures. He comes to know what his gestures mean only from the standpoint of others involved in the social act. In a broader context, he comes to know the meaning of his gestures only by taking the attitudes of the community towards them. Thus, significant symbols are social in origin and nature, and they facilitate the human social process by providing an effective mechanism for the mutual adjustment of individuals. They are also the very foundation of minds and selves, as we will see in the sections that follow.

To Summarize: An attitude becomes a gesture when it serves as a stimulus for another form involved in a social act. A gesture is the initial stage of the act. A "conversation of gestures" is an unconscious process of mutual stimulation and adjustment. A gesture becomes a significant symbol when it arouses in the individual gesturer the same attitudes which are aroused in the other. Significant symbols are social in origin and character.

Meaning and Consciousness

We have stated that the meaning of an object is to be found in the relation of that object to the organism. In this section we take up the question of meaning further in the context of the social process.

Just as objects have meaning for individuals, so do gestures, especially the gestures of living forms involved in a social act. As we have already suggested, the meaning of a gesture is the response of another living form engaged in the same social act. As Mead illustrates, the response of a chick to the cluck of the mother hen is the meaning of the cluck. Thus, meaning is objectively there in the social act; it is a "development of something objectively there as a relation between certain phases of the social act." It is important to note that meaning is not a mental phenomenon or state of consciousness lying within the individual's mind; it lies in the field of experience.

Meaning, then, is an aspect of the social process or, more specifically, a feature of the social act. It arises within the context of interaction and involves a threefold relationship of the gesture of the first organism, the response of the second to the gesture, and the results of the gesture expressed in the act. To repeat, meaning is to be found in the context of interaction, in the responses of the organism to the gesture; it cannot be found in either the nature of the object or in the psychical structure of the organism.

Just as objects emerge and acquire meaning by virtue of their relations to the organism whose environment they form (as in the case of grass becoming food for the ox), so the mutual adjustments of organisms engaged in a social act generate meanings for the interacting participants. New characteristics of objects "emerge" in this process, and the environment is expanded beyond the limits of the physical universe.

However, such meaning does not necessarily involve consciousness. Consciousness, as awareness of meaning, occurs only when the individual stimulates himself implicitly in the same way that his gesture stimulates others explicitly—in other words, when he engages in significant symbolization. It is in this process that the individual not only acquires the capacity to indicate meanings to himself and to others, but it is through this process that the individual, in concert with others, creates a whole new world of meanings and, therefore, enlarges his universe of experience beyond that given in nature. This is what Mead means when he states that language "does not simply symbolize a situation or object which is already there in advance; it makes possible the existence or the appearance of that situation or object, for it is part of the mechanism whereby that situation or object is created."

Consciousness of meaning becomes possible only within the social process and is not prior to it. The medium through which consciousness of meaning is expressed is language. As Mead states: "The language symbol is simply a significant or conscious gesture." Further, language symbols are necessarily social in origin and character; in other words, they are necessarily shared. It is impossible to possess a symbol that has meaning only for an individual. A solitary symbol is simply a contradiction in terms. In this sense significant symbols are universal in character; they transcend the experiences of particular individuals.

The implications of this are twofold. On the one hand, it is possible to grasp the meaning of particular things and events only by employing universal categories of thought, i.e., shared symbols. On the other hand, it is possible to transcend the particular things or events by using shared symbols to express their general or universal characteristics. For example, to express the meaning of the particular object you presently have in your possession, you may use symbols—such as "module," "sociological," "theoretical"—all of which are universal in the sense that they are held in common and are shared. At the same time, you may want to abstract or "lift out" from this particular object certain general or universal features which will enable you to express similar experiences in relation to a wide variety of other particular things. Such words as "theoretical, "sociological," "learning experiences," etc., can be applied to all sorts of other experiences. These examples illustrate the double character of significant symbols: they are always social, never individual; they are always general, never particular. In this respect the social and the universal features of language are one and the same.

The locus of meaning is the field of experience, not the mind. The meaning of a gesture is the response of the organism to the gesture. Consciousness of meaning occurs with significant symbolization. Symbols are necessarily universal.

Genesis of the Self

Above we outlined the general characteristics of the social self. In this section we will discuss the conditions which make possible the origin and development of the self.

While we are born into a pre-existing society, each of us enters the world initially without a self. The self, we have said, emerges in social conduct, which during the early stages of one's life is unconscious. The needs of the newborn infant—food, comfort, shelter, etc.—are met in a social context. Social interaction takes place between the mother and the child, but, from the standpoint of the child, such interaction occurs on a biosocial level. In keeping with Mead, we could say that the child participates in a conversation of gestures, stimulating and being stimulated by the care of the mother. Such unconscious social activity is a precondition for the emergence of the self.

It is out of such unconscious communication that conscious communication and self arise. An infant is not aware of the meaning of his gestures; he may cry when he is hungry, but the crying is an expression of a physiological, not a conscious, state. He does not say, "Gee, I'm hungry; I think I'll cry, for that will summon my mother to bring food." Yet, his cry does stimulate his mother to bring food, and the life-process is sustained. However, one day, when the child cries and the mother does not appear, he will complete the social act on the level of imagination; he will imagine his mother appearing with the food, and he will at that moment acquire consciousness of the meaning of his gesture (his cry). This is another way of saying that the child is able to take the attitudes of

his mother toward his gesture and that he is beginning to gain facility with significant symbols (language). But before any young mother who reads this text starves her child to death in an effort to speed up its linguistic development, we must hasten to add that the capacity to symbolically complete an inhibited act develops in the child at a certain stage of physiological maturity, and this is determined in large part by the child's genetic endowment. In any event, it is in this process that the difference between man and animals lies. Man and the animals both use signs and gestures, but only man uses symbols with conscious intent, symbols which result initially from the ability to complete an inhibited act on the level of imagination.

It is the inhibited act that gives rise to consciousness and meaning, and consciousness and meaning develop out of unconscious communication within the social process.[8] It is essentially the same process that gives rise to the self, because it is in such a process that the individual acquires the ability to take himself as an object. While taking the attitudes of others toward his gestures, the individual is indicating something to himself at the same time that he is indicating something to another. During this process, the individual necessarily comes back upon himself as an object of knowledge; he indicates himself to himself. At this point, he is not only an agent satisfying his needs but is a self-conscious being, taking the attitudes of others toward himself. Self, self-consciousness, and language (significant symbols), then, are phases of the same process, and it would be quite correct to say that they mutually imply each other.

In addition to language as a social condition under which the self arises as an object, Mead draws attention to two other situations in which this happens, namely in play and the game. The genesis of the self involves the ordering of social experiences in terms of a role. This process we refer to as role taking. In the early stages of development, the child plays at being various other individuals, taking first this role and then another. He plays at being mother, father, fireman, postman, and so forth. The child takes the particular attitudes of others and plays at various individual roles; he takes the role of the particular other. It is through play that the child learns to organize attitudes into specific clusters which we call roles.

In the organized game the child must be pre-

8 George H. Mead, "What Social Objects Must Psychology Presuppose?" **Journal of Philosophy**, VII (1910), 179.

pared not only to take the role of other individuals individually, but he must also take the attitudes of the organized group as a whole. The team can be seen as a "cluster" of roles, a cluster, however, that is organized and structured; it is the "structure" of the whole that calls out the attitudes which a child must take in order to play the game. Complex, coordinated activity, as takes place in a game, is sustained not by the particular attitudes of individuals *per se*, but by general principles or rules. We can say that the attitudes have been "generalized," because they reflect the organization of the whole social group and cannot be reduced to the attitudes of individual members. When the individual takes the organized attitudes of the whole social group toward himself, he takes the attitudes of the "generalized other;" and only when he is able to take the attitudes of the generalized other toward himself is he able to acquire a fully developed self.

To Summarize: Consciousness and self emerge out of unconscious social activity. Significant symbols and language emerge with the ability of an individual to complete an inhibited act on the level of imagination. Significant symbols make self-reflection possible. The development of the self involves the importation and organization of attitudes, first in the form of particular roles, and second in the form of the "generalized other."

The Generalized Other

As we have noted, the "generalized other" is the organized set of attitudes of the social group or community taken as a whole. It was Mead's contention that the importation of the generalized other into the experiences of the individual is a necessary condition for the development of a complete self. In Mead's view, the individual acquires selfhood by virtue of taking the attitudes of the generalized other. This is another way of saying that the self or personality is a structure of attitudes adopted from the community. We can go one step further and say that the imported self and the generalized other are phases of the same reality—an organized set of attitudes reflecting the organization of life in the community.

Mead was convinced that there was nothing in the biological inheritance of man that could organize his social experiences for him. Such organization must come from the outside, since it is not evident in the child at birth or during the early stages of development. By importing the attitudes of the generalized other, the individual structures his experiences and provides coherence to his life. It is in relation to the

generalized other that the human individual is able to act intelligently in his environment, including his physical environment, for it is the generalized attitudes of the community that imbue his universe with meaning. At one and the same tine, such attitudes the self and the environment.

It is the generalized other that makes linguistic communication and thought possible, for significant symbols are themselves expressions of the generalized other. This is especially true in abstract thought. As Mead notes, "abstract concepts are concepts stated in terms of the attitudes of the entire social group or community." And it is equally true in "private" conversations that one has with oneself. And it is no less true with scientific thought; universal categories are social in origin and character.

While the generalized other provides organization for the self, it also represents the control of the community over the individual. By internalizing the attitudes of the community, one adopts its patterned life and becomes subject to its laws and regulations. On the other hand, one acquires a measure of control over things, as for example, when one asserts a property or civil right. In such instances one is evoking the attitudes of the generalized other.

To Summarize: The individual acquires a self by importing the attitudes of the generalized other. The generalized other provides organization and meaning to an individual's experience. Categories of thought are phases of the generalized other. The generalized other represents the control of the community over the individual and ensures an orderly, organized collective life.

Phases of the Self ("I" and the "Me")

The self is not merely an importation of the organized set of attitudes of the community. There is also involved in the self a response of the individual whose self it is. Mead distinguished between the "me" (representing the individual's importation of the organized set of attitudes of the community) from the "I" (which is the response of the individual to the attitudes of the generalized other). The "I" and the "me" are parts of the whole self which arises in the process of symbolic communication. By taking the attitudes of others we introduce the "me," and we react to it as an "I."

The "I" is the response of the individual to the organized attitudes of the community, but it is always something uncertain and unpredictable. It is the impulsive, imaginative, novel aspect of the organism and represents the assertion of the self over against the attitudes of the community, the latter serving as a social control which sets the limits for the spontaneous and creative "I." It is through the "I" that new attitudes are introduced into our common fund of attitudes which make up our institutions. Normally institutions are flexible enough to incorporate such new expressions of thought and action.

The "I" and the "me," although appearing in experience as separate and distinguishable characteristics of the individual, are parts of a single whole and belong together, and together they constitute a personality or self in the experience of the individual. Essentially, the self is a social process with two distinguishable phases, one phase answering to the organized life of the community and ensuring responsibility in the conduct of the individual, and the other phase providing the basis for novelty in experience. In other words, the self embodies in one and the same process (or structure) an internalization of the social attitudes of the community and the expressions of the impulsive, creative, subjective aspects of the individual. Mead sees no contradiction between the social and individual aspects of experience; in fact, one is seen as necessary for the other. The impulsive, creative inclinations of the individual realize themselves only by structuring experiences in relation to the attitudes of the generalized other. Only by assuming the attitudes of the community can an individual get a complex situation into his experience, and this provides the backdrop or foil over against which the individual plays out his creative tendencies.

There is one further point that needs to be made with regard to the character of the "I." Mead recognized that the self could not appear in consciousness as an "I," but only as the objective "me." In Mead's words, "such an 'I' is a presupposition, but never a presentation of conscious experience, for the moment it is presented it has passed into the objective case, presuming, if you like, an 'I' that observes—but an 'I' that can disclose himself only by ceasing to be the subject for whom the object 'me' exists."[9] Thus, the "I" can never become an object of knowledge. To let Mead speak, "it is only the 'me'—the empirical self— that can be perceived. The 'I' lies beyond the range of immediate experience." Further, "the self-conscious, actual self in social intercourse is the objective 'me' or 'mes' with the process of response continually going on and implying, a *fictitious* 'I' always out of

sight of himself."[10] Mead gives the "I" a central position in his social psychology, criticizing positivistic psychology for ignoring the creative aspect of the self, but he is forced to conceptualize the "I" as a theoretical presupposition, an implied reality always prior to the moment and observable only in retrospect, at which time it no longer exists as an "I" but as a "me."

To Summarize: The self presents itself in two distinguishable phases—"I" and the "me," the latter representing the organized attitudes of the community, the former expressing the creative, uncertain response of the individual. The "I" realizes itself within and in relation to the community. There is no contradiction between the "I" and the "me." The "I" exists only at the moment of experience and can never be an object of knowledge.

Self and Social Process

In the preceding sections we identified some of the salient features of the social self. In this section, we focus on some aspects of the self in relation to the social process, in particular to the essence of the self, unity and scope of the self, differentiation of the self, and the problem of individuality.

In Mead's view, the essence of mind is its rationality, and, since the self is a mental construct, the self is essentially a cognitive, rather than an affective, structure—a rational rather than an emotional phenomenon. Mead rejects any attempt to root the organizing principle of the self in the pre-social nature of the human being, whether that nature is conceived primarily as a biological or an affective substratum of life. In other words, Mead does not accept the view that the instincts (or primitive impulses) or the feelings of man constitute the primary basis of the self. Even the theories of Cooley and James, which conceive the self as an organization of reflective experience in terms of an emotional core (or "self-feeling") were unacceptable, since they could not account for either the self or the emotional core. The organization of experience had to come from the outside, from the social process, and the expression of that experience took the form of significant symbols. The essence of the self had to be cognitive, and its character was social. And it follows that, since institutions are essentially established phases of the social process, they too are cognitive structures. The objective self and the institution are the embodiments of

---

9 George H. Mead, "The Social Self," **Journal of Philosophy**, X (1913), 374 (emphasis added).

10 George H. Mead, "The Mechanism of Social Consciousness," **Journal of Philosophy**, IX (1912), 406.(emphasis added).

human reason and constrain the emotional and impulsive tendencies in man.

We have already alluded to Mead's assertion that the unity of the self reflects the unity of the social process, that the complete self mirrors the social process as a whole. It necessarily follows that the enlargement of the self occurs with the expansion of the social process. The expansion of the social process, then, holds out considerable potential for the individual; at the same time it is a precondition for the enlargement of the self and establishes the limits of the self. The self, then, cannot exceed or transcend the social process, cannot live a life of uniqueness and novelty outside of it. Yet, Mead did insist that each of us injects novelty into the stream of society some of the time, and some individuals, such as artists and scientists, are expected to do so as a matter of course. How, then, can the self and the social process be enlarged? In Mead's view this could occur with the enlargement of the mind. There are two characteristics of the mind that make such enlargement possible—its emergence and its universality. The first leads to novelty (not novelty for its own sake, but for the sake of problem-solving), and the second leads to transcendence. When patterned or impulsive conduct breaks down, the human individual, through the exercise of reflective intelligence, invents or discovers alternative modes of conduct. However, to "validate" and to "preserve" the discovery, it is necessary to express it in significant symbols, which by their very nature are universal and social in character. The experience becomes universalized in the social process, and the process becomes enlarged.

Just as there are different parts of society, different social groups, organizations, classes, etc., so there must be different parts to the self. The self reflects the differentiated, structured life of the community and therefore is itself a differentiated structure. Further, the individual participates in a number of social groups within the community and stands in a relation to each of these in much the same way that he stands in relation to the whole community. The process of generalizing attitudes and importing them into the structure of the self is qualitatively the same in the two cases. Thus, it would be quite in keeping with Mead's theory to say that each of us possesses several "mes" each reflecting a significant group in the life of the individual. Such "mes" are necessarily integrated into a comprehensive "me" which reflects the attitudes of the whole community. We may want to refer to the first as a "mini-me" (a term we just invented,

so please help to universalize it) to distinguish it from the more comprehensive "me" of the complete self.

If the socialized individual is a reflection of the society of which he is a part, in what sense is it possible to talk about individuality? Mead answered this question first by saying that, while each individual reflects the organized life of the community, he does so from his particular standpoint, from his location in the social structure. Each individual occupies a place in the community which is different from that of any other individual; thus, he reflects the structure of the whole from a slightly different perspective. What we internalize, then, differs slightly in its particularities from that of every other individual. But does that mean that individuality is nothing but a unique reflection of the social process? Are we nothing but unique constellations of social roles which, like snow flakes, are carved from the same social stuff? Mead's answer to this question can be found in his conceptualization of the "I" and the "me." The latent individuality of the "I" comes into being only in the response to the "me"; it is the "me" that makes the "I" possible by providing the objective content which the "I" can fashion into a unique response. There is nothing inherent in social institutions that opposes the full expression of the individual; on the contrary, social institutions are the very embodiments of the expression of the "I's" of previous generations. Therefore, institutions are constituent of individuality. There is a third sense in which individuality expresses itself in the social processes, and that is as a functionally differentiated part of an organized whole. Differentiated roles provide opportunities for individuals to develop their unique capacities and talents. It stands to reason that, the more functionally differentiated a society is, the more provision there will be for individual expression. In Mead's view, functional differentiation in society is itself the expression of individuality in the evolutionary process.

To Summarize: The essence of the self is cognitive. The enlargement of the self and the extension of the social process occur through the expansion of the mind. The self is a differentiated structure. Individuality stems from one's particular location in the social structure, from the assertion of the "I," and from participation in one or more differentiated social roles.

Social Organization

To this point, we have talked about the social process, and much less about society. This is due, in no small measure, to the fact that Mead himself conceptualized social life as a process. Yet, in the latter parts of **Mind, Self, and Society** there emerges a vision of society as a socially structured whole.

First, it is important to note that, in Mead's view, all living forms live in societies, which is to say that living forms exist in groups and that the contacts and interrelations among the organisms constitute an essential condition of life. As we have already mentioned, underlying the social life of all living forms are the fundamental biological and physiological impulses—from those of hunger and sex, to those associated with nutrition and protection, to those having to do with position and balance—that require a social nexus for expression and completion.

While all social life is sustained by such impulses, the principles of organization differ significantly between the societies of human and animal forms. Functional differentiation—whether based simply along lines of sex or along lines of more complex communicative processes—is a general feature of all societies, but the basis of such differentiation is qualitatively different in animal and human societies. In Mead's view, the societies of lower animals are differentiated physiologically; members of such societies are constructed differently and perform different functions by virtue of their biological and physiological differences. Mead reasoned that human individuals all possessed essentially the same physiological characteristics, which means that the functional differentiation and social organization of their societies could not be based along physiological lines.

Mead felt that human individuals had, in the course of evolution, developed a form of symbolic communication that set them apart from the rest of the animal kingdom. To be sure, insects and vertebrates possess elaborate communication systems, and, in the case of the latter, a form of natural inter-stimulation occurs, as for example in the herd instinct. But such communication, in Mead's view, is an unconscious process and does not involve an awareness of the meaning of the gestures that trigger the response of the organism. The basis of human social organization is to be found in the process of self-conscious, symbolic communication. "In man," Mead writes, "the functional differentiation through language gives an entirely different principle of organization which produces not only a different type of individual, but also a different society" (**MSS**, 244).

Before going on with our discussion of social organization, we may want to pause to ask the question of how human individuals acquire the differentiated roles they perform in society. Are the differences among us to be explained solely in terms of sociolinguistic processes? Are these differences mere consequences of arbitrary and accidental socialization experiences? Is our self an accident of social location? Mead does not provide a formal answer to such questions, but in his discussion of the evolution of the ideal society, he calls for the removal of social barriers to the process of democratization, which, in his view, does not mean the levelling of social differences, but, rather, the removal of unnecessary constraints so that the individual can attain the level of development that "lies within the possibilities of his own inheritance." It would appear that one's natural endowments, whatever they may be, play some part in shaping individual differences.

In any event, Mead regards the process of symbolic communication as the basis for the structuring of human society. Human societies are organized in terms of "generalized social attitudes," which define the appropriate and required modes of conduct in different situations. A discernible cluster of such attitudes constitutes, in Mead's terms, a social institution. The "generalized other" can be seen as a configuration of social institutions.

But are social institutions fashioned arbitrarily according to the whims of individuals who live out their lives within them? Why is it that certain institutions—religious, familial, economic, political—tend to be found in all societies? Mead's answer to this question is that certain forms of institutional life are universal, particularly religion and economics, because they answer to certain fundamental attitudes in man. Mead recognized that the family emerged from the biosocial process to satisfy such needs as sex, procreation, protection of the young, etc., and that these needs we clearly share with the lower animals. But animals do not establish religious and economic institutions. Therefore, we cannot explain their origin and character in terms of our primitive impulses. They are to be explained in terms of fundamental attitudes of human beings, such as "kindliness, helpfulness, and assistance," in the case of religion, and recognition of the benefits of exchange, in the case of economic institutions. In both cases, symbolic communication and cooperative social activity are presupposed. While Mead did not explicitly analyze these fundamental attitudes in terms of socio-psychological processes, one cannot help but see the process of "taking the attitudes of the other" as the basis of universal religious and economic expressions.

Whatever the role of socio-psychological processes, it is clear that Mead regarded society primarily as an established phase of the social process, and regarded social institutions as analyzable units within that process. However, Mead does appear to have an image of society as a structure that is differentiated along functional, behavioural lines. Mead provides us with few conceptual tools or insights for understanding what these functional differentiations will be. He seems to have faith that they will sort themselves out in the evolutionary process as society adapts to the conditions of life.

To Summarize: All living organisms live in societies which are sustained by fundamental biological and physiological impulses. Animal societies are functionally differentiated along physiological lines; human societies are differentiated through language. Human societies are organized in terms of generalized social attitudes and social institutions which arise in response to fundamental social attitudes.

Social Integration and Progress

Mead presupposed a form of cooperative social activity as logically prior to minds and selves. Such was the society of living forms brought into being by the fundamental biological and physiological impulses of the pre-human organism. The mechanism of social integration of such a society is given in the very process of formation. While human societies spring from such biosocial networks, they cannot be explained in terms of them, for the society of man is an "emergent" in the same sense that mind and self are emergents, from the biosocial process.

Just as the principle of social organization of human society is to be found in the process of symbolic communication, so, one would assume, the mechanisms of social integration would be discovered in the linguistic inheritance of the community. In many respects this is true, and one might well be led to the view that there is little to be gained from an independent examination of the process of social integration. The organized attitudes of the generalized other necessarily presuppose an integrated social process; the two are different ways of saying the same thing. In a static society there would be little point in separating the questions of integration and organization, but Mead clearly saw society as an ongoing, dynamic process in which the process is constantly modifying the form.

Society, in Mead's view, evolves so as to effect a more adequate realization of the life-process. In the life-struggle, humans, like the creatures that preceded them in the evolutionary chain, develop the most effective means of survival available to them. Reflective intelligence is the key to man's success, but mind itself is constantly evolving, ever seeking more effective modes of adjustment. Thus, human societies are never fully formed; they are continuously evolving toward a more perfect adaptation to the conditions of life. It is in this sense that the question of integration arises, and for Mead, integration and progress are essentially one and the same process.

While Mead did not discuss the mechanisms of integration in a formal way, it is possible to identify in his work at least four discernible patterns of development in the evolution of society—developments in science, religion, economics, and politics—each of which exhibits a tendency toward the universalization of human experience. Underlying these patterns can be found different socio-psychological mechanisms. These might be described as: transcendence, identification with others, exchange, and self-realization.

We have already mentioned the process of enlargement of the mind as a means of transcending localized attitudes. The scientist is an example of someone who can exceed the limits of the local community, and, in the process, can present an enlarged universe of discourse to its members. Statesmen and politicians, who can take the attitudes of entire groups in addition to their own, can often bridge communication gaps between groups, and, by universalizing their experiences, lead the groups into larger cooperative activities. In the first example, the enlargement of mind leads to the presentation of an abstract world of thought which is virtually unlimited. In the second example, the enlargement of the mind leads to a more inclusive empirical community.

Integration is also achieved through the extension of fundamental attitudes, such as those of neighbourliness, kindness, and concern for others, attitudes which are embodied in universal religions. The expression of these attitudes leads to an identification of individuals with one another, which, Mead felt, was a natural tendency in human beings. The full realization of this tendency would be the establishment of a universal community of mankind.

Another fundamental attitude that tends to lead to the creation of larger, more encompassing social wholes is that of exchange. Unlike contract theorists, who regarded economic exchange primarily in terms of the self-interestedness of individuals, Mead looked at the process from the standpoint of the person who is able to "put himself in the place of the other" (**MSS**, 292), to interpret the other's needs and to act accordingly. It is this tendency that leads to the division of labour and to the allocation of functionally differentiated roles, since each individual will tend to do that which he is most capable of, and new roles will emerge in an effort to solve the problem of human need.

The last mechanism expresses itself initially in acts of dominance of one group over another. The subjugation of peoples necessarily leads to the development of administrative structures, then to the creation of functional divisions within society, and finally to the democratization of political life. In the process communities are united into more encompassing social units. The socio-psychological mechanism underlying this process is that of self-realization. To Mead, the initial act of self-assertion signals the "expression of self-consciousness reached through the realization of one's self in others" (**MSS**, 284). As society develops, the basis of organization shifts from force to function, and the individual attains self-realization, not by asserting himself over against another individual, but, rather, by excelling in the performance of his social function. Self-assertion of this type is the expression of superiority in acts and deeds and is quite different in character from the self-assertion of the bully who realizes himself through the subordination of others. The political expression of the tendency toward self-realization in the modern world is the development of democracy, in which the artificial barriers to social intercourse are stripped away, and each individual is able to become that which he is most capable of being.

Mead was quite convinced that the evolutionary process, as it expressed itself in the universalizing tendencies in science, religion, economics, and politics, was leading toward the ideal society. Universality, then, is the measure of progress.

To Summarize: Integration and progress are achieved through the tendency toward universalization in the institutions of society. Underlying this pattern are socio-psychological mechanisms which can be described as transcendence, identification with others, exchange, and self-realization.

Conflict and Reconstruction

In the closing sections of Part IV of **Mind, Self, and Society**, Mead outlines his vision of the ideal society, the society toward which the evolutionary process is

necessarily tending. Such a society would be differentiated along functional, behavioural lines; each of its members would attain full self-realization and self-consciousness; all would possess a "perfected social intelligence;" institutions would be flexible and accommodating to change; and the general thrust of change would be in the direction of a form of international civilization. Underlying this image, and, indeed, underlying the entire body of Meadian theory, is a presupposition of natural harmony and cooperation among men. What then, does Mead have to say about conflict?

In Mead's view, conflict arises from two sources: the expression of "anti-social" impulses and behavioural tendencies, and the disjunction between and among individual selves. In both cases the resolution of conflict involves a refashioning of the social process and a reconstruction of the self.

Fundamental impulses, by their very nature are social, But, considered in a non-ethical sense, certain primitive impulses, such as those of self-protection and self-preservation express themselves in hostile, anti-social attitudes towards others. Individuals initially become aware of themselves by asserting attitudes associated with such "hostile" impulses. However, as individuals enter rational social organizations, or as groups enter unions of association, the "hostile" impulses become fused with "friendly" impulses, and often express themselves through the "primary constituent ideals" of the larger organization—those of social protection and social assistance. Thus, "anti-social" impulses become converted into social motives. In the process, the self, since it is an expression of the social process as a whole, necessarily is enlarged. The full development of the self calls out this kind of enlargement and necessarily tends toward a resolution of conflict stemming from "anti-social" impulses.

The second form of conflict, which tends to arise in more highly developed societies, results from incompatibilities either among the different aspects of an individual's self (what we have called "minimes") or among different individual selves.[11] In both these situations, conflict is resolved by modifying the social situation and restructuring the self in the direction of a more encompassing social whole, by creating a generalized other that encompasses the particularities of the discordant elements. Put very

11 Later sociologists will refer to these types of disjunction as forms of role conflict; see Robert K. Merton, **Social Theory and Social Structure** (Glencoe: The Free Press, 1957), 225–280.

simply, conflicts between and among individuals and groups are resolved by "taking the attitudes of the other." Mead had faith that such social modification and reconstruction would occur in the direction of increasing adaptation to the conditions of life. The reflective and problem-solving character of the mind makes this possible. In the process, both the self and society would be brought ever closer to the "ideal."

From the foregoing, it is evident that, in Mead's view, there can be no fundamental, unbridgeable disjunction between and among individuals, classes, groups, societies, etc. Fundamentally, social and individual life constitute a continuous whole, and, while conflicts do arise in social life, they naturally and necessarily are resolved through the self-conscious, problem-solving activity of the human mind. Conflict and discord are possible in the Meadian world of symbolic interaction, but they are conceived as temporary disjunctions which necessarily tend toward resolution. Social conflict is to be resolved in the evolutionary process.

To Summarize: Conflicts arise either from the expression of "antisocial" impulses or from a disjunction within and among selves. In both cases, conflict is resolved through social transcendence and self-reconstruction in the direction of the ideal human society.